The Possible Worlds of Hypertext Fiction

The Possible Worlds of Hypertext Fiction

Alice Bell

First published 2010 by
PALGRAVE MACMILLAN

Palgrave Macmillan in the UK is an imprint of Macmillan Publishers Limited, registered in England, company number 785998, of Houndmills, Basingstoke, Hampshire RG21 6XS.

Palgrave Macmillan in the US is a division of St Martin's Press LLC, 175 Fifth Avenue, New York, NY 10010.

Palgrave Macmillan is the global academic imprint of the above companies and has companies and representatives throughout the world.

Palgrave® and Macmillan® are registered trademarks in the United States, the United Kingdom, Europe and other countries.

ISBN 978–0–230–54255–6   hardback

This book is printed on paper suitable for recycling and made from fully managed and sustained forest sources. Logging, pulping and manufacturing processes are expected to conform to the environmental regulations of the country of origin.

A catalogue record for this book is available from the British Library.

Bell, Alice, 1979–
   The possible worlds of hypertext fiction / Alice Bell.
      p. cm.
   Summary: "Written in hypertext and read from a computer, hypertext novels exist as a collection of textual fragments, which must be pieced together by the reader. The Possible Worlds of Hypertext Fiction offers a new critical theory tailored specifically for this burgeoning genre, poviding a much needed body of criticism in a key area of new media fiction"—Provided by publisher.
   Includes bibliographical references and index.
   ISBN 978–0–230–54255–6 (hardback)
   1. Hypertext fiction—History and criticism.   I. Title.
   PN3448. H96B46 2010
   809.3'911—dc22   2009048419

10 9 8 7 6 5 4 3 2 1
19 18 17 16 15 14 13 12 11 10

Printed and bound in Great Britain by
CPI Antony Rowe, Chippenham and Eastbourne

For Douglas, Janet and Tom,
and in memory of Barbara May (1917–2007)

Contents

List of Figures

List of Tables

Acknowledgements

Some sections of this book have been published elsewhere and I thank the publishers for allowing me to use this material. Reworked sections from my (2007) article, '"Do You Want to Hear About it?" Exploring Possible Worlds in Michael Joyce's Hyperfiction, *afternoon: a story.*' In: M. Lambrou and P. Stockwell (eds) *Contemporary Stylistics.* London: Continuum, pp. 43–55, have been used in Chapter 3 by kind permission of Continuum International Publishing. Some sections in Chapters 4 and 5 have been adapted from my forthcoming article, 'Ontological Boundaries and Methodological Leaps: The Significance of Possible Worlds Theory for Hypertext Fiction (and Beyond)'. In: R. Page and B. Thomas (eds), *New Narratives: Theory and Practice.* Lincoln, NE: University of Nebraska Press. I am grateful to the Press for authorising the use of that material in this book.

I am extremely grateful to Mark Bernstein at Eastgate Systems Inc. for allowing me to use numerous extracts and screenshots from four Eastgate hypertext fiction novels. Their inclusion facilitates the analysis throughout this book.

I would also like to thank William A. Nance for helping me to secure rights to reuse the image of 'Ralph the Flying Pig' in Chapter 6. The visual image is central to my argument in that part of the book and is published by permission of Texas State University–San Marcos.

My sincere gratitude goes to Lucy Allen (at www.lucyallen.co.uk) for designing the cover image. I am in awe of her talent.

For expanding my mind and making me a better researcher, I would like to thank the following people: Joanna Gavins, Brian McHale, Joe Bray, Astrid Ensslin, Marie-Laure Ryan, David Ciccoricco, Peter Stockwell, Marina Lambrou, Ruth Page, Bronwen Thomas, Lesley Jeffries, Alison Gibbons, Andrea Macrae, Sara Whiteley, James Boon, Will Slocombe, Jan Alber, Monika Fludernik and Richard Holeton. They have each read versions or extracts from this project and provided constructive criticism which has undoubtedly made my work more robust and accurate. My thanks also go to my colleagues in the English department at Sheffield Hallam University for fostering a stimulating environment in which to work. Barbara MacMahon who has answered several of my, often embarrassingly naive, linguistics questions and queries warrants a special mention.

Finally, without the familial and social network that surrounds me, this book would simply not have been possible. I would therefore like to thank them for their eternal encouragement. My family inspire and support me unremittingly and have given me the confidence to pursue my interests, both academic and otherwise. Words cannot begin to convey my gratitude to them. A special mention goes to Toddla T for providing a healthy supply of music throughout the course of this project. His creativity and enthusiasm never cease to impress me. Although I cannot name them all here, I am indebted to all of my friends for their kindness. They provide support in numerous ways and through various means, but each brings comfort, joy and fun. Their presence continually reminds me that theirs is the world to which I always hope to belong.

1
Introduction: The Universe of Hypertext Fiction

Background and Rationale

This book offers a new critical approach for the analysis of hypertext fiction. The term 'hypertext', coined within the work of Nelson (1965, 1970, 1974, 1981), can be most simply defined as 'non-sequential writing' (Nelson, 1974). Nelson's (1981) vision of hypertext is that of a system that 'branches and allows choices to the reader' (2), so that the user can move within a hypertext system according to their rationale. Facilitated by a digital environment, hypertext allows documents to be linked according to concepts and ideas rather than alphabetical or numerical sequences. In hypertext, documents are structured according to context and purpose and horizontal or vertical hierarchies are forsaken in favour of 'intertwingularity' (Nelson, 1974: 45), an apparently neologised blend of 'intermingled' and 'intertwined' which suggests complex configurations and multiple combinations. The World Wide Web is the most celebrated and renowned example of a large scale hypertext system in which individual electronic documents are linked to form a vast network containing everything from textual documents and visual media to executable programs and intricate applications. The popularity and extent of World Wide Web 2.0 technology heralds the emergence of more technological sophistication and greater user-accessibility.

Representing a very specific application of hypertext technology, 'hypertext fiction' is a term that is used to describe novels or short stories that are written in hypertext and sometimes contain accompanying image, film and sound. Such works of digital literature can be accessed on the World Wide Web but they are also distributed via self-contained storage devices such as CD-ROMs. Emulating the structure of the World Wide Web, hypertext fictions consist of individual windows of text, each known as 'lexia', which are connected by hyperlinks. Structurally, they are often multi-linear so that a number of different possible routes exist within the same work. Hypertext fictions are, like the World Wide Web, interactive. The reader must participate in their construction, choosing which path to take from the choices with which they are presented. Unlike the World Wide Web, however, most hypertext fiction novels are fixed in length and cannot be added to once published. Some user-generated fictions, such as Coover's (1994) *Hypertext Hotel* and Penguin's (2007) *A Million Penguins* project, expand to accommodate inputs from multiple authors. However, these are relatively few in number and usually culminate in an imposed conclusion at some point. Most hypertext fictions are published as self-contained works which do not expand according to external forces such as user requirements or changes in technology. The expansive attributes enabled by hypertext linking lie within the confines of independent work only, as opposed to a larger system in which they are housed.

Hypertext Fiction in Context

A full survey of the hypertext canon is beyond the remit of this text and has been more than comprehensively addressed in Ensslin's (2007) extensive review of the field. As a means of contextualising the approach and accompanying analyses contained within this study, however, a brief overview of the chronological development of hypertext fiction is required at this point.

As others have pointed out (e.g. Moulthrop, 1991b; Douglas, 1992; Aarseth, 1997; Landow, 1997; Phelan and Maloney, 1999; Koskimaa, 2000; Bolter, 2001) a number of print works, retrospectively collected under the term 'proto-hypertext', are often seen as the literary precursors of hypertext fiction. Saporta's (1963) *Composition No. 1* exists as a collection of 100 loose pages, which can be read in any order; Cortazar's (1966) *Hopscotch* can be read following the numerical sequencing of the chapters or from an alternative reading order provided at the beginning of the novel; Coover's (1969) short-story, 'The Babysitter', is comprised of fragments of text that readers are invited to piece together in any order they choose. Comparisons might also be made between hypertext fiction novels and Choose Your Own Adventure novels associated with children's literature. In each case, different reading orders deliver or imply different narrative outcomes so that the reader is assigned responsibility, as in a hypertext fiction, for selecting which path to follow.

While proto-hypertexts share some of the structural attributes with hypertext fiction, however, digital hypertext is not, like the texts cited above, a collection of textual fragments which can be joined in any order, allowing for an unlimited number of configurations. Rather, a hypertext fiction contains fragments that are linked in predetermined paths. The reader of both types of text is allotted a degree of responsibility, but their omniscience is quite different in each case. The reader of a proto-hypertext can access each fragment of text at their will; they can flick forwards and backwards through the leaves of the novel. The hypertext fiction reader, on the other hand, can only unveil one lexia at a time and is often ignorant of the forthcoming sections and reading paths. In each case, the reader is granted some agency but the reader of a hypertext fiction is always constricted by the integral capacities of the digital medium to hide their forthcoming reading experience.

The existence of proto-hypertext at least implies that some twentieth-century writers were experimenting with narrative form. In a digital context, the possibilities were expanded. Many early hypertext fiction novels were written and published before the key developments in World Wide Web technology, which took place in 1991, and certainly before the explosion of general World Wide Web usage in the mid to late 1990s (see Berners-Lee, 1999; Connolly, 2000). Appropriate computer software was therefore required to facilitate hypertext writing.

Storyspace Hypertext

Since its introduction in the late 1980s, Bolter, Joyce and Smith's Storyspace software has been the dominant format for CD-ROM-based hypertext fiction. Storyspace is hypertext editing software designed specifically for the writing and reading of hypertext fiction but it can be used for all types of creative writing, both fictional and non-fiction. Eastgate Systems is, to date, the sole producer, publisher and distributor of Storyspace hypertext fiction worldwide – although the texts are also available for purchase through larger online merchants such as the Amazon.com franchises.

Two of the developers, Bolter and Joyce, categorise Storyspace as 'a simple system for hypertextual fiction' (1987: 44) but stress that it 'permits significant structural experiments' (44). Visually, Storyspace may seem like a primitive piece of software relative to some of the technological advances made in recent years and authors choosing Storyspace are comparatively limited with respect to the non-textual features that they can use. Yet a project produced in Storyspace is able to house extensive material and generate very intricate structural configurations.

Figure 1.1 provides a visual representation of a typical Storyspace hypertext structure, taken from Stuart Moulthrop's (1991a) *Victory Garden*.

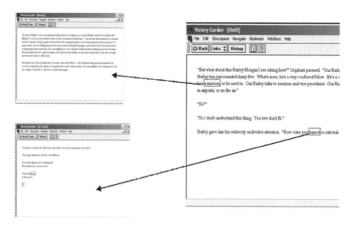

Figure 1.1   Screenshots of Storyspace hypertext fiction

While the screen shot shows all three lexias, during reading each lexia is displayed individually. As opposed to the numeric sequencing that is associated with most print novels, lexias are entitled rather than numbered. The first lexia in the sequence in Figure 1.1 is entitled {Unfit} (lexia titles will appear in curly brackets throughout this book). The reader may access the next default lexia in a near-linear fashion by clicking the 'Enter' key on their keyboard. Alternatively, words and sometimes sentences are hyperlinked to provide access to other lexias within the text. As shown in Figure 1.1, if readers click on the hyperlinked phrase, 'a mission', they will be taken to a lexia entitled {Bounty} and if they click on the hyperlinked word, 'turned', they will come to a lexia entitled {U Turns}. In some Storyspace hypertexts, the reader can type a response to the novel in a text box below the narrative and different structures will result from their inputs. In Storyspace hypertext fiction novels, lists of lexia titles are also available for readers to browse in a navigational drop-down menu, so that they can be accessed out of their allotted reading sequence. Some Storyspace hypertexts contain hidden or secret lexias that can only be accessed in reading sequences. Joyce's (1987) *afternoon*, for example, contains a secret lexia which is not listed in the lexia lists. Overall, irrespective of the structuring and associated navigational mechanisms, hypertext fiction novels exploit hypertext capabilities, so that a number of different reading configurations exist within the same text. The reader is assigned responsibility for choosing which path to follow so that they must interact with the text throughout the entire reading experience.

Since Storyspace works are predominantly text-based, the texts chosen for analysis in this study are limited to what Ensslin (2007) categorises as 'hypertext' as opposed to the more multi-medial 'hypermedia' or 'cybertext'. In her seminal study, Ensslin provides a comprehensive framework in which she defines digital literature according to 'generations' (19ff), 'the temporally over-lapping techno-historical stages of this literary genre' (19). Ensslin's taxonomy is useful because, while she notes that 'the progress of technological developments does alter the genre in a techno-methodical … way' (19), her classification system is based upon the respective *characteristics* of each work as opposed to relying on the date of publication or the software in which the work is produced.

According to Ensslin's framework, '*[h]ypertext* refers to a largely script-based form of interactive computer-based literature [in which] … [p]ictorial devices are employed sparsely if at all' (20). As Ensslin's definition implies, while some Storyspace novels contain photographs and graphic images, most of the earliest examples make relatively conservative use of non-verbal media. The relative simplicity of hypertext's mediality distinguishes it from 'hypermedia' literature, defined by Ensslin as 'semiotic systems [which] comprise text, graphics, digitized speech, audio files, pictographic and photographic images, animation and film' (21) and 'cybertext', which she defines as 'a term coined by Espen Aarseth (1997), who sees hypertexts that are programmed in particular ways as autonomous "text machines" that assume power over the reader by literally "writing themselves" rather than presenting themselves as an existing textual product' (22). Examples of 'hypermedia' thus include: McDaid's (1992) *Uncle Buddy's Phantom Funhouse*, a novel published in HyperCard which contains short animations and sound; web-based Sawhney and Balcom's (1997) *HyperCafe* which contains short pieces of film; and M. D. Coverley's (2000) *Califia* which, though underpinned by Storyspace software, utilises sound, images and animation. Stuart Moulthrop's (1995) *Hegirascope*, a Web-based work, is perhaps the best known cybertext. *Hegirascope* exploits web-browser technology so that the pace of the reading is predetermined. Each lexia is displayed on screen for only eighteen seconds before the browser refreshes causing the next lexia to appear. As Ensslin's definition of cybertext suggests, in *Hegirascope*, it is the text rather than the reader that controls the reading experience.

More recently, Ensslin (forthcoming) has sub-divided 'cybertext' to include a more specific type of digital literature, namely 'physio-cybertext'. This is digital text which responds to and subsequently incorporates into the narrative the physical inputs of the reader. In Pullinger et al.'s (2004) physio-cybertext, *The Breathing Wall*, for example, the pace of the reader's breathing determines the paths that are available to them so that an apparent synergy between the reader's physiological state and the text's narrative appears to be forged.

The Limits of Storyspace Criticism

As the preceding overview suggests, a vast array of tools and forums are available for digital writing. Yet hypertext fiction novels are still published using Storyspace. Between 1989 and 2001, 26 Storyspace hypertext fictions were published (Bernstein, 2002: 180) and the software is still available for purchase from Eastgate. As this book will show, Storyspace hypertext has undergone extensive theorisation by the field. Similarly, while a number of hypertext fiction novels exist on the World Wide Web, Storyspace hypertexts are usually cited by those who work outside the field as texts which exemplify hypertext fiction writing (e.g. Geyh et al., 1997a, 1997b; Abbott, 2002).

Yet while Storyspace hypertext fiction is well established as a literary form both within and outside its discipline boundaries, analyses of individual works are still relatively uncommon. In a special edition of the *Journal of Digital Information* dedicated to hypertext fiction and criticism, the editors assert that the journal should 'contribute to this area by publishing criticism of specific works and discussions about the state of hypertext criticism' (Tosca and Walker, 2003). Somewhat ironically, however, the articles largely comprise the latter: Higgason (2003a) calls for 'a body of criticism [which] can provide various readings of the texts'; Miles (2003a) concedes that the field is 'hobbled by the lack of examples of such simple things as what an individual hypertext might mean'; and Larsen (2003) notes that 'to understand nuances in Dante's language, culture and story, we have a myriad of commentaries, translations and keys. Where are these supporting works for hypertext?'

Just as significant as the lack of critical material is the absence of a systematic and transparent methodological approach to hypertext fiction analysis. Though some readings do exist, few elucidate a methodology that can be replicated by others. Close readings of hypertext fiction that are more methodologically transparent are slowly emerging, either in the form of field-specific journals such as *dichtung-digital* and the *Electronic Book Review*, or as individual projects (e.g. Van Looy and Baetens, 2003; Bell, 2007 and forthcoming; Ciccoricco, 2007; Ensslin, 2007 and forthcoming; Ensslin and Bell, 2007; Taylor and Pitman, 2007; Pressman, 2009; Page and Thomas, forthcoming). However, profiles of replicable methods are relatively few in number.

Aims and Outlines

This book attempts to remedy a methodological shortfall within hypertext theory by providing a critical theory for the analysis of Storyspace hypertext fictions. In addition, it begins to rectify the analytical gaps in the field by providing four readings which are methodologically transparent, systematic and replicable. Providing a theoretical and methodological context to the study, Chapter 2 traces the development of hypertext theory from what has retrospectively been categorised as a trajectory from the first wave to the second wave. In particular, the discussion shows how a number of second-wave hypertext theorists have shown self-reflexivity to be an inherent characteristic of Storyspace hypertext fiction. Since readers are required to participate in the construction of the text, they are habitually alerted to the artificiality of the narrative. In addition, the discussion shows that many Storyspace novels also house narratives which utilise self-reflexive devices. Thus, ontological self-consciousness prevails both inside and outside the texts. Since self-reflexive devices are not exclusive to hypertext fiction and, in particular, are often associated with postmodernist print fiction, the chapter also argues that hypertext fiction might not constitute a radically new literary genre which requires new theories of fictionality, but rather that it adds new dimensions to fictional self-reflexivity by coupling it to and expanding it within a different kind of context.

Chapter 2 also shows why, as a method that is fundamentally concerned with the ontological domains and structures that are built by fictional texts, Possible Worlds Theory is an appropriate methodological framework with which to analyse the ontological self-consciousness of Storyspace hypertext fiction and shows why Ryan's (1991) model, in particular, offers a useful methodological starting point. However, while Ryan's framework offers an appropriate point of departure, the critique, supplementation and application of Possible Worlds Theory, which forms an integral part of the methodological discussions throughout the book, represent the second and equally significant function of this study. Primarily, Chapter 2 will show that, while some debates remain unresolved, the theoretical foundations of Possible Worlds Theory have been well documented in both a philosophical and narratological context. Conversely, practical applications within the latter context are significantly lacking. In addition to addressing the methodological shortfalls evident within hypertext theory therefore, this book also attends to the analytical gaps which are apparent in Possible Worlds Theory. By creating a dialogue between two fields, it also offers a systematic and replicable approach which, through being profiled in this study, can then be used by others for the analysis of other hypertext fiction works. Moreover and more specifically, the analyses show how an ontologically centred approach is entirely apposite to the narrative and often semantic concerns of hypertext fictions in general.

By showing how the ontological mechanics of each novel are intrinsically related to their thematic concerns, Chapters 3, 4, 5 and 6 each demonstrate the suitability of a Possible Worlds Theory approach to Storyspace hypertext fiction. The four texts chosen for analysis in the study have each received a varying amount of critical attention but they are all well established within the relatively immature canon of digital literature. From a methodological perspective, they have been chosen as texts which are representative of the field. This aspect of their canonicity is important because it means that many of the conclusions arrived at in this study can potentially be applied to other Storyspace works. Conveniently, their publication dates represent a chronological spread across the Eastgate catalogue of Storyspace hypertext fiction. Paradoxically, however, the texts have been selected for analysis because of their generic diversity. As novels which are thematically divergent, each demands a different type of critical reading. Consequently, the analyses collected in this book are used as a way of profiling the dexterity of the demonstrated approach across a diverse sample of the Storyspace hypertext spectrum.

Chapter 3 presents an analysis of Michael Joyce's (1987) *afternoon: a story*. It begins by showing how a modified form of Ryan's (1991) Possible Worlds Theory can be used to analyse the ontological self-consciousness that the narrator is responsible for instilling at the beginning of the text and, in so doing, profiles an ontologically centred model of fictional communication. The chapter also shows how Possible Worlds Theory can be adapted to analyse the narrative contradictions that the novel contains. Through the analysis of the conflicting first-person perspectives in *afternoon*, the chapter also argues for the addition of a 'World View' category to Ryan's (1991) Possible Worlds Theory framework. Hermeneutically, the chapter shows that the ontological self-consciousness and associated epistemological indeterminacy in *afternoon* is connected to the protagonist's inability to confront his reality, as well as the readers' experience of its hypertextual narrative.

Chapter 4 offers an analysis of Stuart Moulthrop's (1991a) historical novel, *Victory Garden*. The chapter begins by showing how Possible Worlds Theory can be used to explain how all historical novels are epistemologically reliant on the reader's knowledge of the world that they inhabit. From a theoretical perspective, the discussion also attempts to resolve existing inconsistencies within Possible Worlds Theory with respect to transworld identity and counterpart theory. The second half of the chapter shows that *Victory Garden* subverts many of the epistemological devices on which historical fiction relies as a means of deliberately drawing attention to its own artificiality. In particular, the analysis shows that the text problematises the ontological distinction that other parts of the text work so hard to enforce and concludes that while the text draws a sharp correlation between fiction and reality, it also raises questions about the legitimacy of fictional and historical discourses. Correlations are also drawn between *Victory Garden* and the generic category of 'historiographic metafiction' (Hutcheon, 1988, 1989).

The analysis of Shelley Jackson's (1995) *Patchwork Girl* in Chapter 5 reveals how Possible Worlds Theory can accommodate the ontological and epistemological parallels that are enforced by texts which invoke and subsequently rewrite works of classic canonical fiction. It begins with a discussion of transworld identity and counterpart theory to show how concepts that are traditionally associated with historical fiction in Possible Worlds Theory can also be used to analyse intertextual references to other fictional characters as well as the appearance of an author figure in the text. The analysis reveals that *Patchwork Girl* fulfils the criteria of a postmodern rewrite (Doležel, 1998a). In particular, it shows how *Patchwork Girl*'s ontological landscape is predominantly shaped by the incorporation of other sources and concludes that the text works via a combination of epistemological and ontological interdependence.

In Chapter 6 Richard Holeton's (2001) *Figurski at Findhorn on Acid* is analysed as an 'absurd situation novel' (Slocombe, 2006). The effect that visual images have on the text's ontological landscape is also explored. It begins by showing how Possible Worlds Theory can be used as a method for analysing the ontological and epistemological interplay which is ultimately responsible for generating the absurdist humour in the text. This chapter then focuses on the use of visual images in the novel and thereby begins the development of Possible Worlds Theory for the analysis of multimodal hypertext fiction.

Drawing together a number of consistencies found within the four analyses, Chapter 7 concludes the study by consolidating the findings and evaluating the effectiveness of the Possible Worlds Theory approach for Storyspace hypertext fiction. Offering directions for future research, it also suggests ways in which other forms of digital literature might also benefit from a similar, if not identical, method of theorisation and examination.

2
Theory: Hypertext Fiction and the Significance of Worlds

This chapter provides an overview of hypertext theory as it has developed from the exaggerated claims about the capabilities of the medium to a more systematic and replicable analytical approach to Storyspace fiction. It thus tracks the development of what has been retrospectively termed the transition from the first wave to the second wave of hypertext theory. The second part of the chapter profiles the theoretical approach that will be used for the four analyses and suggests ways in which Possible Worlds Theory is an appropriate framework through which to analyse hypertext fiction in general.

First-Wave Hypertext Theory

Hypertext theory has always accompanied hypertext novels and many hypertext fiction authors, including Joyce, Moulthrop and Jackson, have made significant contributions to the field (e.g. Joyce, 1987, 1988, 1997; Moulthrop, 1989, 1991b, 1994; Jackson, 1995, 1998). However, some of the primary, or what has recently been termed 'first wave' (e.g. Pang, 1998; Bell, forthcoming), hypertext theory has been scrutinized by what might be appropriately termed a 'second wave' of hypertext theory for its potential theoretical and methodological limitations.

Initially, a number of first-wave theorists explore some potential and attractive similarities between the hypertext structure and form and the hypothetical textual models described in poststructuralist theory. As a consequence of hypertext's branching structure and multi-linearity as well as the choice that was permitted because of its interactivity, discussions boast the potential changes that hypertext will bring to readers, writers and texts. First-wave theorists claim that 'the new dialectic of hypertext will compel us, as Derrida put it, to "reread past writing according to different organization space"' (Bolter, 1991: 117) and that hypertext 'might come close to realizing Roland Barthes' vision of "the Text"' (Moulthrop, 1991c: 130). The term 'lexia', which is used to describe individual chunks of text in a hypertext, is also appropriated from Barthes' work. In addition to Derrida's (1979, 1981) concept of a decentred text (e.g. Bolter, 1991, Landow, 1994, 1997, 2006) and Barthes' (1990 [1974]) 'writerly' text (e.g. Delany and Landow, 1991; Moulthrop, 1991c; Landow, 1992, 1994, 1997, 2006), hypertext is also compared to Deleuze and Guattari's (1988) conception of a 'rhizome' text (e.g. Landow, 1994, 2006) and as a medium which might facilitate Cixous' (1991) idea of *l'écriture féminine* (e.g. Landow, 1992, 1994, 2006; Page, 1999).

Yet while many of the poststructuralist models are seductively suggestive of the hypertext form, beyond very superficial similarities the comparisons are unfeasible and consequently unsuccessful. If hypertext is, as Delany and Landow (1991) most famously declare 'an almost embarrassingly literal reification or actualization' (10) of contemporary literary theory, it is most likely because it resembles a form of writing that was not available to theorists working with print. As Bolter (2001) points out, 'if poststructuralist theories ... seem to resonate with hypertext, it is important to remember that these theories developed among writers who were primarily working in and with earlier technologies. ... To deconstruct a text, one used a vocabulary appropriate to the computer precisely because this vocabulary contradicted the assumption of print' (181). While initially theoretically appealing, therefore, hypertext does not fully possess the capabilities associated with the poststructuralists' ideals. Perhaps more importantly, from a methodological point of view, little is to be gained in terms of generating critical analyses by locating the hypertext structure within an abstract theoretical model. It does not aid a literary critical understanding of individual novels and instead abstract structures are used only metaphorically and the hypertext form is allied to a theoretical blueprint from which few, if any, analyses have since materialised.

In a more influential approach, first-wave theorists move the focus on the reader to their logistical role within the hypertext (e.g. Delany and Landow 1991; Liestol, 1994; Snyder, 1996). Yet, while the role of the reader is important and, as the discussion below will show, is crucial to much second-wave theory, many first-wave theorists position the readers of hypertext relative to their print counterparts and thus unrealistically elevate the authority and power of the hypertext reader. Delany and Landow (1991), for example, define hypertext as 'the use of the computer to *transcend* the linear, bounded and fixed qualities of traditional text' (3, my italics) producing a 'textual structure that can be represented on the screen in different ways, according to the reader's choice of links to follow' (3). Delany and Landow's description emphasises the respective peculiarities of each medium: readers of print text are bound to an enduring structure and length which offers little or no flexibility, whereas readers of a hypertext are attributed with power and authority in what they imply is a superior textual experience. Similarly, in his seminal overview of hypertext theory and practice, Landow (2006) claims that in '*all* hypertext systems ... the reader is not locked into any kind of particular organization or hierarchy' (38, my italics). Again, Landow's description of hypertext as structurally liberating implicitly favours choice over prescribed or premeditated order.

Yet while hypertext theorists often perceive a high level of reader omnipotence in all hypertext manifestations, hypertext fiction novels often invert many of the attributes found within an informational hypertext. In an informational hypertext, clarity is often desirable, but in a literary text this is not always so. In an informational hypertext, the link is more often than not suggestive of what the reader will find at the destination. However, in a hypertext novel, words used as hyperlinks are often not indicative of the destination nodes to which they lead, so that any semantic associations are usually made, not in anticipation of the destination lexia, but in retrospect. Moreover, hyperlink words are sometimes hidden in hypertext novels – *afternoon*, for example, has no visible links so that readers must experimentally click within each lexia. In this case, the text inhibits rather than empowers them in their role as link chooser.

As an inevitable consequence of the form and structure, readers of hypertext do have some agency. They can click back and forth through the predefined structures and any reading can be extended or terminated according to the reader's desire. However, readers are sometimes unaware of how long each path will last so that they are not necessarily able to make informed decisions about their experience in the text. Overall, while hypertext fiction does offer choice, the reader's degree of control, which was envisaged by many first-wave theorists, is inflated and readers are erroneously attributed with unrealistic powers in their actual capacity to manipulate and operate within the text.

Some of the theoretical inaccuracies of the first-wave are remedied in their engagements with individual novels. Somewhat paradoxically, however, while many first-wave theorists see the reader as a powerful agent in hypertext reading, when the focus shifts to individual hypertext reading experiences, their claims are less universal. With the fragmentary form of hypertext fiction comes multiple reading paths and potential narrative ambiguities or contradictions. This has resulted in first-wave theory focusing on the reader's response to the multiple paths which often involves rather subjective accounts of their reading experiences as well as strategies that might be used to assert mastery over the hypertext form.

Analysing four different reading experiences in *afternoon*, for example, Douglas (1994) documents an approach in which she continues to read the text until a path is found that satisfies her own personal curiosity. The exploration of the text is based on what Douglas perceives as the reader's desire to find closure in a hypertext fiction. 'Our sense of closure', she concludes 'is satisfied when we manage to resolve narrative tensions and to minimize ambiguities, to explain puzzles, and to incorporate as many of the narrative elements as possible into a coherent pattern' (185). Douglas anticipates that readers will seek a definitive ending and one which represents 'the most *plausible* conclusion to the narrative's network of mysteries and tensions' (170). According to her prognosis, while a reader is aware that there are a number of possible paths within the text, once their own personal curiosity has been satisfied, they are less inclined to explore the fiction further.

Landow (1997) also suggests that readers seek solace from the ambiguities that hypertext narratives can produce and, in reflecting on his own experiences, he attributes general characteristics to hypertext reading. He suggests that 'after reading awhile one begins to construct narrative placements, so that one assigns particular sections to a provisionally suitable place, ... Then having assigned particular sections to particular sequences or reading paths ... one reaches points at which one's initial cognitive dissonance or puzzlement disappears, and one seems satisfied. One has reached – or created – closure!' (193). Yet while hypertext fictions may well cause confusion for readers by retracting what has been said, giving different versions of the world or different versions of events in that world, in their implicit drive towards closure, the theorists undervalue the reader's response to narrative irresolution and ambiguity by assuming that all are driven towards the same end – a single and unambiguous ending.

Walker's (1999) analysis of *afternoon* has similar limitations. Her approach is to 'piece together a story' (111) and therefore find some kind of linear succession of events within the text. As Walker rightly asserts, *afternoon* 'can be read in several different orders, and the succession of events is not always clear' (111) and she notes that the text houses many devices that 'destabilis[e]' (114) the narrative, but her analysis shows how narrative theory can be used to neutralise these obstacles so that '*the* story' (111ff) can be found.

As the examples show, first-wave theorists perceive confusion and disorientation as an inevitable consequence of hypertext fiction reading. However, they also suggest that ambiguities can be abated by reading on until personal curiosities have been satisfied. More importantly, while their accounts are based on their own experiences, they imply that all hypertext readers seek satisfactory narrative resolution. Yet, while their respective approaches can be used to understand the resulting effects of hypertext narrative, the methodological approaches are less useful to others. Unlike more recent studies (e.g. Gardner, 2004; Pope, 2006), they lack empirical evidence to substantiate their claims. More importantly, it is precisely because devices are used to generate ambiguity that finding a definitive order or successions of events is problematic. Since choice is granted to the reader, Storyspace hypertexts often demand to be read in a number of different ways and it is such indeterminacy which is vital for a complete comprehension of the text's narrative structure and thematic concerns. Determining the chronology of a hypertext fiction prioritises one order of events over another, which is an approach that is difficult to substantiate in a multi-linear text.

Similarly, choosing one final path for analysis from the many on offer defies and ignores the uniqueness of hypertext fiction texts. It is an unsuitable approach because it attempts to distort it into a text which more closely resembles linear narratives. As Miles (2003b) warns, hypertext theory should be careful not to 'punish the object because it doesn't give you the mastery and the pleasures that you have taken as your right'. Instead of condemning the unconventional 'because a work does not do what we think it is supposed to do', Miles suggests that critics should attempt to understand how features such as concurrency and resistance to deterministic closure add to the text and its meaning. As Miles notes, although potentially perplexing, narrative instability and ambiguity are often integral to hypertext fictions and, in order to completely appreciate these texts, a means of analysing such features is required.

The role of the reader represents an important facet of hypertext fiction and its reception and, as this book will show throughout, the reader's position in the text is crucial to second-wave analyses. However, from a literary critical perspective, focusing upon the respective power struggles that might take place between a reader and a particular type of text does not provide insight into how we might interpret a particular type of narrative. Similarly, measuring the reader–writer relationship may be an appropriate method of comparing the structure of hypertexts with other types of text, but the semantic dimension of each hypertext fiction is largely disregarded and a study of this kind forms theoretical and abstract observations about the hypertext form and its reading which are unsatisfactory in a literary critical context.

Second-Wave Hypertext Theory

Somewhat inevitably, a second wave of hypertext theory seeks to rectify many of the theoretical inaccuracies and methodological limitations that have been identified in the first wave. In particular, while first-wave theory sees the medium as creating a powerful role for the reader, second-wave theory has shown that the structure of the text, and the reader's role within it, represent a means of prohibiting her or him from fully engaging with the narratives that hypertext novels contain. Aarseth (1994), for example, defines hypertext in terms of its capacity to cause feelings of estrangement. He notes that as a consequence of the reader's choices, 'the main feature of hypertext is discontinuity – the jump – the sudden displacement of the user's position in the text' (69). Considering the role of the reader in hypertext narratives, Snyder (1996) also notes that 'the need to make choices never lets you forget that you are participating in the making of a fiction' (89). Similarly, Ryan (1998) recognises that hypertext fiction narratives appear more artificial to readers because their absorption in the narrative is continually disrupted by the proactive role they have to play. Rather than an 'immersive' (Ryan 1998: 143) world, Ryan suggests that a hypertext behaves more like a game, which 'emphasizes the active participation of the reader' (143). In Ryan's analogy, the 'reader is not allowed to lose sight of the materiality of the language and of the textual origin of the referents' (142) because the hypertext structure continually reminds her or him that the text constructs an *artificial* domain. Thus readers' immersive experience in the fictional world is disrupted by the active role they are required to play.

In more recent work, Ryan (2001, 2006) has devoted book-length investigations into the nature of immersion and interaction in electronic texts. In her (2001) study, she shows that varying degrees of what she defines as 'spatial', 'temporal' and 'emotional' immersion apply when reading digital works and in so doing she highlights the anti-immersive attributes of electronic literature. With regard to hypertext, she notes that 'immersion remains a rather elusive experience' (19) because 'every time the reader is asked to make a choice she assumes an external perspective on the worlds of the textual universe' (20). Similarly, in her most recent study, Ryan (2006) suggests that certain types of text seem to anticipate if not enforce a particular type of narrative. In particular, she suggests that hypertext is 'better suited for self-referential fiction than for textual worlds that hold us under their spell for the sake of what happens' (109). The reader, she argues, is inevitably held back from the narrative because the hypertext's 'external/exploratory interactivity ... promotes a metafictional stance, at the expense of immersion in the virtual world' (109). In each investigation, Ryan identifies an almost inevitable partnership between the hypertext form and alienation from the fictional worlds they describe.

Aarseth, Snyder and Ryan each recognise that the reader's external position is emphasised in hypertext narratives because her or his role as co-constructor draws attention to the artificiality of the reading experience. Moving away from first-wave claims about the power of the reader, therefore, they emphasise the reader's role in the fiction-making process. According to their theoretical conjectures, readers cannot fully engage with hypertext narratives because they are held back by the interactive role they are required to play. Yet because their work is concerned with developing *theories* of hypertext, they often, like many of the first wave, focus on mechanisms that occur *outside* the text. That is, they are committed to making general conclusions about the hypertext medium rather than linking them to the narratives that they contain. Thus, while the aforementioned studies produce more accurate observations than the first wave's misinterpretation and overestimation of the reader's role in Storyspace hypertext, their work has a predominantly theoretical focus and, perhaps with the exception of Ryan (2001, 2006), contains few sustained applications to individual works.

In studies which have a more analytical focus, hypertext theorists have shown how the interactivity of the hypertext medium has been utilised in some hypertext novels to yield particular types of narrative. Moving further away from the first wave which emphasised the uniqueness of the medium from a material perspective outside the texts, second-wave analyses consider how the medium affects or corroborates with the narrative inside texts. Making similar conclusions to Aarseth, Snyder and Ryan, Bolter (2001) recognises that the hypertext medium causes feelings of estrangement because 'whenever the reader comes to a link and is forced to make a choice, the illusion of an imagined world must break down, at least momentarily, as the reader recalls the technical circumstances of the electronic medium' (138). However, he also points out that the narrative devices *within* hypertext novels are often used to intensify that experience. In particular, he suggests that while 'it may be possible for a reader to ignore these [reading] circumstances, ... interactive fictions are [usually] calculated to make the reader aware of their links, their technical circumstances' (138). Bolter's observations improve on the general observations of the first-wave theory because his conclusions are drawn from engagements with individual texts. Focusing on Storyspace novels in particular, he suggests that alienation is achieved by the reader's interactive role and also by narrative devices such as contradictory stories, non-chronological ordering of events, overtly visible navigation tools, and the use of intertextual references (121–38). In each case, he argues, the 'rhetorical displacement draws attention to itself and therefore away from any simple illustration the narrative might create' (138) so that the reader is always aware of the inherent artificiality of the narrative that they are uncovering.

As each theorist above notes, estrangement in hypertext is usually a consequence of two separate but integrally related characteristics. First, the reader's role outside the text draws attention to the artificiality of the narrative because they are always aware that they are involved in the construction of the text. In addition, as Bolter in particular notes, self-reflexive devices within some Storyspace novels draw further attention to the physical and hermeneutic role of the reader. Thus there is an interdependent connection between the medium and the narrative which has a significant effect on the reader's experience.

The Question of Uniqueness

The self-reflexive tendencies of Storyspace hypertexts that have been identified so far are certainly not unique to digital texts. Estrangement can be found throughout print fiction beginning with the self-reflexive playfulness of *Tristram Shandy* to the more experimental strategies that McHale (1987, 1992) has found in postmodernist literature (cf. Waugh, 1984; Hutcheon, 1988, 1989). Some hypertext theorists have made explicit connections between hypertext fiction and particular types of print literature. In his examination of hostile reader responses to Storyspace hypertext, Punday (2004) reflects that he 'was struck by how similar they were to the complaints made about narrative engagement in the self-conscious, playful metafictional narratives prominent in America in the 1960s and 1970s. I have in mind stories and novels in which the narrative is interrupted to reflect on itself to such a degree that forward progress becomes impossible' (88). Ryan (2006) also suggests that Storyspace hypertexts often remain 'faithful to post modern aesthetics' (144) because of their tendency for epistemological and ontological contradictions.

Koskimaa (2000) makes similar comparisons between hypertext novels and other types of contemporary fiction, but he is more committed to the distinctiveness of the digital medium. He identifies a tendency within certain types of fiction for what he calls *ontolepsis*, 'a narrative device which strongly foregrounds fictional ontology' through 'the "leaking" of ontological boundaries'. Ontolepsis, according to Koskimaa's analyses, is used as a means of categorising narrative devices which result in incompatible or contradictory versions of a fictional world including embedded narration and alternative versions of narrative events. While he recognises that such ontological self-reflexivity can be found in a range of different text types, he suggests that ontolepsis is a likely, if not inevitable, component of hypertext fiction. 'In postmodernist fiction' he argues, 'it [ontolepsis] is used as a metafictional device to foreground ontological questions, ... In hypertext fiction *ontolepsis* is an integral, unavoidable part of the representational logic' (Koskimaa, 2000). According to Koskimaa's typology, while postmodernist fiction authors deploy similar narrative devices to those found in hypertext fiction, they do so voluntarily. He suggests, however, that hypertext fiction authors inherit self-reflexivity from the medium in which they are writing. Thus, while there may be fundamental similarities between print and digital texts, Koskimaa suggests that there are also some subtle but very significant differences.

It is an inevitable consequence of the generic diversity of Storyspace novels that it is difficult, if not impossible, to classify all hypertext as postmodernist. More importantly, without analyses to substantiate such a view, it would be wrong to attribute software with the ability to create a particular type of writing or period style such as metafictional writing or postmodernist fiction. Further, while some theorists have allied some Storyspace novels with postmodernist print fiction, others contradict such claims. Aarseth (1997), for example, suggests that 'although *afternoon* is playing postmodernist games, these are marginalized by the modernist devices' (87–8). Pressman (2007) draws similar conclusions in her analysis of the text. Whether all Storyspace hypertext can be defined as postmodernist or not remains to be seen and such a strict generic classification is not the principle aim of this study. However, as the theorists above suggest and as the four analyses will show, the alienation that the medium causes for the reader outside the text and the narrative devices that draw attention to the artificiality of the narrative inside the text often resemble those that can be found within other types and forms of contemporary fiction.

As the superficial associations between Storyspace hypertext narratives and some types of print fiction imply, hypertext may not necessarily offer new narrative devices. It does, however, offer authors an alternative context in which to place them. Irrespective of whether the devices that hypertexts contain are familiar or unique, the novels require a method with which they can be analysed if they are to attain and retain their place within a literary canon. Thus, while observations about the displacement of the reader in hypertext are significant because of the common features that they isolate, without indicative examples of how and where such displacement operates within specific texts, they remain somewhat ineffective. Similarly, while a number of features have been identified as idiosyncratic of Storyspace hypertext narratives, hypertext theory still lacks an appropriate and systematic framework with which the narrative devices can be analysed.

Hypertext Fiction and Possible Worlds Theory

As the discussion has shown, since readers are required to participate in the construction of all hypertexts, often choosing from a number of different possibilities, their role in the fiction-making process is emphasised. In addition, however, because readers of Storyspace hypertexts experience different events, different versions of events, or a different ordering of events, depending upon the path they choose to take, the narrative structure of the novels further foregrounds the artificiality of the text. The reader is always aware that the current reading path can be replaced by an alternative so that it is apparent that it is only ever a temporary *construction*. In addition to the branching structure that the Storyspace software facilitates, as the theorists above verify, many Storyspace hypertext novels also contain additional self-reflexive features within the narratives which draw further attention to their artificiality. Thus several devices combine to draw attention to the ontological status of the fictional world that the reader helps to materially and mentally construct.

As a consequence of the ontological self-reflexivity that can be observed within Storyspace hypertext, a number of theorists (e.g. Koskimaa, 2000; Ryan, 2001; Bell, 2007 and forthcoming) identify Possible Worlds Theory as a suitable analytical framework from which such texts can be analysed. Ryan's work is particularly pertinent in this respect because she is influential and prolific within both hypertext theory and Possible Worlds Theory in literary studies. Superficially substantiating the theoretical connections made between hypertext fiction and other types of referential literature, Possible Worlds Theory has also been used to analyse postmodernist print fiction (e.g. McHale, 1987, 1992; Ashline, 1995; Punday, 1997).

The fundamental basis of all facets of Possible Worlds Theory can be traced to Leibniz's (1710 [1952]) philosophical tracts in which he proposes that God firstly conceives of every possible world and then chooses one for us to inhabit; this becomes the actual world. He pledges that 'even though one should fill all times and places, it still remains true that one might have filled them in innumerable ways, and that there is an infinitude of possible worlds among which God must needs have chosen the best, since he does nothing without acting in accordance with Supreme Reason' (128). According to this doctrine, the Christian God did not create one world and subsequently perfect it. Neither did she or he indiscriminately choose a domain for humans to inhabit. Rather, the Christian God chose the world from a collection of possible worlds using a process of rational and deliberate reasoning. According to Leibniz, therefore, the world that we inhabit is surrounded by a number of other possible worlds; worlds which might have been or which could be.

In a logical and philosophical context, Leibniz's principles are developed into a system that can be used to evaluate the truth value of statements by measuring them against a modal system (e.g. Kripke, 1963, 1972; Hintikka, 1967, 1989; Lewis, 1973, 1983a, 1983b, 1986; Plantinga, 1974, 1979, 2003; Rescher, 1975, 1979). Taking influence from Leibniz, at the centre of the modal system is the 'actual world' which is the world to which we all belong. The actual world is surrounded by an infinite number of alternative states of affairs, which are known as possible worlds and they are generated by mental processes such as hopes, fears, wishes, dreams, hypothetical propositions and so on. Within philosophical logic, a statement that is true in all possible worlds represents a *necessary proposition*; a statement that is true in at least one possible world represents a *possible proposition*; a statement that is true in the actual world represents a *true proposition*. As this exposition shows, it is essential that every proposition is assigned to a particular world or worlds. A proposition cannot belong in-between these domains, nor can a proposition be judged outside of the possible-worlds referential frame (see Divers, 2002; Nolan, 2002 for detailed overviews of Possible Worlds Theory in philosophical logic).

Yet while this brief overview of Possible Worlds Theory in philosophical logic suggests that it comprises a relatively coherent and homogenous field, a theoretical schism does exist which has influenced many of its applications. At the centre of the debate is the ontological status of possible worlds. Kripke (1972), for example, argues that 'a possible world isn't a distant country that we are coming across, or viewing through a telescope. ... *A possible world is given by the descriptive conditions we associate with it.* ... Possible worlds are *stipulated*, not *discovered*' (44). He thus maintains that possible worlds do not actually exist; we cannot physically access them. Instead possible worlds are regarded as the product of human mental processes and as such are immaterial. Possible worlds are, according to Kripke, 'ways the world might have been' (18), rather than alternatives that physically exist elsewhere.

Conversely, according to the modal universe constructed by Lewis, the ontological status of all domains is relative. He (1983a) argues that '"actual" and its cognates should be analyzed as *indexical* terms: terms whose reference varies, depending on relevant features of the context of utterance. The relevant feature of context, for the term "actual", is the world at which a given utterance occurs' (184–5). According to Lewis, therefore, someone inhabiting one of the worlds that we regard as "possible" will necessarily regard that world as "actual". Thus, in Lewis's system of reality, the ontological status of all domains is relative; possible worlds and the actual world are therefore ontologically indistinguishable across the entire system of reality because their ontological status depends on the position from which they are viewed.

Nolan (2002) categorises the schism in Possible Worlds Theory as the difference between 'theories which take possible worlds to be "concrete" and those which take them to be "abstract"' (19). While differentiating between theorists who regard possible worlds as concrete existents (e.g. Lewis, 1973, 1983a, 1983b, 1986) – what we might call Concretists – and theorists who regard them as mental abstractions (e.g. Kripke, 1963, 1972; Hintikka, 1967, 1989; Plantinga, 1974, 1979, 2003; Rescher, 1975, 1979) – what we might call Abstractionists – rather simplistically conflates a number of subtly different theories, Nolan's differentiation is useful for illustrating the ontological nature of the disagreement and these terms will be used throughout the rest of this book.

While the ontological debates which exist in philosophical logic might initially appear superfluous to a literary critical context, their disagreements do have ramifications for literary studies. As a product of mental functioning, fictional texts also construct alternative states of affairs and, thus, the worlds that they describe also construct possible worlds. Importantly, the ontological status of fictional worlds and their inhabitants are, as this book will show, absolutely crucial to any literary analysis which uses Possible Worlds Theory as a basis. While we might all agree that fictional worlds are abstract rather than concrete – that is, they do not exist as domains that we can visit or experience materially – Possible Worlds Theory in literary studies has inherited some of the unresolved ontological conflicts from the philosophy on which it draws. Partially, this is because Possible Worlds Theory has been applied within literary studies either without due attention being paid to the unsettled logical debates, or because theorists have allied, either implicitly or explicitly, with Abstractionist or Concretist theorists in order to satisfy their own ontological perspectives with regard to fictional worlds.

More precisely, Possible Worlds Theory was originally developed within the context of literary studies as a means of understanding the ontological status of fictional domains and, consequently, the logical debates surrounding ontology have been crucial to its implementation. Theorists such as Pavel (1975, 1986), Doležel (1976, 1980) and Ryan (1991) have been influential in investigating the truth value of fictional narratives, examining issues such as the ontological distinction between a fictional proposition made in the actual world and an apparently accurate proposition made in a fictional world. Other studies, such as Margolin (1989, 1990, 1996) and Pavel (1979), have focused on the ontological status of fictional worlds and their inhabitants, including the phenomena of a character appearing in more than one text and historical figures from the actual world appearing in fictional narratives. Finally, theorists such as Traill (1991), Ryan (1991), Doležel (1985) and Maître (1983) have devised methods of categorising different types of fictional world according to their relationship with the actual world, with each constructing a taxonomy of fictional possibility relative to genre (see Ryan, 1992; Ronen, 1994 for detailed overviews of Possible Worlds Theory in literary studies).

It is perhaps the diversity of applications within literary studies that has led some to accuse the field of philosophical negligence. Ronen (1994), for example, argues that 'possible worlds is a concept that seems to have been fully incorporated into the literary discipline without a sufficient clarification of its original meaning. The result is a naive adaptation or an inadvertent metaphorization of a concept whose original (philosophical and literary) nonfigurative significance is far from self-evident' (7). Ronen's charges are verified in superficial applications of Possible Worlds Theory which do not acknowledge the conflicting philosophical positions on which they implicitly rest. To avoid producing another inconsistent or theoretically opaque application of Possible Worlds Theory, the analyses will engage with and attempt to reconcile any relevant theoretical debates. Just as importantly, the analyses will be based on a theoretical model which is tailored for and relevant to a literary context.

The modal system is crucial to any analysis using Possible Worlds Theory because, while the unresolved conflicts within philosophical logic suggest an ontological symmetry between possible worlds and fictional worlds, it is important to note that fictional worlds differ from the possible worlds of philosophical logic in a fundamental way. Fictional texts describe both events which are presented as facts as well as alternative or hypothetical states of affairs which are generated by the hopes, fears, wishes, dreams and so on of characters. Therefore, a fictional text constructs not just one fictional world as a particular type of possible world, but an entire fictional system which, like our system of reality, comprises an entire modal system.

Most literary theorists, working within the context of Possible Worlds Theory recognise, either implicitly or explicitly, that fictional texts generate ontological networks. Pavel (1979) notes that 'a number of possible worlds are linked to the actual-in-the-novel world by a usual relation of alternativeness' (190); Eco (1979) distinguishes between 'the possible world ... imagined and asserted by the author' (235) and the 'possible subworlds that are imagined, believed, wished, and so on, by the characters' (235); Doležel (1998a) recognises that a fictional text describes 'fictional facts ... [and] ... private domains, the beliefs, visions, illusions, and errors of individual persons' (151). However, few theorists have developed such observations into an imitable analytical method. Ryan's (1991) seminal work is possibly the only exception.

In her extensive elucidation of Possible Worlds Theory in a literary context, Ryan constructs a modal system which respects the uniqueness of narrative discourse. Her theory begins with the premise that, when we read a fictional text, we inevitably deictically relocate or, to use her terminology, 'recenter' into a different modal system. Crucially, therefore, she distinguishes between two systems of modality: the 'system of reality' (vii), which is the system in which we live and for which the 'actual world' forms the centre, and a 'textual universe' (viii) which is a modal system projected by a text. The textual universe is, like our system of reality, comprised of a 'sphere which the narrator presents as the actual world ... [and] a variety of APWs [alternative possible worlds] revolving around it' (22) which are created by the mental processes of the characters. That is, just as our system of reality is comprised of an actual world surrounded by possible worlds which are caused by the dreams, wishes, hypotheticals and so on of its inhabitants, so too is the textual universe conceptualised as a having an actual world surrounded by possible worlds which are created by the dreams, wishes, hypotheticals and so on of its inhabitants – in this case, the characters.

The textual universe that Ryan presents, though ontologically distinct from our system of reality, has a very similar modal configuration: an actual world is surrounded by alternative possible worlds. Reflecting the similarity as well as the difference between the two systems in her terminology, at the centre of Ryan's textual universe sits what she calls a 'textual actual world'. In her more extensive model, which also encompasses non-fictional texts as well as texts which are generated by lies and errors, Ryan also proposes the ontological category of a 'textual reference world'. This, she defines, as 'the world for which the text claims facts; the world in which the propositions asserted by the text are to be valued' (vii). In analysing our system of reality, the textual reference world is used as a means of distinguishing between what is presented as fact and what actually exists. Thus, it has an essential function for the analysis of non-fictional narratives. As Ryan explains, when someone makes an error, the textual actual world that they present unknowingly conflicts with the textual reference world because they describe something which does not exist in the actual world. Conversely, when someone lies, the textual actual world that they present knowingly conflicts with the textual reference world because they describe something that they know does not exist in the actual world (26–8).

Ryan's distinction between a textual reference world and a textual actual world can be used as a means of assessing the truth value of the claims made in non-fictional texts. In the context of fictional discourse, however, the textual reference world is rendered redundant because, in the textual universe, we can never know whether the descriptions of a textual reference world verify or contradict its actual status because it does not actually exist. As Ryan verifies, in fiction, a 'TRW [textual reference world] does not exist independent of its representation. TAW [textual actual world] thus becomes indistinguishable from its own referent ... [and] this ... makes the concepts TAW and TRW largely interchangeable when discussing fiction' (26). Thus, for the purpose of methodological completeness, the textual universe can be notionally conceptualised as comprising a textual reference world, a textual actual world and alternative textual possible worlds but, in the context of analysing fictional narratives, the first two categories are conflated and a textual universe of fiction comprises a textual actual world and alternative textual possible worlds only.

A modal system based on Ryan's approach is particularly useful to this study because it acknowledges the capacity of a fictional text to project an entire alternative system of reality. During the course of the proceeding analyses, some adjustments, supplementation and modifications will be made. However, as a means of forming an initial framework, the following categories, based on Ryan (1991), will be used:

- The **Actual World** is the ontological domain that forms the centre of our system of reality. In the context of a literary analysis, it is the domain to which the reader belongs.
- **Possible worlds** are ontological domains that represent alternatives to the Actual World. These are created by imaginings, wishes, fears and dreams of inhabitants of the Actual World.
- A **Textual Actual World** is a particular type of possible world which is described and thereby created by an individual fictional text. It is the domain to which the characters of that text belong. It forms the centre of a Textual Universe to which respective alternative Textual Possible Worlds are affiliated.
- **Textual Possible Worlds** belong to the same Textual Universe as the respective Textual Actual World and represent alternatives to what is given as fact in the narrative. Textual Possible Worlds are generated by characters' mental processes such as wishes, dreams or imaginings and therefore constitute possible alternatives to the actual course of events.
- A **Textual Universe** is a modal system comprised of a Textual Actual World and associated Textual Possible Worlds. A Textual Universe is described and thereby constructed by a text.

As the categories above show, as a methodological approach Possible Worlds Theory is extremely proficient at simplifying very complex ontological configurations and also has the necessary terminology for labelling the different ontological domains that are constructed by individual texts. It is precisely because of its capacity for modelling modal structures that Koskimaa (2000) finds Ryan's (1991) version of Possible Worlds Theory particularly useful for analysing hypertext fiction. He argues that while all texts construct alternatives and thereby always implicitly construct a modal system, hypertext fiction makes that system of reality very explicit by literalising the alternative possibilities. 'In hypertext fiction' he argues, 'we have to take the possible worlds model ... for granted – instead of simply imagining that this or that event might have happened in several ways resulting in potentially very different consequences, some of the events really do happen in more than one way'. According to Koskimaa, because Storyspace hypertext fiction novels contain narrative contradictions, Ryan's model can be used as a means of categorising and therefore legitimising conflicting narrative events.

As noted above, Ryan (2001) also sees the potential of her Possible Worlds framework for the analysis of electronic texts because of the tools it provides for modelling the ontological structures that they construct. In an application of Possible Worlds Theory to hypertext fiction, she suggests that using possible-worlds logic 'every lexia is regarded as a representation of a different possible world, and every jump to a new lexia as a recentering to another world, ... This approach is a way to rationalize the texts that present a high degree of internal contradiction' (222–3). Like Koskimaa, Ryan uses Possible Worlds Theory as a way of ontologically legitimising the narrative contradictions that are found within many Storyspace hypertexts. Notably, she uses the method as a means of finding clarity, 'significant areas of ontological stability' (237) in the texts.

Both Koskimaa and Ryan use Possible Worlds Theory as a means of legitimising contradictory narratives or ontological ambiguities. In some ways, connections can be drawn between their use of Possible Worlds Theory and the approaches of the first-wave hypertext theorists, who seek clarity in what are ultimately inconclusive novels. However, Koskimaa's and Ryan's approaches are less interested in determining definitive narrative outcomes than in using Possible Worlds Theory to model intricate ontological structures. Equally, the analyses presented in this book do not attempt to definitively determine what might or might not have happened within Storyspace novels or to eradicate illogical ontology structures. Rather, conducting a number of second-wave analyses, Possible Worlds Theory is used in this book to show, first, how narrative indeterminacy and ontological changeability are generated and, second, how ontological structures are used relative to the themes of each novel.

Fittingly, such an approach, which focuses on the interplay between ontological domains and their internal structures, can ensue without picking definitive reading paths so that lengthy lexia configurations are not necessarily required. Possible Worlds Theory therefore removes the subjectivity associated with first-wave analyses because it is able to accommodate the multi-linear hypertext fiction structure rather than attempting to manipulate it into a pseudo-linear format. An approach that focuses on the ontological peculiarities of hypertext narratives therefore remedies a logistical problem associated with hypertext fiction scholarship generally. As an unavoidable consequence of the multi-linearity of hypertext fiction and the different experiences readers have therein, a common point of reference can be difficult to establish. Readers of Storyspace will experience events in different orders, prioritise some events over others or simply miss out events in their reading. Thus, because of the exponential number of combinations that are possible, any attempt to analyse lengthy lexia sequences will always prove difficult. Higgason's (2003b) definition of hypertext fiction as a 'scholar's nightmare' reflects the logistical problems associated with hypertext fiction analysis.

Offering a means of solving this methodological challenge, the approach profiled in this book moves away from conceptualising hypertext novels in terms of facts or order of events. As the preceding discussion suggests, disentangling the order in which events might or might not have occurred works against many Storyspace narratives. While any analysis inevitably involves selecting specific parts of a text, the examples in this book are given as being *indicative* or *representative* of the way in which each text works as a whole so that the approach can be replicated in other parts of novels. This book thus provides a systematic, comprehensive and overt application of Possible Worlds Theory to Storyspace hypertext fiction. More importantly, however, the applications that follow in the next four chapters are intended to stimulate others within the much anticipated but long overdue context of hypertext theory and analysis.

3
Communication, Contradictions and World Views in Michael Joyce's *afternoon: a story*

afternoon: a story, published in 1987 by *Eastgate Systems,* was one of the first Storyspace hypertexts to emerge. Now, its notoriety extends beyond the field of hypertext studies to the canon of contemporary American fiction (Geyh et al., 1997a, 1997b). Its structural and narrative complexities result in an ontological indeterminacy which is perplexing but which resonates with its thematic concerns. Within the text, navigation is enabled by using 'Yes' and 'No' buttons displayed at the bottom of the window or by the convention of hyperlinks. The links in this novel however are hidden from the user interface so that readers must locate them by clicking experimentally within the lexias, seeking to find words that will provide access to others. As explained by the detailed instruction in the preface, only 'words that yield' {a hypertext} will allow access to other parts of the text. Further restricting the reader's capacity for exploration, the reading paths in *afternoon* are limited by 'guard fields' which prevent readers from accessing specific lexias until they have visited others. Both 'words that yield' and 'guard fields' place temporary restrictions on the structure of the text and readers are often ignorant of the rules governing the reading paths. They represent one of the many ways in which the reader has limited power within and incomplete knowledge of the hypertext and the Textual Actual World that it houses. Utilising the potential of the hypertext form and structure, *afternoon* also offers a number of totally different events or versions of events, depending upon the reading path taken, so that particular events may or may not happen in the course of a reading. Similarly, different scenarios are detailed from alternative perspectives so that a definite series of events is difficult to decipher.

Despite the narrative multiplicity, it is possible to gain an overall impression of the Textual Actual World and its inhabitants. The novel is set in modern-day America and centres around four central characters. Peter is the protagonist. He works with Wert, who may be his wife's new lover, and Lolly his secretary and confidante. Lolly also counsels Nausicaa, who may be Peter's lover. Wert and Nausicaa may also be having an affair. The text pivots around a number of separate incidents, of which the most influential is a car accident, in which Lisa, Peter's ex-wife, and Andrew, his son, may have been involved. As this short synopsis demonstrates, the text houses many unresolved mysteries and the story of *afternoon* is often unclear.

Most discussions of *afternoon* identify a correlation between the reader's search for certainties within the multi-linear narrative and Peter's reluctance to determine the facts of the accident or the affairs (e.g. Douglas, 1992, 1994; Gaggi, 1997: 123–6; Murray, 1997: 57–8; Walker, 1999; Bolter, 2001: 124–8). Adhering to a first-wave agenda, however, the accounts often search for definitive conclusions or show how readers might adopt a particular reading strategy in order to reach narrative resolution. Rather than searching for certainties or offering strategies which might aid such an agenda, this chapter will examine the interplay between possibilities and actualities in the text and show how they work both structurally and thematically. The different paths are certainly important, but their resonance lies in their coexistence rather than their individual credentials as a privileged or authentic solution to what is essentially an inconclusive collection of narratives. In particular, this analysis focuses on the use of ontological boundary violation, narrative contradiction and narrative perspective to show how each device is used to thwart the reader's search for the truth and therefore adhere to the narrator's apparent agenda.

The Entrance to the World of *afternoon*

While *afternoon* houses 539 lexias and 951 links, there is only one entrance to the text. Readers enter the novel through a default title page and subsequent opening {begin} lexia. The {begin} lexia is crucial to the reader's entire experience of the text because of the ontological landscape that it instils and the relationship between reader and narrator that it initiates. It contains the following text:

I try to recall winter. "As if it were yesterday?" she says, but I do not signify one way or another.

By five the sun sets and the night freeze melts again across the blacktop into crystal octopi and palms of ice – rivers and continents beset by fear, and we walk out to the car, the snow moaning beneath our boots and the oaks exploding in series along the fenceline of the horizon, the shrapnel settling like relics, the echoing off far ice. This was the essence of wood these fragments say. And this darkness is air.

"Poetry" she says, without emotion, one way or another.

Do you want to hear about it? {begin}

Primarily, the lexia contains an interchange between two people delivered in first-person narration. A winter scene is described and finally a question is asked. Throughout the lexia, there is consistent use of the definite article, as in 'the sun', 'the car' and 'the shrapnel'. This implies that this winter scene is known to the reader. Similarly, the use of personal pronouns throughout and the associated absence of preliminary proper names provide a very familiar feel to the address; the lack of specificity presumes that the reader knows the referent.

In contrast to the apparent familiarity invoked by the articles and pronouns, however, an elusive atmosphere is also presented. This is largely because the entrance to the text is somewhat poetic and the resulting Textual Actual World is presented rather opaquely. The narrator breathes life into the inanimate objects that surround the two figures. The snow 'moans', oaks 'explode' and rivers are overwhelmed with 'fear'. Yet, contrasting with the dynamism of nature, the two figures are significantly lacking in activity. Their direct speech is delivered without sentiment with the reporting clauses lacking in detail or speech uttered 'without emotion'. Similarly, neither the narrator nor the speaker is named. The speech is reported with a personal pronoun, 'she', signifying the gender of the speaker only. The exact time and location is also unspecified. Rather than being given information from which the reader can start to build a definitive Textual Actual World, this mass of indistinct imagery makes the scene seem increasingly mysterious.

While the indeterminacy of the opening is provoking, however, up until the final line, it is not particularly unusual and its narrative mechanics can be analysed as follows. In the first part of {begin}, a first-person narrator communicates information about the winter scene to an unspecified addressee. Since the reader is also witness to the narration, they also constitute an addressee in the Actual World. Yet while such a superficial application of narrative theory can trace the communication channels, according to the tenets of Possible Worlds Theory, it is impossible for a narrator to communicate with a reader directly because they belong to two different ontological domains. A narrator belongs to a Textual Actual World and a reader belongs to the Actual World. Communication between them constitutes a breach of an ontological boundary – something that is logically impossible. Applying Ryan's (1991) model of Possible Worlds Theory to the first part of the {begin} lexia, however, we can legitimise the ontological incongruity of the narrator and reader.

Possible Worlds Theory and Fictional Communication

Principally, Ryan suggests that 'for the duration of our immersion in a work of fiction, the realm of possibilities is ... recentered around a sphere which the narrator presents as the actual world' (22) and, crucially, that 'this recentering pushes the reader into a new system of actuality and possibility' (22). According to Ryan's theory of reading, therefore, when we read a text and consequently access another system of reality, our perspective also moves into that realm. Further, she suggests, when a narrator tells their tale and therefore implicitly addresses an audience, 'whether or not the actual hearers pretend to be part of the projected audience, they do witness in make-believe the transaction ... thus pretending to be themselves members of TRW [textual reference world = textual actual world in fiction]' (75). According to Ryan's theory, whether readers project themselves into the position of the addressee – what she calls a 'substitute hearer' (75) – or whether they see themselves as an additional audience to the communication, they pretend to be part of an alternative system of reality and thus witness the narration within that system.

It is important to emphasise that Ryan's concept of 'recentering' is an epistemological as opposed to an ontological process. Clearly readers cannot become part of the ontological domain to which the narrator and the characters belong as this represents an impossible ontological manoeuvre. However, Ryan's theory can be used to analyse the communicative channels that are opened when we read a text while also keeping the participants in their relative ontological positions. Applying Ryan's theory to the first part of the {begin} lexia, we would conceptualise the reader as recentering into the Textual Actual World of *afternoon* and adopting the position of the substitute hearer within that system of reality.

Ryan's approach is useful because it provides a practical means of conceptualising the communication channels that are opened when a reader reads a text while also maintaining loyalty to, and simultaneously hiding, the ontological status of the participants. In the model, the author and reader belong to the Actual World and the substitute speaker and substitute hearer belong to the Textual Actual World. When reading, the reader recenters into the Textual Actual World either as a direct recipient of the narration or as an additional witness to it. Thus Ryan's communicative model is able to accurately model fictional communication, maintain loyalty to the ontological status of the participants and ensure that the ontological tenets of Possible Worlds Theory are respected.

However, in order to utilise Ryan's model, we must accept that readers do relocate to another system of reality when they read hypertext fiction. While adopting this premise might be largely applicable for the analysis of most types of text as well as some parts of hypertext novels, as the Introduction has shown, readers are often alienated from the Textual Actual World of Storyspace hypertext fictions. Readers might be able to at least partially recenter into a hypertext Textual Universe by conceptualising the worlds that the text describes but, as Ryan (2001, 2006) also acknowledges in her analyses of electronic literature, they are also very much aware of their ontologically alien status in that domain. The fact that the reader must continually choose which link to follow means that they are acutely aware of their position in the Actual World. In addition, as the analysis of the {begin} lexia will show, a second-person address commands that readers do not completely recenter into another system of reality but instead retain their ontological *and* epistemological position within the Actual World. Consequently, for the purpose of this study, a modified version of Ryan's framework is needed for analysing the communication channels because the model must be able to show when the narrator is addressing a textual addressee – known or unknown – and when they appear to be addressing the reader.

Looking beyond Possible Worlds Theory to other theories of narrative, the concept of the 'narratee' as originally conceived by Genette (1980) (also see Prince, 1980 and Chatman, 1978) proves useful. By his own admission (see Genette, 1988: 130–4), Genette's (1980) original definition of the narratee is relatively short and perhaps elusive. However, it can be used here to illustrate the distinction he makes between textual and non-textual entities. He describes the narratee as 'one of the elements in the narrating situation [who is] … necessarily located at the same diegetic level [as the narrator]' (259). In Possible Worlds terms, the narratee is located within the Textual Actual World rather than Actual World space. While Genette suggests that the real reader can identify with the narratee, he makes clear that identification cannot always be presumed (259–60). Thus, while epistemologically, the reader and the narratee fulfil the same role – they each receive the narration either really or hypothetically – they constitute two separate entities. They are ontologically distinct and belong to two different domains.

As the preceding discussion shows, the separation of narratee and reader that Genette proposes relies on an ontological distinction. Translated into a model of Possible Worlds Theory, the reader belongs to the Actual World and the narratee, like the narrator, belongs to the Textual Actual World. Applying the category of narratee to the first part of the {begin} lexia means that the narrator communicates information about the winter scene to a narratee within the Textual Universe rather than to the reader in the Actual World. Within the context of Possible Worlds Theory in a logical context, the category of 'narratee' is attractive because it means that communication is seen to take place between two entities within the same ontological domain as opposed to the alternative ontologically illegal scenario of communication taking place across two different ontological domains – narrator in the Textual Actual World and the reader in the Actual World. As in Ryan's model, the reader pretends that communication is taking place between a speaker and a hearer in the Textual Actual World. However, the model proposed in this book emphasises the reader's epistemological *and* ontological position in the Actual World. While this might initially seem counterproductive in its neglect of the reader's immersive experience in reading, the model accommodates the peculiarity of hypertext fiction. The reader's role as co-constructor of a hypertext fiction means that they are frequently prevented from completely recentering into the Textual Actual World. In addition, as the analysis will now show, the question that is asked at the end of the {begin} lexia demands that the reader retain their position in the Actual World. A model that incorporates a narratee provides an appropriate means of representing that.

Figure 3.1 presents the ontological landscape created by the first part of the {begin} lexia using the proposed Possible Worlds Theory model. The diagram differs from other pictorial representations of worlds within Possible Worlds Theory in which circles or spheres are used to depict ontological domains (e.g. Doležel, 1998a: 186; Ryan, 1998: 162–3). Unlike circular shapes, the rectangular forms may not visually represent what we might recognise as a 'world' shape. However, because one oblong can be placed right next to another, their geometry eradicates a gap that can erroneously imply that an ontological void exists between them. Similarly, oblongs facilitate the visual representation of a definitive

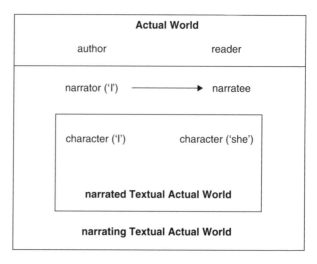

Figure 3.1   The ontological landscape created by the first part of {begin}

boundary between the Actual World and Textual Actual World which is something that will be required throughout this study.

Figure 3.1 shows the position of all participants involved in narrative communication. The reader and the author exist in the Actual World. While they are inevitably involved in narrative communication as the ultimate sender and receiver of information, their roles are performed in the Actual World and thus they always remain outside of the Textual Universe. As the diagram shows, while the narrator and narratee are placed within the Textual Actual World, they do not belong to the same space as the characters. This is because the narrator and narratee's positions are epistemologically peculiar. Whether a character or not, a narrator's role means that they are temporally removed from the action and therefore do not belong to the same space as the events that they describe. As Genette (1980) explains, 'any event a narrative recounts is at a diegetic level immediately higher than the level at which the narrating act producing this narrative is placed' (228), meaning that the narrator is always located at a level above the action about which they are reporting. In order to make this distinction clear, Genette defines the narrator therefore as '*extradiegetic*', a term which acknowledges the separateness of the narrator from what is narrated. It is important to emphasise that a narrator is always placed in a space above the action that they narrate irrespective of whether he or she also appears as a character in that action. Genette (1988) later affirms this point by acknowledging that 'the prefix *extra*diegetic ... seems paradoxical to attribute to a narrator who is ... present (as a character) in the story he recounts (as narrator, of course). But what matters here is that *as narrator* he is "off diegesis," is situated outside of the diegesis' (85). Genette points out that the very act of narrating an event means that a separate space is created in which that narration takes place. Even if the narrator is also a character, they are recounting an experience as well as experiencing it directly and the two functions enforce an epistemological separation.

As a means of representing Genette's diegetic levels visually, the Textual Actual World is split into two separate but closely related domains: a part of the Textual Actual World in which narration takes place and a part of the Textual Actual World in which action takes place (cf. models proposed by Jahn and Nunning, 1994: 285; Dannenberg, 2008: 22–4). These are abbreviated to 'narrating Textual Actual World' and 'narrated Textual Actual World' in Figure 3.1 and they correlate with the *diegetic* and *extradiegetic* levels in Genette's terminology. As the diagram shows, the narrator of {begin} is also present as a character in the narrated part of the Textual Actual World. 'I' therefore corresponds to the same textual entity but, because he fulfils two different roles in {begin}, the 'I' is placed in two different positions on the diagram. As the textual recipient of the narrator's tale, the narratee is also placed within the narrating part of the Textual Actual World. The arrow between narrator and narratee depicts this level of communication. The narratee occupies a position in the narrating Textual Actual World because they are involved in narrative communication rather than in the action that the narrative describes. Yet while the narratee is used to represent the theoretical recipient of the narration, the reader is also the eventual recipient because they are reading the text. Their implicit role in the narrative communication is illustrated by their presence in the diagram but because they are not invoked directly at this point, an arrow is not drawn between them and the narrator.

The modelling of the first part of the {begin} lexia in Figure 3.1 represents a fairly common form of narrative communication in which very little attention is drawn to the textual communication channel between narrator and narratee. The benefit of the model proposed in this book for hypertext fiction analysis becomes apparent when the final line is examined because the question, 'do you want to hear about it?', represents a much more specific form of narration which appears to invoke the reader directly. While the recipient of the first part of the narration in {begin} can be assigned to a narratee, the second-person pronoun heralds the existence of a different addressee. This is because the second-person pronoun is contained within a question to which the reader must respond. In order to proceed to another lexia, the reader must take some physical action – they must reply to the narrator's question, physically responding by choosing a link, pressing 'Enter', clicking on a Yes/No button or typing a response in a box below the text. Thus, while the question could be intended for an as yet undisclosed observer of the scene in the Textual Actual World, the reader's role – as a participant in an interactive document – reduces, if not eradicates, that prospect. The reader is made into the recipient of the narrator's address as a consequence of the interactive role that the hypertext medium ascribes to them. Crucially, their role means that they must retain their position in the Actual World rather than recentering into the Textual Actual World.

As Figure 3.2 shows, as opposed to a channel of communication operating between narrator and narratee in the narrating Textual Actual World, the second-person address in the last line of {begin} appears to establish a direct channel of communication between the narrator in the narrating Textual Actual World and the reader in the Actual World. The hypertext medium further confirms this prospect because the second-person address occurs in a question to which the

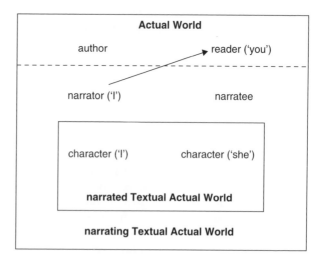

Figure 3.2 The ontological landscape created by the second-person address in {begin}

reader is required to respond. The reader is invited to make a decision regarding their experience of the Textual Actual World – whether they want to hear about the narrator's tale – and they must act in order to move on through the text. While communication between the narrator in the Textual Actual World and the reader in the Actual World is ontologically impossible, the {begin} lexia appears to facilitate it. Although impossible according to possible-worlds logic, an ontological boundary is crossed. If Ryan's theory of recentering were applied, it would under-emphasise if not detrimentally neglect the ontological and epistemological position of the reader at this point. They cannot fully recenter because they have to remain in the Actual World in order to make a choice. The model proposed here, which emphasises the ontological distinction between the reader in the Actual World and the narrator in the Textual Actual World, can more readily accommodate the ontological breach.

In his analysis of second-person narration in postmodernist print fiction, McHale (1992) recognises that a second-person address to a reader has an implicitly 'transgressive nature' (94), leading to 'ontological scandal' (94) in its apparent disregard for the discrete narrative levels. The transgression of ontological boundaries is made all the more apparent in *afternoon* because any decision that the reader makes and associated action that they take can only ever take place in the Actual World. They must type or click. Thus their interactive function separates them from the domain that the narrator describes and emphasises their role in the construction of a fictional world. It reminds the reader of the multi-linearity of the entire text, alerting them to the idiosyncrasies of the hypertext structure and the different narrative possibilities within. While uniting the narrator and reader in a dialogue, therefore, the question also separates the two ontological domains to which they belong. As such the ontological disparity between the reader in the Actual World and the narrator in the Textual Actual World is made very explicit. Applying the model proposed here means that communication is shown to take place between narrator and reader and this compromises the logic of Possible Worlds Theory. However, this channel of communication appears to be opened by the text and the method of analysis proposed here provides an appropriate means of accurately reflecting it.

Somewhat paradoxically, while the dialogue foregrounds the ontological disparity between the Textual Actual World and the Actual World, since interaction does take place, the division between the two domains also becomes less prominent. McHale (1987) describes such instances as creating a 'semipermeable membrane' (34) – a boundary that simultaneously enforces and breaks down the frontier between the two domains. This semi-permeability is shown by the dotted line in Figure 3.2. If the boundary is conceptualised as a semipermeable membrane, readers are aware of the artificiality of the Textual Actual World but they are also engaged in a private dialogue with the narrator. Thus, while the direct address in {begin} foregrounds the boundary for the reader in the Actual World, it also draws the narrator and the reader closer together. Indeed, irrespective of the ontological mechanics, there is also something quite intimate about being addressed directly by the narrator and being personally invited into her or his world. In addition to its self-reflexive function, therefore, the use of the second-person address in this case also begins to establish an important relationship between the reader of the text and the narrator of the scene.

Since the second-person address occurs at the beginning of the novel, the familiarity of the narrator is rather unsettling because the reader is unacquainted with the narrator and ignorant of his agenda. Somewhat ironically, therefore, the vagueness with which the Textual Actual World is presented by the narrator in {begin} actually impairs the reader's ability to make an informed decision. The narrator asks whether the reader wants to hear about 'it', but because this is at the beginning of the text, the reader is lacking the detail required to know what 'it' is. The Textual Actual World is therefore both ontologically separate and epistemologically opaque at this point. Similarly, because a relationship has not yet been established between the narrator and the reader, readers have no way of knowing whether the narrator will accept their instructions or continue in spite of them. They are ultimately powerless in any role beyond that of link chooser, primarily because of their lack of knowledge about the Textual Actual World and its rules, but more specifically because of the narrator and his agenda. Thus, while readers are empowered by their role as respondent, they are also limited in their ability to make an informed decision.

The Significance of the Ontological Breach

Ontologically, while the invitation by the narrator marks the occlusion from the Textual Actual World, hermeneutically, it also reveals important details about the 'I' of the {begin} lexia. In taking on the role of guardian of the text, the narrator implies that he holds control of the narrative and may divulge information about his story only if he wishes. Yet while the question might initially imply omniscience and omnipotence, the fact that the narrator has to ask whether we want to hear his tale also signals some degree of inferiority and hesitancy. He deems it necessary to confirm our interest in his 'story' before he will continue.

The reticence shown by the narrator in {begin} is also shown by his reaction to the reader's reply. If the reader chooses a negative response to his question, by typing 'No' in the feedback space or clicking the 'No' button, the narrator immediately concurs, 'I know how you feel' {no}. Choosing a negative response to the question represents a rejection of the alternative affirmative. This is a literal possibility in terms of the path, but also a part of the Textual Actual World that is yet to be unearthed. It is a path with alternative possibilities that has not yet been explored and it exists only as something to be explored later. The narrator's condoning response seems to recognise if not favour this. Similarly, the familiarity with which he addresses the reader and the way in which he claims to know how she or he feels immediately draws the two parties together and, by condoning the reader's disinterest in the scene, he allies with them in their apparent reluctance to address the conflict in the opening lexia.

By contrast, choosing an affirmative response, by typing 'Yes', clicking the 'Yes' button or pressing the 'Enter' key, leads to a lexia containing a haunting declaration: 'I want to say I may have seen my son die this morning' {I want to say}. The text appears to retreat from the immediate concerns of the {begin} lexia and the reader is alerted to the protagonist's search for the truth about the day's events. The volatile relationship of the {begin} lexia may be related to his eerie admission, but our desire to hear more about the pressing concerns of {begin} is ignored. In either response therefore, any apparent power that is granted to the reader by the narrator's question is immediately retracted because the narrator ignores our instructions – albeit only temporarily. In addition, although the fork occurs at the very beginning of the novel, it is extremely significant because it epitomises a theme to which the narrative often returns – the protagonist's refusal to address his life. While readers may search for answers within the text, the narrator appears to thwart that investigation from the outset.

Embedded Worlds

After exploring the text further, it is revealed that the anonymous narrator in the opening lexia is the protagonist, Peter, and throughout the novel he is shown to be extremely unreliable in this role. Not only is he unable to confront his Actual World and communicate accurate information about it to his addressee(s), but he also appears unable to fulfil the role of omnipotent and omniscient narrator that he creates for himself in {begin}. The most striking evidence of this is the other narrators which operate throughout the text. In both individual lexias and also lengthier sequences, other voices seem to take control of the narration. Some simply tell their own story, thereby offering new or additional information about specific characters. One lexia sequence details Peter's secretary Lolly's upbringing in the South Mississippi delta. Another tells of Nausicaa's history from drug addiction to recovery. Each provides an individual narrative, describing a particular aspect of the Textual Actual World. Others are more ontologically disruptive. In a lexia entitled {ex-wife}, for example, an observer takes over the narrative and, though unnamed, she or he appears to be someone other than Peter. The narrator begins *in medias res*:

> She'd prefer that little be said about her. Consider her name, ...
> "Lisa ..." Her mother's friends would say, "Sounds a little French doesn't it?" ...
> When they had a child she named him Andrew because it seemed timeless and unlikely to be popular {ex-wife}.

This lexia provides details about the naming of Peter's ex-wife, Lisa, and the impact this has in the choice of their own child's name, Andrew. Significantly, the pronoun used in the final paragraph suggests that this narrator is not Peter. The use of the third-person, 'they', when referring to Lisa and her then husband, Peter, makes a pronominal distinction between the narrator of {ex-wife} and the subjects of that narration and so implies that it is not Peter. Thus, an additional narrator appears to be introduced and the ontological landscape established in lexias such as {begin} is changed. Characters, such as Peter, Lisa and Andrew, exist in the same ontological domain: the narrated Textual Actual World. However, this domain is now narrated from multiple perspectives. Peter sometimes assumes the role of first-person narrator in the narrating Textual Actual World but in the {ex-wife} lexia, the narration is adopted by an unknown third-person so that an additional perspective is presented.

As Figure 3.3 shows, the introduction of a third-person narrator means that the text contains at least two narrators: Peter as narrator and an additional, currently unknown, narrator. However, while another entity has

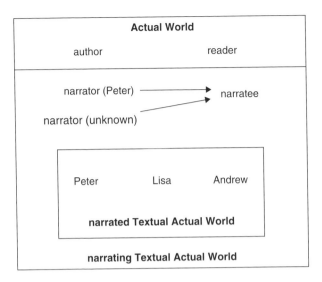

Figure 3.3   The ontological landscape created by {ex-wife}

been added to the narrating Textual Actual World, this is not particularly disturbing to the ontological landscape. Another narrator is added and an additional perspective is posited but the ontological structures remain consistent with those of the {begin} lexia for example. The frequency of link choice, reading paths and narrative contradictions within *afternoon* may mean that changes in perspectives do not represent a particular challenge to readers. However, it is precisely such complacency that the text exploits. It encourages conclusions to be drawn about the ontological landscape before subverting or unsettling them in the other areas of the novel.

Like many other examples in *afternoon*, readers discover the true status of the narrator of {ex-wife} in a lexia which is situated elsewhere in the text so that an explanation will likely be found when readers are in a different reading path or exploring the text in a more experimental fashion. The lexia which clarifies the status of {ex-wife} is entitled {gift of hearing} and reads:

"'She'd prefer that little be said about her' indeed! ... For all your supposed variations, you've written nothing but the same old patterns: the wooden wife, the receptive whore, the all accepting female mind! ...

No. No, you have no right to such a term, not even in passing, not even as part of some supposed narrativistic point of view. ... I mean what could you possibly know of women's friendships, of women's fears, of women's minds?"

Apart from the first sentence, this lexia largely comprises direct speech. It is a critical rebuke from one person directly to another with speech marks indicating that the exchange is verbal. Crucially, the opening sentence is exactly the same as the opening sentence of the {ex-wife} lexia: 'she'd prefer that little be said about her'. This is given as a quotation, signalled by single quotation marks, and its appearance here has consequences for the ontological configuration of *afternoon* as a whole. In the Actual World, the quotation acts as a trigger to remind readers of the {ex-wife} lexia. Even if they cannot remember the exact context, they may well remember the sentence, if not acknowledge that they have encountered it before. The repetition of material is not uncommon in *afternoon*. The clause, 'I want to say', for example, is repeated throughout the text in a number of different contexts. In {ex-wife}, while the sentence, 'she'd prefer that little be said about her', is not repeated as much throughout the text, its recurrence produces the same effect. It provides a dreamlike sense to the text and an accompanying déjà vu feel to readers' experience because it refers to another part of the text which readers may or may not be able to place. The lexia title, {gift of hearing}, also implies listening and perhaps surveillance and suggests that the quoted sentence might have come from elsewhere, as in an overheard conversation. Thus, even if readers have not encountered the {ex-wife} lexia directly, the punctuation signifies that the sentence is to be taken as a quotation. The speaker's references to 'writing' and 'narrativistic point of view' also suggest that they are talking about a written account, particularly some kind of fabricated or fictional narrative. The combination of all these features suggests that the speaker has heard or, more accurately, read the depiction of Lisa and Peter given in the {ex-wife} lexia.

The quoted text in {gift of hearing} is significant because it challenges the status of the {ex-wife} lexia, while simultaneously raising questions about the ontological position of its speaker. Readers do not know how or why the speaker has access to {ex-wife} and consequently the function and ontological location of that narrative is unclear. It appears as if someone else – another textual entity – has read the same text as the reader and therefore someone else has access to the narrated Textual Actual World created in {ex-wife}. In the Actual World, this is disruptive and ontologically challenging because this additional narrator is nomadic – he or she cannot currently be placed in relation to the rest of the text. Readers do not know why this character has access to the text or from what position he or she is reading.

The ambiguity that the additional narrator causes is immediately resolved because the only available hyperlink leads to the following text:

> "Fuck this! – I say – I don't need this…" I stop this short. It is what she wishes me to do. {salt washed}

In this succeeding lexia it is revealed that the text in {ex-wife} forms part of a dialogue between Peter and a female confidante. Peter is restored as the first-person narrator in {salt washed}. Working backwards, his confidante is the critic in {gift of hearing} and Peter is the narrator of his own tale in {ex-wife}. Therefore, what appeared to be two different narrators – Peter as first-person and an unnamed third-person – are actually the same. Readers learn from {gift of hearing} and {salt washed} that sometimes Peter adopts the first-person and sometimes Peter talks about his life using the third-person. However, when Peter uses third-person, other characters have access to this narrative.

The {gift of hearing} lexia therefore reveals that {ex-wife} comprises part of a written narrative and as Figure 3.4 shows, it represents an additional Textual Actual World that is embedded within another.

The surrounding narrated Textual Actual World is the domain to which Peter and his female confidante belong and in which {gift of hearing} and {salt washed} are situated. The action described in the {begin} lexia also belongs to this Textual Actual World because Peter is narrator of this domain. As Figure 3.4 shows, the Textual Actual World to which the Peter of the {begin} lexia belongs surrounds an additional Textual Actual World because Peter's narrative in {ex-wife} constructs an additional fictional domain which is embedded within the original. In this embedded domain, Peter is still the narrator because he narrates his own tale albeit using the third-person. However, as the diagram also shows, there are multiple recipients of Peter's embedded narrative. The first is the corresponding narratee who is situated in the embedded narrating Textual Actual World. As in all narratives, embedded or not, this hypothetical entity is used as the textual incarnation of the actual recipient – in this case, the female confidante referred to in {salt washed}. Thus, because the female confidante also receives Peter's narration, she is an additional recipient. Finally, the reader in the Actual World ultimately receives this narrative.

While the analysis shows that Peter's embedded narrative has several recipients, the multiple addressees are not the cause of the resulting ontological effect. The ontological disturbance is caused because an

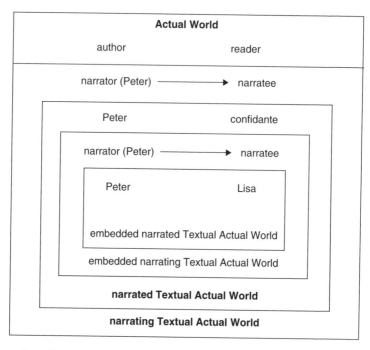

Figure 3.4   The ontological landscape created by {ex-wife} with clarification from {salt washed}

additional embedded ontological domain is introduced into what has largely been presented as being one Textual Actual World. The {ex-wife} lexia appeared to be an alternative perspective in the same Textual Actual World as the one in which Peter's first-person narrative is situated but this is shifted by the {gift of hearing} and {salt washed} sequence so that an additional ontological domain is created. Moving the narration and action in the {ex-wife} lexia into an ontological domain quite separate to its initial position means that, rather than it forming part of the original Textual Actual World, it comprises a Textual Actual World *within* a Textual Actual World. McHale (1987) uses the metaphor of 'Chinese box worlds' to describe the recursive structure that occurs when additional narrative levels are introduced (112ff.). He suggests that while some texts contain ontological structures that can be clearly ascertained, 'postmodernist texts ... tend to ... deliberately mislead the reader into regarding an embedded, secondary world as the primary' (115). McHale suggests that such deceptive recursive structuring is a typical feature of postmodern fiction. Yet irrespective of whether we classify *afternoon* according to this period style, the resulting effect is the same because as McHale argues, when the truth is revealed it 'intensif[ies] ontological instability, titillating and horrifying the reader' (116).

The effect of the ontological revelation in *afternoon* is certainly unsettling because the addition of another Textual Actual World unexpectedly destabilises the original landscape. In response to the ontological shift, readers must reconsider where the characters and the worlds sit in relation to each other, causing disorientation or confusion if only temporarily. This creates a feeling of uneasiness because the reader's original relationship to the text is disturbed. Implicitly trusting that the narrator was describing the original Textual Actual World, readers realise that they have been deceived. Any uncertainty does lessen when a stable ontology is established. However, readers will likely feel suspicious and perhaps question the status of the rest of the text because the evidence suggests that the entire Textual Universe is no longer stable – it has been and might again be subject to unpredictable change. Thus while reconciliation can be reached by seeing the {ex-wife} lexia as creating a world within a world, the ontological ambiguity that such a shift creates means that the ontological status of the different narratives within the whole text is called into question. After an encounter such as the unanticipated embedding of ontological domains, of which there are others, readers cannot be sure how much of the rest of the text is the Textual Actual World in which Peter resides and how much is the Textual Actual World of his own construction. That is, how much of the world is textual reality and how much is textual fiction. Thus, in addition to the epistemological barriers enforced by the text's vastly complex structure, readers are also inhibited in their search for the truth by the unpredictability and volatility of its ontological structures.

The Significance of Embedded Worlds

Significantly, while the ontological shift is disruptive, the narrative's thematic concerns remain unaffected by this device. That is, if readers encounter {gift of hearing} and {salt washed} but not the {ex-wife} lexia, they will still learn that Peter has to articulate his past as a written story, rather than providing an oral account. From this perspective, it is of no consequence as to what is described by Peter's narrative. The significance lies in the fact that the counselling session revolves around a story; Peter can only confront his life by fictionalising it. Without seeing the textual source – Peter's written account in {ex-wife} – the significance of the change in narration from third- to first-person will be missed and the ontological significance of the quotation will also not be perceived. In fact, the ontological trickery will be entirely removed because readers will not experience the required renegotiation. However, hermeneutically, Peter's procrastination is evident in either case and it becomes increasingly clear that he cannot confront his own reality directly.

Logical Contradictions in *afternoon*

The embedding of ontological domains, though significant, is not the sole source of ontological disruption in *afternoon*. Similarly, Peter's marital status, while the source of some emotional difficulty for him, is not the only event in his life which he can cannot confront directly. Irrespective of the paths that the reader chooses, they will often return to the declaration in the {yes} lexia: 'I want to say I may have seen my son die this morning'. Throughout the text, this statement is used to signify Peter's inability to articulate or find out about the possible death of his son. Coupled with the procrastination shown by Peter throughout, however, the structure of the text also offers additional means of representing Peter's reluctance as well as obstructing the reader's search for answers.

Utilising the ontological multiplicity that the hypertext form facilitates, *afternoon* houses a number of totally different and sometimes contradictory events depending on the path taken. Crucially, they are each presented with equal validity but present irresolvable ontological conflicts. Some lexias suggest that Peter's wife and son have been involved in the car accident. Peter recalls 'I felt certain it was them. I recognized her car' {Die}. Other lexias suggest that the accident might have been 'an awful dream' {no, luv} or a case of 'mistaken identity' {what I see}. Providing another alternative, other lexias suggest that the accident may not have involved Andrew and Lisa at all. The {1/} lexia implies that Peter's car has collided with Wert's truck. Each scenario perceptibly contradicts the other so that readers are unsure as to the status of events.

Logical Contradictions in Possible Worlds Theory

As the examples show, *afternoon* contains events that result in internal narrative contradictions. From a methodological point of view, two important laws prohibit contradictions in Possible Worlds Theory and these must be negotiated before it can be applied. First, the Law of Excluded Middle states that the proposition: p OR ~p is true. This means that either something happened or it did not; an in-between state is impossible. In the case of *afternoon*, this would mean that the accident involving Andrew either happened or it did not; a state of irresolution is not permitted. Second, the Law of Non-Contradiction states that the proposition: p AND ~p is false. This means that it is impossible to have a world in which two contradictory states occur simultaneously. In the case of *afternoon*, this correlates to the accident involving Andrew both happening and not happening simultaneously. In either scenario, such propositions which break either the Law of the Excluded Middle or the Law of Non-Contradiction are illogical and, in possible-worlds logic, they result in what is known in Possible Worlds Theory as an impossible world.

Yet, while impossibility is illegal within propositional logic, as the existence of narrative contradictions in *afternoon* show, it is entirely possible within a literary context. Consequently, theorists working within Possible Worlds Theory in literary studies have debated the relevance of the two laws that restrict them to analyses of fictional narratives. Ashline (1995), for example, notes that 'the logically impossible is a salient feature in the fictional universe of many works of recent literature' (215) so that 'the once sacred laws of logic have been opened to violation' (215). He defines such texts as causing 'impossible fictions' and suggests that they are a salient feature of 'so-called "postmodernist fiction"' (215). While Ashline perceives contradictory narratives as being representative of a particular period style, namely postmodernism, Doležel (1989) defines contradictory narratives as creating 'self-voiding narratives' (238). He explains that 'fictional worlds constructed by self-voiding narratives are introduced, presented, but their fictional existence is not definitively established' (238) because devices such as irony, self-reflexivity and narrative contradictions weaken their authenticity. He argues that self-voiding narratives make it impossible to decide between 'what exists and what does not exist' (238) because 'on the one hand, possible entities seem to be brought into fictional existence since conventional authentication procedures are applied; on the other hand, the status of this existence is made dubious because the very foundation of the authenticating mechanism is undermined' (238).

While Ashline and Doležel suggest that logical deviance is limited to particular types of text, Ronen (1994) regards such violations as an unavoidable component of all types of fiction. She argues that 'the literary interpretation of possibility is ... bound to make use of possible world notions in a way that intensifies the autonomy of fictional worlds at the expense of doing justice to the *logical* meaning of possibility' (61, my italics). Ronen suggests that all fictional worlds compromise possible-worlds logic to some extent because the autonomy of a Textual Actual World is the primary concern of a text. This is, she suggests, because the concerns of fiction are not those of possible-worlds logic. Most obviously, fictional texts construct worlds that readers interpret and enjoy rather than measure propositions against.

From an interpretative point of view also, Ronen suggests that readers are adept at conceptualising worlds which do not necessarily obey the logic laws of the Actual World so that contradictions are not necessarily epistemologically problematic. 'The coherence of fictional worlds', she argues, 'does not collapse when a world of the fictional type contains inconsistencies or impossibilities. That is, the understander of fiction can make propositions about fiction that are either logically consistent or inconsistent' (93). Ronen emphasises that a fictional text can create any manner of worlds, logically possible or otherwise. They might contravene the laws of logic but, while readers might not regard them as corresponding with their experience of the Actual World, they are still able to imagine, conceptualise and comprehend this type of domain. Ryan (1991) also emphasises the varying perspectives that fiction can bring to readers. While she suggests that the 'refusal to organise the textual universe around a single factual sequence amounts to a rejection of plot, a rejection of the mode of intelligibility immanent to narrative organization' (166), she also notes that 'the textual universe is freed from the dictatorship of the modal structure, in which one world is signalled out to rule over all the others' (166). Thus, logical deviance can stretch the constraints of Actual World logic in interesting and refreshing ways resulting in a simultaneity that can never be experienced directly.

While the tenets of possible-worlds logic must be respected, loosening their constraints so that Possible Worlds Theory can be used to analyse texts which defy some of its rules means that its analytical scope is widened. Possible Worlds Theory is therefore not restricted to texts which adhere to Actual World logic or which describe ontological landscapes that are relatively unproblematic. As Ronen and Ryan note, texts do produce unusual ontological structures and logically impossible scenarios which, although impossible in the Actual World, can be processed by the reader. More importantly, while they may challenge some of its axioms, the remit of Possible Worlds Theory is such that it has sufficient conceptual basis and associated terminological vocabulary to analyse and define these ontological configurations. Thus, somewhat ironically, while some texts represent a challenge to its underlying logic, Possible Worlds Theory is an analytical approach that is well suited to texts that describe unusual narrative situations, challenge Actual World logic and produce illegal ontological landscapes.

As a step towards relaxing the laws of possible-worlds logic for application to a literary context, Ronen offers a potential solution to logical contradictions in fiction. She suggests that 'impossibilities can be neutralised relative to different spheres (one proposition does not contradict another – each is valid in another subworld); and indeterminacies (p and ~p) can be made valid when each interpretation of an indeterminate proposition obtains a different ontic sphere' (55). In this approach Ronen classifies each contradictory state as an independent 'subworld'. This allows each conflicting proposition to be true in a particular 'ontic sphere' with each alternative asserting equal validity and authenticity within a particular domain. Maintaining logical integrity, this approach means that contradictions are 'neutralised' or 'made valid' rather than deemed to be illegal. Applying Ronen's solution to this book's terminology, rather than contradictions causing a contradictory Textual Actual World, the Textual Universe would contain multiple Textual Actual Worlds which contradict one another. This approach projects an immediate logical advantage in that it does not dismiss contradictions but instead seeks to extrapolate each possibility or actuality as constituting its own ontological domain.

While Ronen's approach stretches the potential constraints of Possible Worlds Theory by rectifying logical inconsistencies, its hermeneutic limitations can be seen once it is applied to *afternoon*. Ensuring that neither the Law of Non-Contradiction nor the Law of Excluded Middle is broken, each narrative possibility, such as Andrew dying and Andrew not dying, is thought of as creating an independent Textual Actual World within the Textual Universe. In one Textual Actual World, Andrew dies and in another he lives. Yet as the analysis of the {begin} lexia shows above, readers are aware of the alternative possibilities from the very beginning of the novel and the narrative contradictions within the novel are too prevalent to be ignored. If contradictions are neutralised by allotting them to different Textual Actual Worlds, the richness of the narrative is lost because complex events and intricate descriptions are translated into propositions with the sole purpose of resolving logical conflicts and identifying incompatible events.

Similarly, while this approach satisfies possible-worlds logic, it misrepresents the text as well as the reader's experience thereof because it assumes that the reader treats each narrative independently, forgetting the one when others are found. Analysing contradictions in postmodernist fiction, however, McHale (1987) provides a fitting analogy with the written word which has been crossed out. He describes it as 'physically cancelled, yet still legible beneath the cancellation, these signs *sous rapture* continue to function in the discourse, even though they are excluded from it ... [so that] they both cannot be admitted, yet cannot be excluded' (100). McHale suggests that once two alternatives have been posited, it is thereafter impossible for either to be discounted or rejected. In fact, he suggests, the contradictions are meant to be noticed because conflicting narratives have an inevitable ontological consequence. By subverting and thereby undermining world-building conventions, texts which contain narrative contradictions 'lay bare the process by which readers, in collaboration with texts, construct fictional objects and worlds' (100) and thereby draw attention to the conditions under which fictional worlds are usually *constructed*. Ultimately, this results in the artificiality of the fictional world being foregrounded.

The same process that McHale observes in postmodernist fiction can be seen to happen in *afternoon*. While, logically, we know that there can only ever be one true course of events, *afternoon* offers multiple outcomes and thus we are prevented, if not discouraged, from isolating one as definitive. Ryan (forthcoming) sees this as an inevitable attribute of hypertext reading suggesting that 'hypertext aesthetics favors the serendipitous emergence of meaning over a goal-oriented, deliberate retrieval of information' (n.p.) so that, contrary to providing certainties, hypertext encourages readers to prioritise the overall meaning of the text over establishing definitive conclusions. She also suggests that 'the price to pay for guaranteed narrative coherence is the self-renewing power and the emergent meaning of classical hypertext fiction' (n.p.), so that choosing to identify one path results in a hermeneutic compromise.

As the preceding discussion suggests, narrative contradictions do exist in fiction and require a theory with which they can be analysed. In Possible Worlds Theory, splitting the Textual Universe into several Textual Actual Worlds is perhaps unnecessarily reductive, but allowing contradiction to exist within one Textual Actual World requires that one of its fundamental laws must be broken. A violation of the Law of Non-Contradiction means that something both happens and does not happen at the same time. This represents quite a challenge to our own logic because this is something that is impossible in the Actual World. A violation of the Law of the Excluded Middle means it is impossible to establish whether something has happened or not. This projects an immediate advantage over the former approach because it represents an inability to choose between the alternatives that are offered. Not only is this congruous with our experience in the Actual World, it is much more appropriate in a literary critical context because it aligns more readily with the ambiguity found within fiction. In the context of *afternoon*, it allows narrative contradictions to be interpreted alongside other ontological and epistemological inconsistencies that are present within its Textual Universe.

The Significance of Logical Contradictions

Our inability to decipher exactly what has happened in the Textual Actual World of *afternoon* is pertinent because it parallels the protagonist's behaviour. Despite the fact that Peter has seen the aftermath of a car accident and suspects that his son may have been involved, he is unable to confront the situation. While he makes a number of attempts to discover the identities of the crash victims, they are half-hearted and his inquiry is not pursued with much vigour. He visits the scene of the accident but is unable to ask the bystander who was involved and instead remains silent, learning nothing {can I help you?}. By his own admission, he cannot yet face the truth: 'I am still too afraid to have them check for Andy' {3}; 'I do not call the hospital. I take a pill' {I call}; 'part of me does not yet want to know' {I would have asked}. Peter refutes his Actual World in favour of ignorance, so that, in Peter's mind at least, it does not yet currently exist. The narrative logic of the text parallels Peter's reluctance, or inability, to open up the truth by creating an additional layer of uncertainty. Hermeneutically, the narrator, the ontological domain to which he belongs and the reader are all united in a relationship of ambiguity and irresolution.

As the preceding discussion has shown, refusing to choose between the alternatives and thereby allowing contradictions to exist in the text means that Possible Worlds Theory has to be compromised, or perhaps more accurately, amended, when applied to some texts. However, this strategy maintains loyalty to *afternoon* because it does not attempt to mould its multiplicity into a singular narrative – something that the hypertext form itself inherently counters. Further, relaxing the laws inherited by the analytical framework also widens the remit of Possible Worlds Theory generally by a wider range of texts to be analysed using this approach. If Possible Worlds Theory is to become a comprehensive theoretical approach which can encompass all types of text, some of its logical axioms may have to be relaxed and its categories carefully redefined.

Multiple Perspectives and the Manifestation of World Views

As the analysis of the Peter's narrative shows, our impression of the Textual Actual World has to be continually renegotiated in order to accommodate what are often unanticipated changes in narrator or to accommodate narrative contradictions. In the {ex-wife} lexia, what once appeared to be multiple perspectives materialise as one – those of Peter. As has been documented above, however, in some parts of the text, other characters do act as additional narrators so that different perspectives are offered. The use of multiple first-person narrators is not necessarily unusual in a literary text; different characters can often be used to narrate a particular aspect of their life. However, some parts of *afternoon* detail the same part of the Textual Actual World from various perspectives and this results in conflicting accounts which, like the narrative contradictions, prevent the reader from gaining a consistent and coherent impression of the Textual Actual World.

While there are a number of scenes which are presented from different viewpoints, an encounter between Peter and his friend Wert is the most ambiguous. Throughout *afternoon*, the narrative often returns to a scenario in which Peter and Wert are sitting in Wert's office, discussing the possibility of Wert having slept with Peter's partner. Table 3.1 provides the text from a number of lexias, which refer to this particular discussion.

While the lexias are distributed throughout *afternoon* and therefore not necessarily connected to each other with hyperlinks, there are a number of ways in which the lexias can be ordered so as to create chronological coherence. The configuration of {three}, {asks}, {As if}, {he says} creates a logical dialogue between the two men as does {he says}, {three}, {asks}, {As if}. The latter sequence can also be shortened to {asks}, {As if}, {he says} so that the repetition of the question is not detailed.

Yet while the lexias can be ordered mechanically readers are unlikely to experience the scene in this way. Rather, because the lexias can be reached via a number of different routes, Peter and Wert's dialogue will probably be experienced as snapshots rather than an ongoing scene. However, while the reader may encounter the different lexias sporadically, each contains a textual marker which links it to the same conversation. The most overt connection is the question about how one man would feel if the other slept with his ex-wife. In some lexias, such as {asks}, the reference is explicit and reported using direct speech: 'how would you feel if I slept with your ex-wife?' In others, such as {he says} and {he, he says}, the query is implicit with the qualifying clause absent: 'How would you feel?'. In

Table 3.1 Title and contents of each lexia detailing Peter and Wert's conversation

Lexia title	Full text from lexia
{three}	I am boring him. He would rather consider the probabilities of one of us sleeping with the other's wife.
{yes6}	"Are you sleeping with her?" he asks. There are candies in the dish before me. I pick one up and unwrap it carefully.
{asks}	He asks slowly, savouring the question, dragging it out devil-ishly, meeting my eyes. "How … would you feel if I slept with your ex-wife?" It is foolish. She detests young men.
{As if}	It is foolish. He doesn't know her, has never met her. She detests young men. "As if I were your father" I say.
{he says}	"No seriously… How would you feel? I would like to know this." The jelly-filled hard candies in the crystal bowl on the table are, curiously, wrapped Polish hard candies Wert keeps in his office. For a moment I wonder if he has requested that they serve these to him here.
{he, he says}	"No seriously… How would you feel? I would like to know this." The jelly-filled hard candies in the crystal bowl on the table are, curiously, wrapped Polish hard candies Wert keeps in his office. For a moment I wonder if he has requested that they serve these to him here.

{As if}, we can infer that the question has been asked because the speaker's response incorporates text from some of the other lexias; the statements 'It is foolish' and 'She detests young men' provide subtle intratextual references to the free indirect discourse found in {asks}. In other lexias, a more explicit form of acknowledgement is employed; the content of {he says} is replicated in {he, he says} and the duplication of the third-person pronoun, 'he', in the title playfully emphasises the repetition of material which is found in the other lexia. Additional markers include the references to 'candies' in a number of lexias, which spatially locate the exchange, and the repetition of the verbs 'feel' and 'sleep' in various forms which sets up a further reference chain between each description.

Douglas (1994) uses the {asks} lexia in her analysis of *afternoon* to show how the context in which a scene is encountered dramatically alters its resultant meaning. Offering an explanation for how readers make sense of the personal pronouns in the {asks} lexia, she suggests that they 'need look no further than the preceding or succeeding places [lexias]' (15).

While this might be a legitimate explanation for readers who follow the default path, as Thomas (2007a) notes, Douglas 'does not seem to allow for other ways of navigating the text' (368), so that she neglects the other routes through which readers might approach each lexia, including following a link from another part of the text or using the drop-down menu to select a reading point. The lexias are scattered throughout the novel and often interrupt other reading paths, so that the structural configuration of the text means that the re-representations of the Peter–Wert scene will be experienced fragmentally. In such instances, consulting the preceding lexia will likely not provide an adequate solution to the referential ambiguity. Further, Douglas's approach implies that the default reading paths remain static. Yet the guard fields in *afternoon* affect the configuration of permitted reading routes, so that what preceded or succeeded a lexia during one encounter with the {Asks} lexia might not do so in the next. Once a reading path has been chosen, particular lexias might not or cannot be visited according to the order in which they might have originally occurred.

Thomas's method might initially appear to adhere to the same approach as Douglas because she recognises that 'different interpretations of this lunchtime conversation ... necessitate asking how did we arrive at this scene, and where might this take us?' (368). However, her approach goes further than Douglas's because she locates the lexias within the wider context of the entire reading experience and thus acknowledges that the conversation will have different implications depending on the other parts of the text that the reader has explored. Thomas concludes that the scene will have 'far reaching implications of understanding both of the relationships between the central characters and what may or may not have happened to the narrator's ex-wife and child' (367) and points to a number of conclusions that might be made by readers on their encounters with the scene. Engaging with Thomas's conclusions, my analysis will show how the six lexias in Table 3.1 contribute to the ambiguities in the text by positing a range of different perspectives.

The representation of Peter and Wert's conversation is significant because while many of the lexias in Table 3.1 can be correlated coherently, there are a number of significant discrepancies between them. In {three} and {asks}, the speaker asks either about a 'wife' or an 'ex-wife'. This might represent either two different points in time within the same Textual Actual World: one in which the narrator and his partner are together and one in which they have separated. Alternatively, it could represent two different narratives entirely: one in which the couple are divorced and one in which they are not. An additional inference we could make in this instance is that the different designations could be attributed to a mistake on the speaker's part. They may have inadvertently used 'wife' because the split is very recent or it may be intentionally provocative; referring to the ex-wife as 'wife' signifies infidelity much more explicitly. In the other lexias, the female is referred to using the pronoun, 'her', which is a more indeterminate form of reference and allows for both possibilities. That the female remains unnamed hides not just her status, but also that of her (ex-)husband.

In addition to the ambiguity created by the noun phrases, the status of the narrator is also questionable. Most of the lexias are probably narrated by Peter because, throughout the novel, his narrative often returns to his relationship with Lisa. However, in a text which often plays with narrative perspective and ontological structures, it is entirely possible that someone else is narrating one or more of the six lexias in Table 3.1. Further, even if most of the narration is attributed to Peter, there is a deictic shift in {yes6} which suggests a definite change in perspective. The question, 'Are you sleeping with her?', is likely a response to Wert's provocation in {asks}, {he says} or {he, he says}. In this case therefore, 'he' refers to Peter as the person asking the question and the 'me' and 'I' of the first-person narration can be attributed to Wert. The pronoun changes are subtle but significant because they demonstrate that the scene is described by two different narrators. More specifically, it shows that there are two first-person narrators present in this scene.

Importantly, as the analysis of {ex-wife}, {gift of hearing} and {salt washed} shows above, some of the most significant changes in perspective are those in which the narrator's status and their subject matter is ambiguous. When different narrators provide disparate accounts, a similar indeterminacy is apparent. However, while multiple perspectives, narrative contradictions and embedded ontological levels each contribute to an ambiguous and unstable Textual Actual World, the devices are enabled by different kinds of narrative mechanics. When characters write their own story, additional ontological levels are introduced; when events both happen and do not happen, a number of potentially conflicting Textual Actual Worlds emerge. When different versions of a particular event are presented, however, a Textual Actual World can remain consistent but the perspectives through which it is described are multiple. Thus, worlds-within-worlds and narrative contradictions are primarily ontological because they establish different ontological configurations, whereas different perspectives on the same world are primarily epistemological because they offer diverse views about a world.

Analysing Conflicting Perspectives with Possible Worlds Theory

Possible Worlds Theory and the possible-worlds logic on which it is based is an ontological approach which is primarily interested in the truth-value of statements and, within that context at least, the epistemological origin of individual propositions is beyond its methodological remit. However, the analysis of the six lexias above shows that the Peter and Wert scene is presented in a number of ways, through at least two different perspectives, and this has hermeneutic ramifications. While the short analysis of the lexias above shows that each lexia can be assigned to a particular narrator using a process of inference and deduction, like an approach that simply seeks to order the lexias chronologically, limiting the analysis to determining the speaker ignores the resulting effect that the multiple perspectives generate. In a fictional text, the epistemology of propositions is important but in logic it is not. The different agendas therefore represent another potential clash between possible-worlds logic and Possible Worlds Theory in a literary context.

Ronen (1994) articulates the primary difference between the worlds of logic and the worlds of fiction in terms of epistemology. She emphasises that 'information about them [fictional worlds] is *always* perspectivally determined. Unlike other worlds where perceiving and narrating subjects filter or mediate information, in the case of fictional worlds, domains of entities are constituted *through* perceiving and narrating acts' (195, my italics). Recognising the significance of narrative perspective in the construction of fictional domains, Ronen notes that fictional worlds are always brought into existence through narration. Thus, a fictional domain does not exist independently of its representations but rather is constructed *through* representation. This maxim is important within the context of literary analysis because it highlights the subjectivity and associated fallibility of Textual Actual World construction. Within the context of a text such as *afternoon*, which contains multiple first-person perspectives, this is particularly pertinent because it shows why, unlike in logic, it is not always possible to make definitive conclusions about a Textual Actual World. Conflicting perspectives may be provided so that the Textual Actual World and the viewpoints that it contains can be difficult to distinguish between.

Ronen's observations about the epistemological status of fictional worlds suggest that the 'perspectival' aspect of world building is exclusive to the fictional realm. She also implies that in 'other worlds' – that is, in the system of reality to which you and I belong – it is possible to distinguish between an ontological domain and a particular view of it. Some factions of Possible World Theory, such as those categorised as Abstractionist and Concretist, reflect Ronen's view because they rely on a system of reality with one Actual World. Propositions can be evaluated against the Actual World, making it possible to distinguish between what is true in that world and what is not (see Chapter 2 for full elucidation of Abstractionist and Concretist perspectives). However, one faction of Possible Worlds Theory is less convinced by the epistemological accessibility and therefore ontological exclusivity of the Actual World and, in the context of a literary analysis which requires a more flexible approach to ontology, it can be used to form a more appropriate analytical strategy for fictions which contain multiple first-person narrators.

Goodman (1978, 1983, 1984), a Constructivist within Possible World Theory, offers an approach to modality that refutes the existence of an objective Actual World centre within our system of reality. Emphasising the many constructions, embodiments or descriptions of the Actual World that exist, his position suggests that all ontological domains are, like fictional worlds, always experienced subjectively. Goodman (1983) argues that 'what we often mistake for the actual world is one particular description of it. And what we mistake for possible worlds are just equally true descriptions in other terms. We have come to think of the actual as one among many possible worlds. We need to repaint that picture. All possible worlds lie within the actual one' (57). Goodman speaks about the Actual World and possible worlds as if they have the same ontological status. According to this system of reality, possible worlds are individual depictions of events or individual perceptions rather than logically possible alternatives. In addition to individual perceptions, Goodman also proposes that 'versions' of the world exist. His definition of a version is unclear but versions appear to be similar to perceptions in that they are developed according to a 'given science, a given artist, or a given perceiver or situation' (Goodman, 1978: 3) and are created both via 'statements … and in nonverbal media' (Goodman, 1978: 39). Versions, in the preceding quotations, correspond to different interpretations or representations of the Actual World such as scientific theories, news stories, music, fictional narratives or any other form of depiction claiming to be factual or fictional. However, representative of the ambiguity that can be found in his work, such forms of communication could also be described as possible worlds because, as perspectives on the world, they could also constitute 'one particular description' in Goodman's terms.

As the account suggests, Goodman's approach differs significantly from other facets of Possible Worlds Theory because he rejects the concept of a *singular* Actual World. The system of reality that he proposes is relative. Each person is modally centred within their own perspective of the Actual World and so that theirs may be incompatible with any others. As Goodman (1978) asserts 'many world versions are equally right' (39) so that no one world can be privileged over any other – none can be deemed *the* Actual World. According to Goodman's conjectures, there is no objective Actual World but instead multiple versions. Thus, he sees our system of reality as a collection of multiple Actual Worlds each constructed subjectively. Each Actual World constitutes an individual person's view of the world and, according to Goodman's Constructivist position, it is precisely because each person has his or her own view of the world that an objective Actual World is not feasible or, more importantly, accessible. From this perspective, distinguishing between epistemological perspectives and ontological domains is problematic because experiences of the Actual World can never be evaluated against anything other than other experiences. Within the context of possible-worlds logic, therefore, the structure of Goodman's system of reality is at odds with the singular Actual World that is proposed by Abstractionist and Concretist theorists.

Ronen's (1994) analysis of what she calls Goodman's '*anti-realist* view' (23) suggests that his approach is unsuitable for any type of application. She warns that 'the kind of view that Goodman promotes contradicts a sense of division throughout the culture between fiction and reality; treating all worlds as versions of an equal status defies the very ideas that a culture differentiates among its various ontological domains' (24). According to Ronen, Constructivism is analytically inadequate because in refuting an Actual World centre, it appears incapable of distinguishing between actual and possible and thus between reality and fiction. The opaqueness of Goodman's writing and the apparent variability of his categories have resulted in a Constructivist approach which, as Ronen notes, does not appear to be immediately useful in a literary critical context. However, some useful distinctions can be made through meticulous inspection of his work.

Ryan (1998) establishes a valuable differentiation between epistemological and ontological concerns by suggesting that Goodman's 'versions' can take two discrete forms. She argues, 'a version can create "our worlds" by offering something to contemplate to the imagination; or it can create "our world" by shaping our personal representation of what lies at the center' (150). According to Ryan's interpretation,

Goodman's modal system can be split into 'versions' as what *might be* real (possible worlds) and 'versions' as individual perceptions of what *is* real (individual Actual Worlds). While this is a subtle distinction, Ryan is able to discern two types of ontological domain from Goodman's rhetoric. Moreover, while Goodman's work initially appears to deny the existence of a singular Actual World, Ryan's analysis suggests otherwise. As she points out, 'a version, by definition, is a version of something' (148). Thus, somewhat paradoxically, Goodman's deployment of the term 'version' actually relies on the existence of an original. Adopting Ryan's interpretation, we can conclude that Goodman does not deny that there is a world behind versions but only that it is not possible to reach it or test the different versions against it.

As the preceding discussion shows, Goodman's apparent refutation of *the* Actual World as well as the perceptible similarity between 'versions' and 'possible worlds' that he posits complicates the ontological status of many of his categories. The different responses to his position, as shown in Ronen and Ryan's accounts, also demonstrate that his evasive interpretation of Possible Worlds Theory generates debate and contradiction amongst literary theorists. In its current state, therefore, Goodman's modal system is too ill-defined and contentious for an unmitigated application within literary studies. It is perhaps for this reason that, to date, his approach has not been fully implemented within that context. Yet Goodman's Constructivist perspective, though largely inconsistent with other facets of possible-worlds logic, is not necessarily entirely incongruous with the model of Possible Worlds Theory proposed in this study. In fact, Goodman's analysis of our system of reality and its emphasis on the epistemological nature of ontological domains can help inform the analysis of the elusive Textual Universe purported in *afternoon*.

Applying Goodman and Constructivism within a Fictional Context

Ryan (1991: 109ff.) offers a means of analysing the fictional perspective which, because of its emphasis on fictional beings as carriers of subjectivity, resembles Goodman's system of reality to some extent. She presents the Textual Actual World as the ontological centre of the Textual Universe but she also conceives of a number of categories which 'relate to the private worlds of characters' (1991: 111) in order to make a distinction between 'what exists absolutely in the semantic universe of the text, as opposed to what exists in the minds of characters' (112).

Principally, Ryan sub-divides the private worlds of characters into three types. First a 'knowledge world (K-world) [is] cut out from the general realm of perception' (111) and so corresponds to a view of the world. Second, 'a wish-world (W-world) [is] extracted from subjective value system judgements' (111) and so corresponds to an ideal form of the world. Thirdly, 'an obligation-world (O-world) [is] dictated by social rules of behaviour' (111) and so corresponds to what is required in the world. While Ryan places each within the same 'epistemic system' (111), she also stresses that there is an integral difference between the categories. Crucially, 'these constructs ... are conceived as either images of TAW [Textual Actual World] (K-world) or as models of what it should be (W-world, O-world)' (111).

The distinction that Ryan makes between 'images of TAW' and 'what it should be' is important because it differentiates between what is potentially *actual* and what is currently only *possible*. A wish is different to a particular account precisely because a wish is something that does not exist in the Textual Actual World; it is desired. As a proposition, therefore, it constitutes a Textual Possible World because it does not correspond to the current state of the Textual Actual World. Similarly, an obligation expresses an impeachment to act and so is a form of potential *future* commitment. Again this does not correspond to the current state of the Textual Actual World but comprises a possible scenario – a Textual Possible World. Yet, while a W-world and O-world can be defined as Textual Possible Worlds within a Textual Universe, a particular account of the world is always *thought* to be true. It portends to the epistemic as opposed to the ontological. It may be verified by the text and become the Textual Actual World or it may be proved as false and become a Textual Possible World. Whether verified or not, however, it is a view of a world. While my analysis of Ryan's framework suggests that there is a subtle but important existential difference between the three categories, the current terminology hides these respective characteristics because the single-letter prefix of either 'W', 'O' or 'K', followed by the root, 'world', currently emphasises the *ontological* nature of all three.

As a more appropriate term, 'World View', allies with the German, *Weltanschauung*, meaning world view or perspective. This is a deliberately different denotation from the alternative 'View World', which, like K-world, implies that it is always an ontological domain. Taking influence from Goodman's Actual World model and his 'versions' of worlds, the term 'World View' can be used to denote a perspective *on* a world. Since a World View represents a *view* of the world, as opposed to a world state, and is therefore epistemic rather than ontological, it is fluid. It can change in light of new information or under different circumstances. It can be used to refer to either a spatial, temporal or political view. It can also be applied to different circumstances. Its designation as a projection of a particular view acknowledges that they may be multiple but it does not necessarily enforce hierarchy or necessitate judgement about authenticity or legitimacy. Each 'World View' might be equally valid.

Importantly, a World View is, like Ryan's K-world, different to other domains that can also be constructed by characters. In Ryan's framework, for example, F-universes are 'formed by mind's creations: dreams, hallucinations, fantasies, and fictional stories told to or composed by the characters' (119). However, unlike an epistemological perspective, this type of domain is always ontological in nature and corresponds to what has been analysed as a Textual Actual World within a Textual Actual World in {ex-wife} and {salt washed} above. The different perspectives given in the Peter–Wert conversation are very different to the fictional narrative that Peter constructs. As Ryan acknowledges, 'heroes of fictional fictions may write fictions. This type of recursive embedding differs from the one we have observed in K-worlds in that it does not propose ever new points of view on the same system, but transports the experiencer to ever new realities' (119). The distinction that Ryan asserts between a K-world and F-universe makes visible the epistemic as opposed to ontological nature of a World View. It is a 'point of view' as opposed to something that constitutes an 'ever new reality'.

Thus, while perhaps terminologically misleading, the theory behind Ryan's K-world provides a means of analysing epistemology in a system of reality and can inform its application as 'World View' here. Applying her term to our own experiences in our system of reality, Ryan notes that 'in a first-person perspective, K-worlds may be either complete or incomplete with respect to their reference world, but never mistaken, since we have no external access to the reference world' (115). Our inability to distinguish between the Actual World and our perspective from which we view it, which Ryan emphasises, echoes Goodman's conviction that the Actual World is only ever experienced as a particular version. Ryan points out that from our perspective, in our system of reality, our K-world – or our World View – *is* the Actual World because we regard our own beliefs and experiences as accurately representing that domain. In addition, because we do not have any other direct access to the Actual World we always experience the Actual World from our point of view. Thus, as Ryan explains 'in a third-person perspective, the modal operators of the K-world are computed by comparing the truth value assigned to propositions by the subject with the objective truth value in the reference world (which may turn out to be the truth value assigned by a third party)' (115). She explains that when we experience the third-person perspective – that of another person – in the Actual World, we judge its truth claim relative to our own experience and therefore conception of the Actual World. Thus we can assess the validity of other people's point of view by judging them according to our beliefs but, again, we can never experience other people's perceptions directly.

Somewhat exceptionally, in a fictional context, we *do* experience an ontological domain through another person's perspective – that of a narrator. In first-person narration, one character is solely responsible for the construction of a Textual Actual World so that we cannot distinguish between the Textual Actual World and the narrator's view of it. In this case, when only one World View is given, this then constitutes the Textual Actual World. Even if other characters express their opinions or views on a scenario – other World Views – these will always be communicated through the first-person narrator so that this information is always filtered. We might compare the different perspectives, but the Textual Actual World is still given according to the World View presented by the first-person narrator. Thus, the World View of the narrator is equal to the Textual Actual World. Similarly, in third-person narration, we also experience the Textual Actual World through the perspective of another: a third-person narrator. In this case, readers can determine whether different World Views correspond to the Textual Actual World by comparing the perceptions of characters with the status of the world as defined by the authoritative narrator (see Doležel, 1998a: 145ff.; Palmer, 2004 for similar approaches). During the course of a reading, it might be necessary to assign different World Views to their respective ontological status of Textual Actual or Textual Possible as and when a particular World View is confirmed or falsified. In this case, epistemological beliefs become ontological domains; one World View becomes the Textual Actual World and all others are classified as Textual Possible Worlds.

As Ryan also recognises, however, there are problems associated with finding an authoritative source in some fictional narratives because narrators can offer misguided or erroneous perspectives on the world that they describe. Ryan notes that 'the existence of unreliable narrators in fiction represents a possible gap between the world projected by the narrator's declarations ... and the facts of the TAW [Textual Actual World]' (113). Yet, while she recognises the fallibility of narration so that 'the actual facts potentially conflict with the narrator's declarations' (113), she also suggests that facts are usually easily decipherable. The approach she advocates is one in which 'the narrative actual world is determined by what the author wants the reader to take as fact' (113). In such scenarios, readers can recognise when a narrator is unreliable and therefore acknowledge that a World View of a Textual Actual World does not necessarily give an accurate reflection of that Textual Actual World.

While it may be easy to distinguish between fact and falsehood in some texts, it is not necessarily the case in all. In all forms of narration, we never experience the Textual Actual World directly and, thus, the authenticity of the Textual Actual World is always questionable. In texts that are narrated by multiple narrators, such as *afternoon*, this is intensified because of the conflict to which multiple accounts lead. When multiple World Views are given, each constitutes a particular version of the Textual Actual World. This loosely corresponds to the distinction that Goodman makes between the multiple Actual Worlds that are created by individual perceptions and the Actual World which sits behind them. Thus, in multiple first-person narration, gaining access to *the* Textual Actual World is extremely problematic, if not impossible, because we are faced with several different epistemological perspectives and therefore several different World Views. The World View category is especially useful therefore in texts, like *afternoon*, in which several irresolvable perspectives are offered.

World Views in *afternoon*

Returning to the analysis of the conversation between Peter and Wert more specifically, while the topic is consistent in the six lexias shown in Table 3.1, each offers a different aspect of the conversation and a range of potentially different ontological domains and epistemological perspectives. First, we can assume that the scene is narrated by Peter in {he says} and {he, he says} because he refers to Wert using his proper name. This represents the first World View. However, because {yes6} is presented from Wert's perspective, a second World View is given. Adding an additional perspective to the scene is not necessarily challenging but because there are two World Views the other lexias in which more indirect forms of reference are used could also potentially be seen as originating in either. The lexia, {three} is particularly ambiguous because of the reference to 'wife' rather than the 'ex-wife' that was noted above. Overall, the text prevents readers from making sense of the Textual Actual World by deliberately positing a number of competing commentaries of this scene – multiple World Views – some of which cannot be definitively attributed to either first-person narrator.

Compounding the ambiguity, each lexia presents a slightly different aspect of the scene. In {yes6}, taken from Wert's World View, Peter asks

Wert the question, 'Are you sleeping with her?' In {As if}, probably taken from Peter's World View, we might conclude that the thoughts represent an internal reaction to the question in {asks} with the explicit response 'As if I were your father' offered as the vocalised reaction. Thus, these two lexias either pose the question or answer it. Conversely, {asks}, {he says} and {he, he says}, which could be attributed to either World View, posit the possibility of the other person positing such a question. The narrator asks the other person to imagine a situation by asking 'How *would* you feel?' (my italics). In these instances, the modal verb expresses a potential future in which such a situation could occur – a Textual Possible World – and asks the other to express their opinion about it. Peter is therefore asked to express his feelings about something that might or might not have occurred. Similarly, {three} contains an asser-tion: 'He *would* rather consider the probabilities of one of us sleeping with the other's wife' (my italics). The use of the modal verb indicates that this anticipates the conversation that takes place in {asks}, {he says}, {he, he says} and possibly {yes6}. Consequently, it presents a World View, probably that of Peter, which presupposes what the other person would like to and, in other lexias, inevitably does talk about.

In Ryan's elucidation of her K-world category, she acknowledges that 'the reference world of a character's K-world may not only be TAW [Textual Actual World], but any of the private worlds of the narrative uni-verse' (116). Translated into my terms, this means that while some World Views present the Textual Actual World as it is, others offer a perspective on what another character might be dreaming about, anticipating, wishing for or thinking. This constitutes either a World View of a Textual Possible World or, in the case of thinking, a World View of another World View. In either case, argues Ryan, 'the possibility for a K-World to reflect another character's K-world leads to potential infinite recursive embedding' (116) and in some cases is taken to 'the utmost limits of intelligibility' (116). While {three} only uses one level of embedding – a World View of a potential World View – it still represents a degree of recursion because the narrator is talking, hypothetically, about something that might or might not happen. In *afternoon*, this is made even more challenging because the text contains other lexias such as {asks}, {he says}, {he, he says} or {yes6} where these potential events are invoked.

The Significance of World Views

The various representations of Peter and Wert's conversation are typical of the epistemological and ontological games in *afternoon*. It typifies the chaotic nature of the text, but it also shows how the disorder can be correlated with a failure of communication and comprehension. Peter's unwillingness to face his Actual World is reflected by the text; neither narrator nor narrative will produce certainties. In ontological terms, returning to the scene within a number of lexias, in different orders, with different levels of frequency and with different narrators, means that readers are prevented from categorising events as being Textual Actual World, Textual Possible World or simply different World Views – something which will, perhaps inevitably, have consequences. Thomas (2007a) notes the effect of the Peter–Wert scene on the reader of *afternoon*. She concludes that because we encounter the Peter–Wert scene in multiple lexias, probably during different readings, 'all we have are different possible versions of what may or may not have taken place ... and once we are made aware of the possibility of seeing (and hearing) things differently, whenever and however we revisit the lexia [asks], it is always going to be charged with these alternatives, none of which we can totally discount or set aside' (368). Thomas's interpretation is useful because it acknowledges that, whether readers discount or accept one version or another, the other ones will continue to be visible. Like the more explicit narrative contradictions found throughout the text, they cannot be ignored.

Importantly, conflicting World Views represent a different device to the narrative contradictions that are seen elsewhere in *afternoon*. World Views represent different perspectives and therefore are used as different epistemological perspectives, whereas narrative contradictions represent different outcomes and therefore result in different ontological domains. However, the existence of both devices suggests that establishing an authoritative and reliable source in the Textual Actual World of *afternoon* is not appropriate because its hermeneutic effect is a direct consequence of the epistemological puzzles and resulting ontological ambiguities that it contains. Perhaps as the ultimate confirmation of the ontological and epistemological games which are played in this Peter–Wert scene, if not throughout the entire novel, a lexia entitled {twenty questions} contains the following:

1 What is the answer to number three?
2 Who is sleeping with whom, and why?
3 What is the answer to number one?
4 Define interactivity.

Referring to the potential affair between Wert and Peter's ex-wife Lisa in question two, the four questions confirm the futility of drawing conclusions about *afternoon*. Even if we can answer question number two, 'who is sleeping with whom?', which is unlikely, questions number one and number three form a recursive loop which results in an impasse. The final question, which asks readers to definite interactivity, foregrounds the process in which they are currently involved. It asks them to consider what reading an interactive text involves and what it might mean for the narratives which are contained within. Ultimately, attempting to answer any of the four questions in the {twenty questions} lexia is to miss the point of *afternoon* because the entire text is based around the fact that we cannot get to the truth. This is primarily because the text has an unstable ontological landscape. However, it is also because, as the analyses have shown throughout this chapter, the protagonist does not or cannot confront his Actual World.

Conclusion

The many different self-reflexive devices within *afternoon* mean that the reader is continually reminded of the artificiality of the text and the Textual Actual World that it describes. The ontological foregrounding that is instilled throughout *afternoon* might not prevent readers from feeling concern for the characters or prohibit them from being concerned about the ramifications of the events as a whole. However, the many different paths, the different versions of events and the resultant indeterminacy means that the text continually forces readers to revise their view of the characters as well as their understanding of the ontological structure of the novel. Readers must be aware of the text's vastly complex structure and be cautious about drawing any conclusions, keeping all narrative options open. Hermeneutically, the text exploits the fact that readers cannot find the truth and juxtaposes their relationship to the Textual Actual World with that of Peter's. While they may search for answers within the text, that investigation is continually thwarted by Peter's defiance of his Actual World. His inability to confront the reality of his life can be described as a reluctance to actualise any of his possible worlds. He would rather keep his Actual World opaque, private and inaccessible and therefore a collection of stories, which can neither be substantiated nor disproved. Ultimately, in their pursuit of the story in *afternoon*, readers are at the mercy of the narrator and his troublesome narrative so that they, too, can never be sure what is actual and what is merely possible.

4
Interrupting the Transmission: the Slippery Worlds of Stuart Moulthrop's *Victory Garden*

Introduction

Victory Garden is a historical novel, set in the early 1990s at the beginning of the first Gulf War. The narrative switches between two settings: the Persian Gulf and a university campus in the USA called the University of Tara. While less of the text details the action in Middle East – focusing primarily on the US – the Gulf War is extremely significant in terms of its figurative presence and social resonance. In the two locations readers are given the two views of the war from two different types of character: those who experience it first hand and those who experience it through representations or reports. The difference between the many World Views is most felt through the juxtaposition of Emily Runbird with the other characters. Emily, a former student at the University of Tara, has been drafted to sort military mail in the Gulf as a condition of her government university funding. The rest of her friends remain in the US. They are: Jude Busch who is Emily's brash friend and a student at Tara; Victor Gardner, Emily's former lover who is now being pursued by Jude; Boris Urquhart, a professor at the university, who occasionally shows signs of mental illness and is sometimes the object of Emily's affections; Thea Agnew, a professor at the university, who is Emily's former thesis advisor and mother of Leroy. While most reading paths address a variety of thematic concerns, most of the narrative strands centre on the experiences of these characters. They include: Leroy and Thea's squabbles and reconciliation; Emily and her comrades' experiences in a Saudi Arabian military base; Boris Urquhart and Stephen Tate's academic research into dreams and hallucinations; Victor Gardner and Jude Busch's relationship.

As is typical of hypertext fiction novels more broadly and already shown in *afternoon* in Chapter 3, tracing the chronology of the narrative or finding one consistent narrative is difficult because the text offers a number of different reading paths whose narratives sometimes contradict one another. Most notably, in some readings Emily appears to die in the war and in others she appears to survive. Similarly, a number of different representations of and perspectives on the Textual Actual World are offered throughout. Most of the novel is narrated by a third-person narrator, but reading paths expose readers to different orders of events or narratives with different emphases. The text thus contains a number of competing World Views (for full discussion of World View see Chapter 3), each providing a different perspective on the military conflict. In particular, the Gulf War is seen from many sides of the political spectrum. One default path beginning with {Thea's War}, for example, posits a left-wing stance. The majority of this path depicts a scene between Thea Agnew and her friend Veronica Runbird in which they discuss the motives of the US Government. On television they watch some of the first military attacks in the Gulf and they reflect upon the political climate that has lead to the conflict, concluding: 'It's been so carefully worked out. ... Bush and his people have dreamed about this war for years' {Buildup}. As a hegemonic counter to this in {Rather Not}, a news broadcaster insists that 'it was Iraq who started this war'. Complementing the political debates, personal reflections are provided by Emily's letters home; the {Love, Emily} lexia, for example, is the beginning of a sequence of letters in which Emily describes her personal fears for her safety as well as her ideological position relative to the conflict. Each representation presents a counter to the others and the varying responses and experiences are used to suggest that no sole experience can explain the war systematically or comprehensively.

Most readings of the text recognise the association between the multiple paths, multiple perspectives and the theme of 'representation' within *Victory Garden* as a whole (e.g. Gaggi, 1997; Ciccoricco, 2004, 2007). Critics note specifically that the many different reading paths literalise the epistemological multiplicity that is found both within and outside the text in relation to political and social debates. Particularly relevant is Ciccoricco's (2007) assertion that some self-reflexive elements are used to 'effectively shut readers out, alienating them from the fictional world' (106). In his discussion of *Victory Garden's* hypertextual structure, Ciccoricco suggests that the contradictory narratives 'tend to work explicitly against a reader's immersion in a *singular* fictional world given that they always contain multiple outcomes and, by extension, multiple worlds' (111). He suggests that the ontological multiplicity that is generated as a consequence of the different reading paths might mean that a reader's absorption in any one of those worlds is denied. Yet while he suggests that the reader is often alienated from the text, he also suggests that this is due to an initial engrossment because 'the force of any *local* disruption depends to a degree on the attainment of a *global* immersion. Put simply, an overall textual integrity must first be established if it is to be disrupted in any significant way' (111, my italics). According to Ciccoricco, the reader must be absorbed in the narrative, if only temporarily, in order that he or she can experience subsequent feelings of estrangement. Thus any feelings of alienation are a direct consequence of the disparity between the two states: immersion and expulsion.

Expanding upon some of Ciccoricco's conclusions, this chapter will emphasise the ontological mechanics that establish an interdependent relationship between the Textual Actual World and the Actual World. First, it will show how Actual World events, locations and individuals are used within the novel so that the construction of the Textual Actual World in *Victory Garden* is epistemologically dependent on the Actual World. Following this, some of the numerous strategies that are used to push and pull the reader in and out of the Textual Actual World of *Victory Garden* will be examined to show how an ontological dichotomy is established which ultimately draws attention to the artificiality of the narrative. Finally, the analysis will show how the text uses the Actual World as a means of problematising the epistemological relationship on which other parts of the text so heavily depend. Using Possible Worlds Theory to analyse the different strategies that are employed to foreground the ontological separateness of the Textual Actual World as well as its epistemological congruity with our system of reality, this chapter will conclude that the novel asks us to question our assumptions about the nature of reality and representations in general.

As an ancillary benefit to this study, this chapter will show how *Victory Garden* fulfils some of the criteria set by Hutcheon (1988, 1989, 1996) in her extensive study of 'historiographic metafiction'. The term, Hutcheon (1996) argues, can be used to describe 'novels that are intensely self-reflexive but that also reintroduce historical context into metafiction and problematize the entire question of historical knowledge' (474). As the overview has shown, *Victory Garden* is set against the first Gulf War and this historical context permeates throughout. Yet, as a Storyspace hypertext, the novel also contains devices that draw attention to its ontological status. It is therefore also self-reflexive. Most importantly, as the proceeding analysis will show, it, like historiographic metafiction, problematises the entire ontology of historical discourse.

Historical Fiction, Counterparts and Transworld Identity

As a historical novel, the Actual World context against which *Victory Garden* is set is extremely important. It is with a sense of irony, therefore, that the copyright page contains the following declaration: 'this is a work of fiction: no resemblance to actual persons is intended or should be inferred' {Properties}. This disclaimer is perhaps not unusual in a fictional text. However, in a historical fiction, such as *Victory Garden*, it is remarkable because the novel uses the Actual World as its epistemological template.

Its epistemological dependence on the Actual World is established by casual reference to Actual World events and people throughout. To take one example for illustrative purposes, in the midst of a discussion about the events leading to the Gulf War, Thea and her son, Leroy, debate the political motives behind the conflict. An extract from their conversation is shown below:

> Thea answered ... "Like who backed Saddam for eight years in the War with Iran? Who looked the other way when he 'accidentally' blew up one of our navy ships in the Gulf? Whose ambassador told him we weren't interested in his disputes with Kuwait?"...
>
> Leroy frowned. "You're saying it's our fault Saddam invaded Kuwait? You're saying he has a right to grab all those oilfields?" {Cyclops}.

The scene between Thea and Leroy takes place within the Textual Actual World, but because the characters refer to entities from the Actual World the text demands that readers utilise their knowledge about the Actual World in order to make sense of the characters' debate. Since Actual World individuals and events are used to provide context to their discussion, reference to them is often very casual. In {Cyclops}, the characters refer to 'the Gulf' and 'Kuwait' without glossing these locations. Similarly, no information is provided to clarify the status of 'Saddam', but because of the definite reference, it is assumed that readers will be able to utilise their Actual World knowledge in order to identify him.

While the preceding account provides a very general explanation of how readers make sense of a reference to 'Saddam' and 'the Gulf', Possible Worlds Theory can be used to examine it more precisely. Beginning with the Actual World individual, in the context of a discussion about the Gulf,

Kuwait and Iran, a reference to, 'Saddam', will probably be interpreted by the reader as referring to 'Saddam Hussein' in the Actual World because he was the President of Iraq at the time of the first Gulf War. In Possible Worlds Theory, the link between 'Saddam' in the Textual Actual World and Saddam Hussein in the Actual World is established because of the type of reference that is used. As Doležel (1998a) explains, 'the thread that holds together all the embodiments of an individual in all possible worlds is … the proper name as rigid designator' (18). Applying this to the {Cyclops} lexia, readers will recognise 'Saddam' as a fictional incarnation of Saddam Hussein in the Actual World because they share at least part of the same proper name: 'Saddam'.

While a proper name as a rigid designator offers a potentially useful means of cross-referencing individuals across ontological domains, the limits of the approach can be seen immediately in the preceding short analysis. The reference to 'Saddam' in {Cyclops} is restricted to a first name only so that, while we can assume from the context that it is used to refer to the infamous President of Iraq, the proper name could also potentially refer to any number of Saddams in the Actual World. Doležel admits that rigid designation represents a 'thin and theoretically controversial' (18) issue in Possible Worlds Theory because of the subjective and therefore sometimes tenuous link upon which rigid designation relies. For it to be a useful concept for literary studies, therefore, the basis on which it is to be used must be established.

Counterparts and Transworld Identity in Possible Worlds Theory

Providing a potential means of methodological obstruction, a debate within Possible Worlds Theory exists concerning the extent to which an individual's properties can be deemed to be the 'same' for a proper name to be able to stand as a form of rigid designation. Investigating the issue from a literary context Pavel (1979) recalls that: 'Kripke (1972) appears to think, for instance, that the genetical structure of the fertilized egg which later became Aristotle is a sufficient individuating element. A theologian may consider however that the central fact of individuation consists in God's associating a certain soul to the genetical structure' (183). As Pavel's playful observations point out, different theoreticians have different requirements regarding the properties that an individual must posses for them to qualify as a referent of a proper name. Though he recognises the limits, Pavel proposes that proper names are solely sufficient and argues that 'a being is given a name which refers to him, even if his set (cluster) of properties is unknown, variable or different from what one believes it is. ... Consequently, "Bacon" and "Shakespeare" or any proper name for that matter, are linguistic labels pegged to individuals, independently of the properties these individuals display' (181). Pavel's resolute position of using a proper name as a rigid designator is useful because it potentially eliminates any ambiguity that might ensue if essential properties are used instead. Using this method, individuals are invoked by their proper names and their attributes are susceptible to change or mutation. Yet in instances, such as 'Saddam' in {Cylclops} where the full designation is missing, this is not completely sufficient. As was shown in the short analysis above, contextual information such as the spatial and temporal markers must also be used alongside the proper name in order to affiliate the 'Saddam' in *Victory Garden* with Saddam Hussein in the Actual World.

Ryan's (1991) 'principle of minimal departure' can be used alongside theories of rigid designation to explain how readers process the reference to 'Saddam'. Ryan's principle affirms that when we read a fictional text 'we reconstrue the central world of a textual universe [the Textual Actual World] as conforming as far as possible to our representation of the AW [Actual World]. We will project upon these worlds everything we know about reality, and we will make only the adjustments dictated by the text' (51). According to Ryan's principle of minimal departure, when we – as readers – approach a text, we assume that the Textual Actual World is an epistemological extension of or supplement to the world we inhabit and modifications and supplements are made only when the text specifies. This means that, before we read any work of fiction, we already posses default knowledge about the world that it describes so that every single detail need not be articulated. Consequently, general truths such as logic, physics and biological inventories are assumed to apply unless the text tells us otherwise. It also means that Actual World locations, historical events and infamous individuals are assumed to exist within the Textual Actual World whether or not they are explicitly invoked. As readers move through the text, the Actual World model can be altered or challenged; science fiction and fairy tales being two extreme examples of this. However, the principle of minimal departure means that events, people and locations can be invoked by a text without a direct explanation of their existence or relevance being required. It also explains how casual forms of reference, such as proper names, are interpreted by readers as referring to an Actual World individual unless they are given details which challenge this assumption.

The principle of minimal departure thus explains how a Textual Actual World can utilise the Actual World as its epistemological template or, equally, how readers use their knowledge of the Actual World in the context of the Textual Actual World. In the case of a historical novel, the principle of minimal departure is particularly relevant because of the integral epistemic link between the Actual World and the Textual Actual World that the genre relies upon. As Ryan remarks, 'if it weren't for the principle [of minimal departure], a novel about a character named Napoleon could not convey the feeling that its hero is *the* Napoleon. The resemblance between the Napoleon in the novel and the Napoleon of AW [Actual World] would be ... fortuitous' (52). While *Victory Garden* does not employ an Actual World figure as a character, Ryan's claims still apply because the principle of minimal departure can be used to explain how the novel exploits events from the Actual World, as well as a number of figures and settings associated with those events, as a backdrop to its narrative.

While the disclaimer at the beginning of *Victory Garden* asks us not to infer 'resemblance to actual persons', as a historical novel, the text demands that we do so. Returning to the extract from {Cyclops} above, the 'Gulf', 'Kuwait' and 'Saddam' are not glossed because their inclusion anticipates that readers will come to the text with knowledge of the locations and individuals. As Ryan's example of Napoleon shows, Actual World individuals are used within historical novels precisely because of the information and connotations that they inevitably bring with them. In {Cyclops}, Thea and Leroy refer to 'Saddam' – a notorious figure in the Actual World – because he is integral to the social and political debates in which the characters are engaged. If, as according to the principle of minimal departure, we assume that the Textual Actual World reflects the Actual World unless otherwise specified, then we can assume, taking into account the contextual information in the novel, that 'Saddam' in this context refers to the infamous Saddam [Hussein] in the Actual World. Thus, rather than using a proper name as the sole means of rigid designation, it is more accurate to specify that Saddam Hussein is invoked explicitly, through a proper name, and that he is invoked, implicitly, by his contextual relevance to the text.

Preserving the example of Napoleon, Ryan also provides terminology that can be used to analyse the {Cyclops} lexia: 'under the principle [of minimal departure], the Napoleon of TAW [Textual Actual World] is regarded as a *counterpart* of the Napoleon of AW [Actual World], linked to him through ... *transworld identity*' (52, my emphasis). In Ryan's explanation, the term 'counterpart' is used to define the ontological status of an Actual World individual within a Textual Actual World and 'transworld identity' is used to describe the epistemological relation that unites them. Adopting this terminology means that the Saddam of {Cyclops} is a counterpart of Saddam in the Actual World and they are linked through their transworld identity.

Yet while Ryan potentially provides terminology that might be used in the analysis of historical fiction, an elucidation of her analytical vocabulary is required because of the conflicting theoretical positions on which it relies. Ryan does not engage in the debate explicitly but her use of 'counterpart' and 'transworld identity' is significant because each term originates from a different faction of possible-worlds logic: Concretism and Abstractionism (see Chapter 2 for full discussion). Since the Concretist perspective perceives possible worlds as comprising tangible domains which materially exist, they have the same ontological status as the Actual World. Thus, as constituents of possible worlds, the individuals that populate them also exist in the same way that the individuals that populate the Actual World exist. Thus, as the label implies, constituents of both possible worlds and Actual Worlds are concrete. Consequently, from a Concretist perspective, an entity in the Actual World – animate or otherwise – cannot be the *same* entity as that in a possible world because it is impossible for them to exist simultaneously. As Lewis (1983b) explains, 'worlds do not overlap: unlike Siamese twins, they have no shared parts. … No possible individual is part of two worlds' (39). From Lewis's Concretist perspective, it is impossible for the same individual to exist within a number of different possible worlds. The solution to this logical impasse is to regard each individual within each possible world as a 'counterpart' (Lewis 1973) of the others as opposed to the same individual travelling between domains.

Conversely, from an Abstractionist perspective, possible worlds represent the way things might have been rather than how they actually are within an alternative ontological domain. While the Actual World is a tangible domain, possible worlds comprise imaginary conceptions. Accordingly, their constituents, including the individuals that populate them, are also only *imaginary*. The logical consequence of this philosophical position is that the same individual *can* exist within a number of different ontological contexts. As Kripke (1972) explains 'in talking about what would have happened to Nixon in a certain counterfactual situation, we are talking about what would have happened to *him*' (44). As an Abstractionist, Kripke denies the simultaneous existence of counterparts and instead asserts that the same individual travels between the potentially infinite numbers of possible worlds that make up a system of reality. They posses what Abstractionists refer to as 'transworld identity'.

While the logical tussle surrounding transworld identity and counter-part relations might appear to lie beyond the discipline boundaries of literary studies, possible-world logic does form the basis of a Possible Worlds Theory approach to fiction. As such the field of literary studies has inherited – if only implicitly – a number of the unresolved conflicts along with disparate conceptualisations, varied terminology and potentially incompatible approaches. Acknowledging the potential consequences of the logical debate for literary studies, Ronen (1994) warns that 'different interpretations of possibility in logic and in liter-ary theory result in different conceptions of *trans-world* identity' (57). However, while Ronen recognises the potential for logical incongruity, she also suggests that, once conceptual boundaries have been estab-lished, the relationship between actual and possible individuals can be easily explained. Moreover, she suggests that 'trans-world identity is a relatively straightforward relation when questions concerning existence, identity, and epistemic access to things have already been settled' (59).

If we prudently heed Ronen's guidance on choosing a logical position as a means of refining our methodology here, there are two perspectives from which we can choose. Allying with Concretism means that, as a specific type of possible world, a Textual Actual World and its constituent characters must be regarded as materially existing. This is something that represents a challenge to us because it is impossible. Conversely, if we accept the Abstractionist position and consent that Textual Actual Worlds and the individuals whom they house are imaginary, it becomes more ontologically problematic to draw a correlation between a real historical figure and their fictional incarnation because, from a logical perspective at least, they belong to different systems of reality. As Ronen notes:

> trans-world identity does raise a problem in the context of worlds of different orders, worlds which do not belong to the same logical domain. Such is the case when we have a fictional construct on the one hand and the given world of our experience, on the other hand. Trans-world identity ... thus reflects again in its literary inter-pretations the difference between the way possibility functions in philosophical logic and in literary theory of fictionality (59–60).

As Ronen's observations suggest, the movement of an individual between the Actual World and a possible world or between a Textual

Actual World and a Textual Possible World can be easily theoretically accommodated because they each belong to the same system of reality. However, issues of counterparthood and transworld identity represent a potential ontological challenge when an Actual World individual appears in a Textual Actual World because they belong to different systems of reality – one is Actual and one is Textual. Similarly, a Textual Actual World forms the centre of a Textual Universe which, like our system of reality, is also comprised of alternatives – Textual Possible Worlds. Possible Worlds Theory as applied to fiction must therefore be able to provide terminology to describe the movement of an individual between two systems of reality if it is to be useful to narrative theory.

Doležel (1998a) acknowledges the ontological incongruity between actual and fictional domains and offers a potential solution to the associated logical debate. He stresses that 'all fictional entities are of the same ontological nature' (18) and that 'a mimetic view that presents fictional persons as a mixed bag of "real people" and "purely fictional characters" leads to serious theoretical difficulties, analytical confusions, and naïve critical practices. The principle of ontological hegemony is a necessary condition for the coexistence, interaction, and communication of fictional persons. It epitomises the sovereignty of fictional worlds' (18). Doležel's observation shows that it is necessary to maintain ontological consistency across systems of reality in order that analyses can ensue and warns that a perspective which attempts to 'mix' Actual and Textual Actual is not only logically deviant, but, more importantly, compromises the autonomy of Textual Actual Worlds in general.

Maintaining his commitment to ontological consistency, Doležel (1998b) explains in a separate article that 'Tolstoy's fictional Napoleon or Dickens's fictional London is not identical with the historical Napoleon or the geographical London' (788). In suggesting that Actual World entities are not congruous with their fictional representations, he implicitly discards an Abstractionist alliance which asserts that the same individual travels between worlds. However, the appearance of an Actual World individual within a Textual Actual World has an important epistemological function because such individuals carry information from one domain to the other. As the principle of minimal departure elucidates, readers assume that a Textual Actual World reflects the Actual World unless the text dictates otherwise. For this reason, their ontological origin – as an Actual World inhabitant – is absolutely crucial to historical fiction. Thus, despite the ontological incongruity that Doležel identifies, he also concedes that there is an essential epistemic link between the Actual and the Textual Actual that cannot be abandoned. He stresses 'an ineradicable relationship exists between the historical Napoleon and all fictional Napoleons ... [and] this relationship extends across world boundaries; fictional entities and their actual prototypes are linked by *transworld* identity' (788). In recognising the link between Actual World 'prototypes' and their fictional incarnates, Doležel compromises the rigid logic on which Possible Worlds Theory is based. However, his eventual choice of terminology also means that the autonomy of each individual is maintained.

As the discussion has shown, allying exclusively with one position from possible-worlds logic means that analyses of historical fiction are potentially limited. Ryan implies that logical restraints can be avoided by employing both sets of terminology in her discussions. Doležel (1998b) is more explicit about this kind of strategy:

> Rescher suggests the term 'versions' to designate the different 'descriptive guises' of 'one selfsame individual' in different possible worlds. Lewis, emphasizing that 'things in different worlds are *never* identical,' links the various incarnations of one thing in different worlds by the 'counterpart relation.' It is 'a relation of similarity' and thus seems to presuppose that the counterparts share some essential properties. But it is also flexible enough to link the Hitler of history and a Hitler who led 'a blameless life.' In the end, Lewis disarms all those who might classify him as essentialist with a charming innocence: 'The essences of things are settled only to the extent that the counterpart relation is, and the counterpart relation is not very settled at all.' I feel therefore comfortable using the convenient term 'counterpart' in a radically nonessentialist semantics of fictionality (788–9).

Doležel recognises that his choice of terminology implicitly aligns him with a particular logical perspective. However, in a playful examination of the unresolved logical debate, he also justifies his selection of terms according to his literary critical agenda. While he recognises their logical incompatibility, he adopts a position that is most useful for the analysis of a fictional text. The use of the Concretist term, 'counterpart', to describe an Actual World figure in fiction acknowledges that a fictional incarnation is not the *same* individual as the Actual World inhabitant. However, by describing the process by which they move through and across the different modal systems of reality as 'transworld identity' – a term allied with Abstractionism – their essential epistemic relation is maintained. Like Doležel and Ryan, therefore, these will be used within this study. However, 'counterpart' will be prefixed with 'Actual World' in the case of historical fiction in order to differentiate it from other types of counterpart which will be analysed later in this book (see discussion on Textual Actual World counterparts in Chapter 5).

Historical Fiction and Ontological Boundaries

The theoretical debate presented above illustrates that it is important to establish methodological and terminological transparency within Possible Worlds Theory before any analysis ensues. Now established, an examination of how and why Actual World counterparts are used within *Victory Garden* can proceed. As a historical novel, *Victory Garden* relies upon readers utilising the principle of minimal departure for the construction of its Textual Actual World because it uses the Actual World as its epistemological template and invokes Actual World counterparts, events and locations throughout. Importantly, this process involves the crossing of an ontological boundary because readers must access information from the Actual World in order to bring it to the Textual Actual World. However, this process is not necessarily unusual or challenging for readers because, as McHale (1987) acknowledges, '*all* historical novels ... typically involve some violation of ontological boundaries ... [because] they often claim "transworld identity" between characters in their projected world and real-world historical figures' (16–17, my emphasis). As McHale points out, every single text that utilises an Actual World counterpart causes an ontological boundary to be violated because it takes information from another domain.

Returning to the analysis of the {Cyclops} lexia, the reference to 'Saddam' requires that readers access particular historical knowledge from the Actual World. Ontologically, Saddam Hussein belongs to the Actual World. However, because Thea and Leroy refer to 'Saddam' very casually during the course of their debate, 'Saddam [Hussein]' is also presented as an undisputed component of the Textual Actual World. Information about him is taken from another ontological domain. In this case, the utilisation of an Actual World counterpart is concealed by the text and this, as McHale suggests 'camouflage[s] the seam between historical reality and fiction' (90) so that the reader remains unaware of the world-building process in which they are involved.

Figure 4.1 shows that, in the context of the {Cyclops} lexia, 'Saddam' simultaneously refers to an entity in the Actual World and an entity in the Textual Actual World. Epistemologically, therefore, Saddam's origin

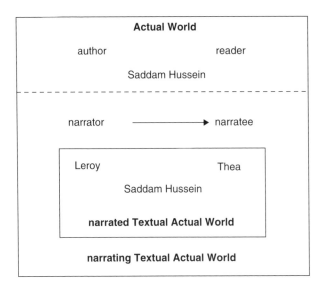

Figure 4.1   The ontological landscape created by {Cyclops}

in the Actual World is required for readers to process the definite form of reference that the proper name carries. They must use information from the Actual World and apply it to the Textual Actual World. However, the underlying process by which readers utilise this Actual World knowledge is not exposed by the text. That is, despite the fact that an Actual World counterpart is utilised within the Textual Actual World, the seam between reality and fiction or, in the context of this analysis, the ontological boundary between the Actual World and the Textual Actual World, is camouflaged by the casual form of reference and the relative lack of attention that is drawn to the process. The dotted line between the Actual World and the Textual Actual World in Figure 4.1 represents the fact that while readers have to remain in the Actual World because of their role of link chooser, the boundary that separates them from the Textual Actual World is softened by this part of the text.

While the {Cyclops} example shows how the seam between the Actual World and the Textual Actual World is occasionally under-emphasised within the novel, a multitude of devices within *Victory Garden* are used to reinforce it. As McHale (1987) notes, postmodernist texts 'foreground this seam [between reality and fiction] by making the transition from one realm to the other as jarring as possible' (90) so that readers are made very aware of the ontological disparity between one world and another.

Though ultimately epistemologically reliant on the Actual World for its construction and occasionally employing narrative strategies which hide the seam between the two, *Victory Garden* generally does contain many devices that expose its ontological status as an artificial construction. Thus, as Ciccoricco suggests above, the text works via a combination of absorption and alienation for the reader, but the cause is a manifestation of the epistemological and ontological interchange on which all historical fiction ultimately relies.

The short analysis of {Cyclops} has shown how Possible Worlds Theory offers a means of modelling the reader's role in historical fiction. In particular, it has shown how the seam between the Actual World and the Textual Actual World is underplayed by some devices. In an attempt to unravel the complex relationship between reality and fiction that *Victory Garden* explores, the remainder of this chapter will show how much of the text contains devices which expose the boundary between the Actual World and the Textual Actual World. It will show that *Victory Garden* is a text which, as the analysis of the {Cyclops} lexia shows, relies very heavily on the Actual World for its construction, but which, as McHale notes in his analysis of postmodernist fiction, also foregrounds this dependence very explicitly. The result is a novel that exposes its own fictionality so as to sabotage any potential claims of historical legitimacy that it or other historical fiction might assert.

Exposing the Ontological Boundary

Utilising the hypertext structure, the seam between the Actual World and Textual Actual World is foregrounded and by the reader's first encounter with the text. *Victory Garden* has multiple entrances from which the reader must choose so that interactivity is required from the very outset and some degree of ontological distancing achieved before the narrative is unravelled. As shown in Figure 4.2, the overview map posits 39 distinct areas, each acting as an entrance to a different part of the text. This large map further subdivides into thirds and each smaller area is labelled according to the lexia to which it leads, as shown in Figure 4.3.

As a navigational tool, the map grants the reader a panoramic view of the Textual Actual World that he or she is about to explore. Crucially, although the titles of each section provide some detail, they actually reveal very little about the contents of the destination lexias or the length and duration of the onward reading paths to which they lead.

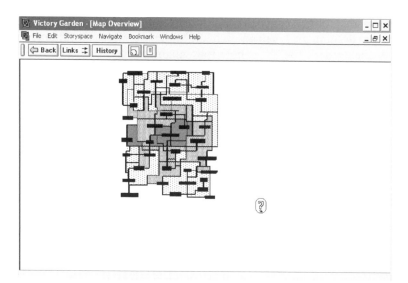

Figure 4.2   Screenshot of {Map Overview}

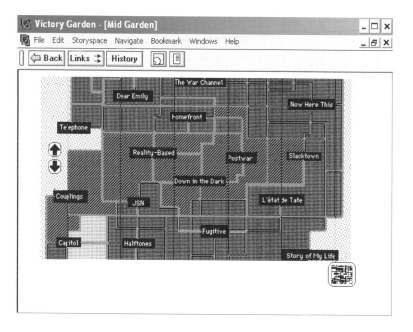

Figure 4.3   Screenshot of {Mid Garden}

In fact they often signify nothing more than the chapter headings of print fictions might – perhaps even less because the absence of numerical sequencing does not show how they might fit together sequentially. The links entitled 'The War Channel' or 'Thea's War', for example, are fairly indicative of their content – a collection of quotations from media representations of the war and the war as focalised through the character, Thea, respectively. However, such semantic associations can only be confirmed in retrospect, after the path has been explored. Other links, such as 'Latticework' and 'JSN' are less revealing and demand that the reader access the lexia in order to discern their narrative concerns. The reader must experiment with the links, stepping in and out of the Textual Actual World before it is possible to understand how the different parts function collectively.

In his analysis of *Victory Garden*, Koskimaa (2000) suggests that 'the use of a representational map is ... one way of making the interface "fuse" to the represented fictional world'. Koskimaa's use of 'fuse' is significant because it implies that complete cohesion exists between the physical representation of the novel in the Actual World and the fictional representation of the Actual World within the Textual Actual World. However, rather than the map causing an amalgamation or unification, somewhat paradoxically, it actually accentuates the onto-logical divide between the Actual World and the Textual Actual World. Maps in the Actual World do depict a space, but they do not provide direct access to the world that they depict; they are simply a represen-tation. In *Victory Garden*, however, the representation of the world – the map – is also literally the space – the Textual Actual World. Thus, the relationship between map and space in this case is ontologically peculiar.

The map in *Victory Garden* acts as a boundary between the reader in the Actual World and the text which describes the Textual Actual World. The reader must appraise the map and make a choice about where he or she will enter the text, returning to this space at the end of each reading. The map in *Victory Garden* is not the same as a contents page or frontispiece – entities that are absolutely separate from the Textual Actual World. The map depicts the space that it provides direct access to and, to some degree, it forms part of the Textual Actual World. However, it also acts as a boundary between the reader, in the Actual World, and the text which describes the Textual Actual World. Readers can dip into the Textual Actual World to read about particular parts of it, but they are continually forced to withdraw from this domain at the end of a reading path and return to their panoramic, *external* view. Through a continual return to the map, readers are regularly reminded of the inherent ontological separateness of the domain to which the map leads. They are always aware that there is a boundary to cross in order to access the Textual Actual World.

As an interactive map, therefore, the entrance to *Victory Garden* explicitly foregrounds its Textual Actual World as a distinct, self-contained system of reality, quite separate from the Actual World to which the reader belongs. Yet the pragmatic function of the individual sections of the map also emphasises the multiplicity to be found once readers have entered the Textual Actual World. That is, the links emphasise that the text is comprised of a number of different narratives. Each reading path can always be replaced with another and the temporariness and contrived nature of the narratives within the novel are foregrounded. Thus, the map in *Victory Garden* performs a number of different functions: it invites the reader to take a panoramic view of the text, encouraging them to explore its contents; it acts as a multifarious entrance to the Textual Actual World, displaying the text's multiplicity; and it separates the Actual World and Textual Actual World so as to define spaces that are ontologically distinct. The artificiality of the Textual Actual World is exposed from the very beginning of the novel, continually reminding readers that what they are reading is contrived and constructed.

Interrupting the Reader

Once inside the text, the autonomy that is granted to the reader by the multiple entrances is removed and they are instead reminded of the autonomy of the Textual Actual World and numerous strategies are in place to draw attention to its artificiality. Throughout the text, the narrator makes direct addresses to the reader, reminding them that the Textual Actual World that they are exploring does not really exist. In particular, the third-person narrator frequently interrupts the narrative to comment on events and explore their relevance within the wider context of the novel. His or her intrusions are relatively frequent but their proliferation does not make individual instances any less ontologically disruptive. As was also apparent in the analysis of *afternoon*, the Textual Actual World of *Victory Garden* is shown as a domain whose content is guarded and controlled by a textual intermediary as opposed to being under the control of the reader.

While the intrusive narrator draws attention to the artificiality of the Textual Actual World, however, unlike in *afternoon*, a narrator is not solely responsible for constructing and simultaneously exposing the artificiality of the Textual Universe. In addition, some lexias are used to signify that the Textual Actual World is communicated via a real-time broadcast with no narrator explicitly present. A lexia, entitled 'Interrupt', is particularly pertinent in this respect. It contains the following message:

```
...temporarily lost our signal from Tara technical diffi-
culties  flashes  of  light  temporary  please  stand  by
technical please...
```

Principally this lexia is distinctive because of the typology. The Courier font is inconsistent with that used in the majority of other lexias and the typeface with its minimalist visual style bears resemblance to fonts used in early text editors or programming software. As soon as the lexia appears, therefore, even before the textual content of the text is read, its visual appearance implies that the text it contains is distinctive. Linguistically also the message signifies that the text may have been generated by a computer system. The syntax is confused and fragmented so that the text appears to have been corrupted. The message is missing the punctuation required to formulate complete sentences and several constituents do not make grammatical sense in their current position so that the intended meaning is ambiguous.

Despite the structural disorder, however, it is possible to interpret a message from the text. The lexia implies that technical difficulties have interrupted a transmission so that someone, somewhere is not able to broadcast. The lexia title, 'Interrupt', corroborates this hypothesis. Looking at the context from which the lexia might have been reached, {Interrupt} can be accessed from {Dropkick}, a lexia which depicts part of a dream sequence. There are several episodes within *Victory Garden* in which academic researchers are experimenting with a dream machine capable of transmitting a dreamer's thoughts. From this perspective, {Interrupt} could constitute an intrusion into a participant's dream so that the error message belongs to the narrated Textual Actual World. However, the experiments have taken place within the university so that they are restricted *within* Tara. It would not make sense for the signal to be lost *'from* Tara' therefore. Alternatively, there are a number of instances within the novel in which characters watch television. The interruption could be interpreted as an interruption to that transmission. However, again, the text suggests that the signal 'from Tara' has been lost so that this supposition is unlikely. We might surmise that the transmission is being made from Tara to somewhere beyond, details of which are located elsewhere in the text. This would imply that there is further information to be discovered about the Textual Actual World and the events that it contains. In a hypertext novel, clarification can often be found in parts of the text which are structurally unconnected to the current lexia, but this ambiguity only complicates any search to establish the logic of the interruption.

While these tentative conclusions represent a number of interpretative strategies that are available to the reader, attributing the {Interrupt} lexia to unlikely or forthcoming events does not address its significance in the wider context of *Victory Garden*. An alternative and ultimately more likely interpretation of the message, which links more directly with the novel's preoccupation with representation, is that the error message is intended for readers of the hypertext. It plays on the fact that reading constitutes a form of voyeurism; we look into other worlds and the {Interrupt} lexia parodies this by literalising it.

As was shown in the analysis of the direct address in *afternoon* (see Chapter 3), real communication between a narrator in a Textual Actual World and the readers in the Actual World is impossible. Texts in which we can be fully immersed or in which we can completely 'recenter' (Ryan, 1991) allow that ontological axiom to be ignored. The {Interrupt} lexia, however, implies that the Textual Actual World of *Victory Garden* is being broadcast to readers and, further, that it is being viewed in real-time. Thus, the disruption that is given in {Interrupt} signifies that a transmission has been corrupted but, more importantly, it also implies that the Textual Actual World is completely autonomous and exists independently of the semiotic channels through which it is constructed. Paradoxically, rather than strengthening the authenticity of the Textual Actual World, the {Interrupt} lexia instead draws attention to the artificiality of this domain because the fiction-as-world metaphor is pushed to its limit. In claiming that the Textual Actual World exists as a domain from which transmissions can be made, the *artificiality* of the entire Textual Actual World is exposed. What would otherwise be an implicit divide between the Textual Actual World and the Actual World is made much more visible. Ultimately, therefore, the lexia which claims, impossibly, to have interrupted the communicative channels makes the reader very aware of their position as an observer of what is ultimately a fictional domain. In claiming to be legitimate and to describe something that actually exists, the text is exposed as a tool for *simulation* – for artificial construction – and by exposing its own methods of construction, the text at least begins to gesture to the ways in which other means of representation might be guilty of making the same false claims.

Blurring the Boundaries

The entrance map and the {Interrupt} lexia are representative of how the ontological boundary between the Textual Actual World and the Actual World is exposed in *Victory Garden*. In other parts of the text, some forms of representation disrupt the communicative channels inside the Textual Actual World so that the distinction between one speaker and another becomes harder to identify.

Continuing the theme of transmission and broadcast that is established by lexias such as {Interrupt}, one such instance occurs across two lexias both entitled {... and ...}. Crucially, the first {... and ...} lexia is always followed by the second {... and ...} lexia so that, unless the reading is terminated, readers will be led from one to the other. The first {... and ...} lexia describes the slow deterioration of a woman, slipping into unconsciousness:

> It was dark. Her head hurt and she couldn't hear anything except a sick constant buzz like when you get real high fevers. Delirious. Now she was confused. Something had happened to her. She didn't know what. She'd been thrown across the room maybe. Right, she knew she'd been thrown through the air, she couldn't say how far, and she knew she landed hard because she couldn't get her breath, she didn't remember coming down but she thought something had happened when she did and she didn't want to move her legs. She could sort of feel them which was good but they felt wet and that wasn't so good ... Maybe there were torches or maybe flames ... She began to feel cold and that gave her a flash of fear, adrenaline kicked out but somehow her body wouldn't catch and now her head was throbbing but the pain was going away in the dark and the buzzing was going away too, dimming out black and silent kind of like falling asleep she was sleepy now and more like passing out drunk or when she has to have a general wisdom teeth impact world smaller small her world going away me too {... and ...}.

This lexia can be reached by one of two reading paths: one describes a missile attack in the Gulf and the other contains Emily's friends' reflections on her death. Given these two contexts, the {... and ...} lexia can be seen to describe Emily's demise. However, the way in which the death is presented stylistically is ontological and epistemologically significant. The lexia begins with two definite statements, 'it was dark' and 'her head hurt'. They each suggest the presence of an omniscient third-person narrator because as un-modalised declaratives they connote certainty and assuredness. However, the narrative voice changes throughout the lexia, so that while it begins with a third-person voice, it actually progresses through more intensely focalised free indirect discourse to a stream-of-consciousness style of narration, which is a representation of direct thought.

After the first two declaratives, most of the scene is consistently focalised through Emily, so that readers experience the scene from a character's perspective. This is instigated immediately after the third statement. The tone of address changes from the un-focalised declarative, 'she couldn't hear anything', to a more colloquial style – 'like when you get real high fevers' – which introduces an informal tone quite different to the formality of the preceding statements. Then follows another switch; the fragment, 'delirious', provides a summation of the character's mental state and thus could be attributed to a third-person narrator. However, the use of the temporal marker, 'now', which follows reverts back to the character by placing the reader directly within their temporal perspective. The uncertainly displayed – 'she was confused' and 'she did not know' – while remaining third-person, represents the apprehension of the focalising character. The frequent use of contractions, such as 'didn't' and 'she'd', also offer a more informal tone which is again indicative of some degree of focalisation. The eighth sentence begins 'right', establishing a shared psychological perspective, as Emily evaluates the scene. An increased sense of uncertainty, usually attributed to a character rather than an omniscient narrator, is affirmed by hesitant declarations such as 'she couldn't say', 'she didn't remember' and 'maybe there were torches'. The narration also contains frequent instances of colloquial modification such as Emily's capacity to 'sort of' feel her legs and her recognition that this is not 'so' good. Thus, while grammatically the narration belongs to a third-person narrator, the increasing focalisation of the narrative introduces free indirect discourse markers.

As the paragraph continues, the narration becomes more frequently infused with Emily's voice so that, by the end of the account, the text is jumbled. The last section comprises an eighty-four word sentence with the punctuation gradually deteriorating until it is completely absent. The syntax is particularly confused and lacks grammatical unity. In the last few words – 'impact world smaller small her world going away me too' – there is an extremely exaggerated mix of different voices and, since there is no punctuation, there are a number of ways in which they can be split into separate phrases. 'Impact world smaller small' and 'me too' are indicative of the direct thought process of the character. The use of 'me' suggests a switch from third to first person. However, the third-person narrator can also be detected in the use of 'her world' with the third-person pronoun indicating reportage, rather than direct quotation. Aside from this brief deictic shift, the lexia ends with almost the exclusive direct thoughts of Emily. Over the course of the narrative, the merging of voices lessens the influence of the omniscient narrator so that readers eventually experience the slippage into unconsciousness almost entirely from Emily's perspective.

As a consequence of the variable focalisation, slipping from one speaker into another, the narrative is unstable. As readers, we are shifted from one viewpoint to another and this jostling changes our relationship to the scene. Ryan (1991) observes that in modes of narration which mix the third and first person, 'the text blurs the distinction between TAW [Textual Actual World] and the worlds at the periphery (i.e. the private worlds of characters) by leaving it unclear who is speaking. ... We never know for sure whether the text describes a factual reality or a character's dream-world or hallucination' (40). Ryan observes that when a first-person perspective infiltrates an un-focalised narrative – as is the case in free indirect discourse – readers are often unable to differentiate definitively between facts and subjective observations. She suggests that this leads to a degree of uncertainty in the authenticity of statements because the characters' own mental conceptions might not reflect the external reality of the Textual Actual World.

As Ryan suggests, the change of address from the third to the first person in {... and ...} signifies a move towards a more subjective form of narration because facts cannot be separated from opinions. Thus, the epistemological status of the Textual Actual World is problematised through the mixing of narrator and focaliser. In terms of authenticity, we may or may not be able to determine the 'factual reality' from a 'character's dream-world'. However, in terms of epistemological immersion in the Textual Actual World, the change in perspective does move from a distanced to a very specific and particularly subjective World View.

Ryan suggests that the characters' private worlds lie at 'the periphery' of the Textual Universe, suggesting that they are situated at a distance from the Textual Actual World so that a move towards the characters' private worlds represents a shift from the centre outwards; readers become more distanced from the events in the Textual Actual World as the narration moves from third to first person. Yet while the *authenticity* of statements may be undermined by a subjective viewpoint – another World View – projecting the perspective into the mind of a character actually signifies a more intimate connection between the reader and the character. In the {… and …} lexia in *Victory Garden*, readers experience a shift, back-and-forth, between a seemingly omnipotent World View of a third-person narrator to the subjective World View of a character. The movement from an un-focalised third person to free indirect discourse to first-person direct thought in the {… and …} lexia means that readers become increasingly drawn into the Textual Actual World as the narrative becomes more intensely focalised. The reader's experience of the Textual Actual World moves from being externally observed to internally experienced, shifting from the relative objectivity of a third-person narrator to the subjectivity of the character. As the psychological viewpoint changes, so too does the emotional immersion and spatial perspective. Thus, the World View of the character is situated, not at the periphery of the Textual Actual World, but firmly within it.

The disparity between Ryan's conjectures about free indirect discourse and my own analysis of the {… and …} sequence ensues because of our differing analytical emphases. Ryan considers the faithfulness of a character's perspective relative to the Textual Actual World in terms of authenticity and therefore its proximity to an objective Textual Actual World centre. According to Ryan's analysis, when a character's voice infiltrates the narrative, a particular 'private world' is invoked; the use of the term, 'world', suggesting that this is always an ontological domain. In these terms, individual views of the world are seen as distanced from the Textual Actual World because, compared to the omniscient view of a narrator, they are relatively unverifiable and therefore potentially non-authentic. My analysis of the {… and …} lexia is concerned, not with authenticity, however, but with the readers' psychological and spatial position in relation to the Textual Actual World and the immersive capacity of the free indirect discourse. In this case, because readers end the scene from the character's perspective, Emily's World View becomes their sole access point to the Textual Actual World and is something that is situated firmly within it. As Ryan's analysis of free indirect discourse observes, the narration does become more subjective as this shift occurs, but the experience also becomes more intense as readers are drawn into empathising with Emily. It constitutes a rare occasion where readers move closer to, if not achieve, recentering (Ryan, 1991). As the syntax becomes confused, the reader becomes confused, positioning her or his perspective epistemologically within the character's view of the Textual Actual World. While the reader knows that this is a subjective account, she or he becomes more deeply immersed within that domain and, consequently, feels empathetic towards her experience. The reader may not believe it to be an accurate description of the world *outside* of the character's mind, but it represents an internal experience *within* the character's mind and because, by the end of the lexia, he or she can only experience the Textual Actual World through her perspective, Emily's perspective becomes the Textual Actual World.

McHale's (1987) analysis of narrative levels more accurately reflects the immersive capacity of the narration in the {... and ...} lexia, but his terminology is not completely satisfactory. He labels mental anticipations, wishes, or recollections of characters as the 'character's subjective domain or subworld' (101), situating this in opposition to 'the world *outside* the characters' minds' (101). McHale's conceptualisation is useful because it distinguishes between inside and outside a character's mind. It also places the private perspective of a character *within* that individual's mind and therefore at a distance from the external environment. However, his use of terminology is inaccurate in the *Victory Garden* example because, while a 'character's subjective domain' might not always represent a particular world-state, the use of 'subworld' suggests that internal reflections do necessitate a separate ontological domain.

Despite this terminological inconsistency, from McHale's perspective, a switch to a character's mental world involves a movement inwards, towards the internal consciousness of the character; the term 'sub' suggests that this is a level lower than or deeper into that of the Textual Actual World. While this level may well be subjective and therefore further away from the facts of the Textual Actual World in terms of authenticity, it is a perspective that is embedded deeper within that domain than that of the third-person narrator because Emily also belongs to the narrated part of Textual Actual World. Readers move from a perspective in which they observe from somewhere above the scene to a perspective which has been established from an experience which is situated within it; from a panoramic view of a non-participating entity to an intensely specific experience of a participating character. Ontologically, therefore, readers move from a presentation of the Textual Actual World that is only situated within the narrating Textual Actual World to the World View of the character who is also situated within the narrated Textual Actual World.

Figure 4.4 represents the variable focalisation of the first {... and ...} lexia. Initially, a communicative channel is established between a third-person narrator and a narratee by the third-person narration at the beginning of the lexia. This takes place within the narrating Textual Actual World. As a consequence of Emily's perspective infiltrating the narration, the third-person narrator's voice begins to

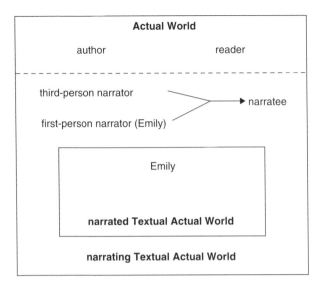

Figure 4.4 The ontological landscape created by the free indirect discourse in the first {... and ...} lexia

merge with Emily's. This duality means that Emily also communicates as an additional first-person narrator. This is represented by the two merging arrows on the diagram. Eventually, towards the end of the lexia, when the direct thought takes over completely, Emily's thoughts become the reader's sole point of access so that she narrates the scene exclusively. At this point, the third-person narrator in the narrating Textual Actual World disappears and the communication between Emily, as first-person narrator, and the narratee remains. The diagram also shows the boundary that separates the readers in the Actual World and the narrator in the narrating Textual Actual World is less prominent; this is shown by the dotted boundary line. A permeable boundary is shown because, for the duration of the reader's experience of the first {... and ...}, there are no devices in place that draw attention to the artificiality of the Textual Actual World. That is, up until the reader has to click to the next lexia, they can ignore the artificiality of the Textual Actual World.

The gradual movement from un-focalised narration to free indirect discourse to direct thought in {... and ...} means that the communication channels are altered steadily and perhaps unnoticeably. More importantly, the ontological boundary between the Textual Actual

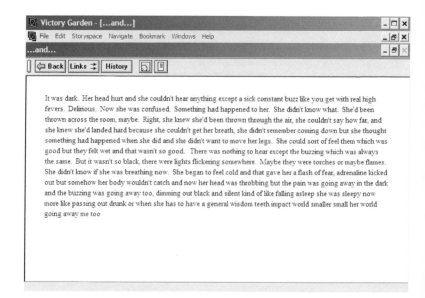

It was dark. Her head hurt and she couldn't hear anything except a sick constant buzz like you get with real high fevers. Delirious. Now she was confused. Something had happened to her. She didn't know what. She'd been thrown across the room, maybe. Right, she knew she'd been thrown through the air, she couldn't say how far, and she knew she'd landed hard because she couldn't get her breath, she didn't remember coming down but she thought something had happened when she did and she didn't want to move her legs. She could sort of feel them which was good but they felt wet and that wasn't so good. There was nothing to hear except the buzzing which was always the same. But it wasn't so black, there were lights flickering somewhere. Maybe they were torches or maybe flames. She didn't know if she was breathing now. She began to feel cold and that gave her a flash of fear, adrenaline kicked out but somehow her body wouldn't catch and now her head was throbbing but the pain was going away in the dark and the buzzing was going away too, dimming out black and silent kind of like falling asleep she was sleepy now more like passing out drunk or when she has to have a general wisdom teeth impact world smaller small her world going away me too

Figure 4.5   Screenshot of the first {… and …} lexia

World and the Actual World is kept hidden. The transparency of the ontological boundary, however, is only temporary because the lexia immediately following the first {… and …} lexia spectacularly reinstates it. The next lexia, also entitled {… and …}, shows the same text as that found in the first {… and …}, but visually distorted. As the screenshots in Figures 4.5 and 4.6 show, the second {… and …} lexia signifies that the first {… and …} lexia has received some kind of impact and been cracked. The second {… and …} lexia therefore provides a representation of the first but one which readers are forced to recognise as artificial. Our own computer screen is obviously not cracked. Instead, *Victory Garden* presents a *simulated* crack.

In the context of the Textual Actual World, the cracked screen represents what can be interpreted as Emily's demise. The screen is broken by an impact, the consequences of which are described in the first {… and …} lexia. However, because *Victory Garden* is read from a computer in the Actual World, the representation of a cracked screen also suggests that the impact is so great that it has impacted on the domain from which the reader is viewing. As has been shown above, lexias such as {Interrupt} suggest that the Textual Actual World is broadcast to the reader via a transmission. The cracked screen continues this motif by

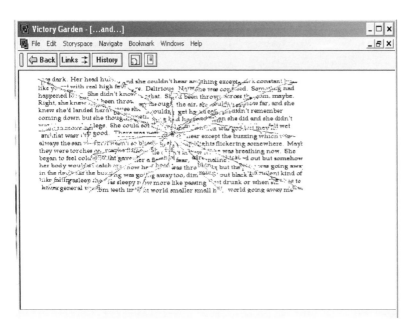

Figure 4.6   Screenshot of the second {… and …} lexia

suggesting that the impact in the narrated Textual Actual World is so great that it actually impacts on the Actual World. It suggests that the reader's access to the Textual Actual World has been interrupted as a consequence of the events that it contains.

Yet while the cracked screen might suggest that events in the narrated Textual Actual World have consequences in the Actual World, this is clearly impossible. Readers have access to the Textual Actual World but the inverse does not apply. Ironically therefore, rather than sustaining a mimetic effect – convincing readers that the Textual Actual World of *Victory Garden* actually exists – the impact actually foregrounds the artificiality of that domain. The boundary between the two domains is no longer concealed but rather firmly reinstated.

Further inscribing the ontological boundary that the second {… and …} lexia instates, the only available screen that leads on from the second {… and …} lexia is a blank, black page as shown by the screenshot in Figure 4.7. In the narrated Textual Actual World, the black screen in {.} suggests that Emily has lost consciousness or died. In the Actual World, this further accentuates its ontological separateness by representing the

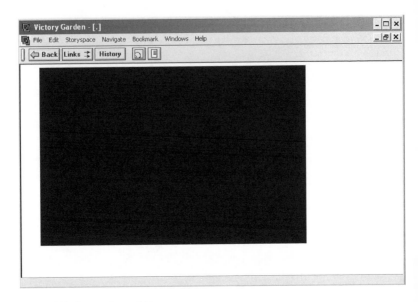

Figure 4.7   Screenshot of {.}

impossibility of the reader's computer having shut down as a consequence of the impact.

Ciccoricco (2007) recognises the role that this sequence of lexias plays
in alienating the reader from the text and argues that 'with the fractur-
ing of this window, our immersion is blocked' (117). He suggests that
readers are no longer absorbed by the text but made aware of their position outside it. In the {... and ...}, {... and ...}, {.} sequence, readers are
alerted to the artificiality of the Textual Actual World, prevented from
becoming immersed and reminded of their ontological position in the
Actual World. However, it is precisely because of their epistemological
absorption in the first {... and ...} lexia that the wrench out of it is so
marked. Ciccoricco concludes that with the cracking of the screen 'the
reader's position parallels that of Emily's friends back home, who are
caught in a continual twenty-four-hour news cycle replete with facts,
opinions, and images of the war' (117). He suggests that the reader
is positioned with Emily's friends 'back home' – that is, in a position
external to the action so that neither reader nor friend can experience
the war directly. As the analysis above shows, the dramatic expulsion
from the Textual Actual World in the second {... and ...} lexia and then
in {.} ensues because the focalisation in the first {... and ...} lexia positions

us within Emily's World View. We are taken into a position within the Textual Actual World before being excluded upon the impact. As our point of access, Emily, loses consciousness, access to the narrated Textual Actual World is denied. Yet this is not an *external* account of Emily's demise; we experience her death directly.

(Re)representing the Textual Actual World(s)

As the analysis has shown so far, *Victory Garden* contains a number of different forms of narration and styles of representation. While ultimately ontologically self-reflexive, thematically they warn us of the very real consequences of military conflict. More importantly, in the context of this analysis, by temporarily immersing readers into the Textual Actual World before pushing them out again, the text warns us of the ease with which we can lose sight of the artificiality of representation. Similarly, while each style of representation has been shown to be ultimately ontologically divisive, collectively they have a more general significance because they show the variety of means through which different events can be portrayed.

A further concern with epistemological plurality is explored in one key part of the text in which, initially at least, the narration appears to be rather unremarkable. However, it is the initial ordinariness of the scene that makes the ontological consequences so dramatic. Throughout the novel, Professor Boris Urquhart's mental state is shown to be unstable. Some of his behaviour is therefore sometimes unusual, classifiable as either pathologically paranoid or else simply eccentric. The scene in question follows Urquhart as he runs, believing that he is being chased. The events can be defined as follows: Urquhart is chased; Urquhart goes to Tate's study; Urquhart walks around the room inspecting a number of objects; Urquhart asks Tate about the photograph on the desk; Tate suggests that Urquhart gets some professional psychological help. While the events might be mechanically catalogued, the scene is resonant and has been analysed by other hypertext theorists from an ontological perspective (e.g. Koskimaa, 2000; Cicoricco, 2007) because it is described three different times by the same third-person narrator one after another. Figure 4.8 shows how the sequence of lexias fits together to describe the scene three times.

Initially, each reiteration of the scene appears to be the same but a closer inspection reveals that small details are changed each time. Temporal markers within the lexias signal that some scenes are a recurrence of others. The narrator playfully alludes to the text's multiplicity

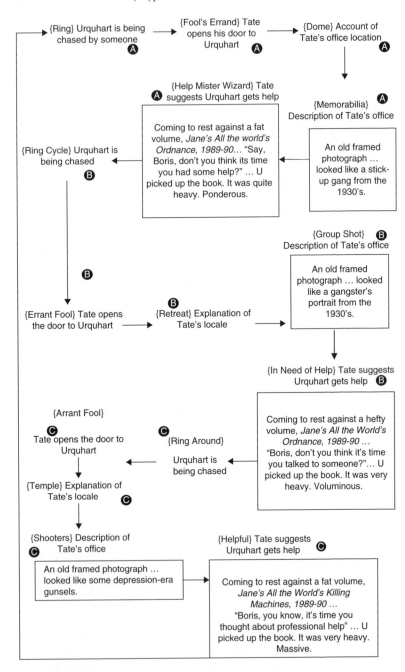

Figure 4.8   The lexia loop

and this is signalled deictically. Reports that 'U is *once again still* always running through that dark field' in {Ring Around, my emphasis} and 'the weather panels were *still* rolled back' in {temple, my emphasis} show that the narrator is aware of the loop in which the reader is caught. In this case, the allusions to other parts of the text form a kind of intra-textual network of references, reminding readers of the integral structure of the hypertext. Similarly, as shown in Figure 4.8, Tate suggests to Urquhart that he seek some professional help, but using three different approaches, either suggesting he 'had some help' {Help Mister Wizard} in Group A, 'talked to someone' {In Need of Help} in Group B or 'thought about professional help' {Helpful} in Group C. In this example, therefore, a more serious tone is introduced by the movement from an informal chat to a professional therapy session.

The objects that are described in Urquhart's office are also altered quite dramatically. When describing the book on the desk, the narrator shifts from 'ponderous' {Help Mister Wizard} to 'voluminous' {In Need of Help} to 'massive' {Helpful}. Each evaluation suggests that the book has a different kind of resonance with synonyms depicting a slightly different size or shape. Likewise, the book on Tate's desk changes from *Jane's All the World's Ordnance, 1989–90* in {In Need of Help} and {Help Mister Wizard} to *Jane's All the World's Killing Machines, 1989–90* in {Helpful}. The word 'ordnance' has military connotations and is essentially euphemistic and 'killing machines' more literal, and therefore explicitly harsh. In Group A, also, the 'stick-up gang' {Memorabilia} in the photograph suggests playfulness. The term alludes to a Hollywood heist or a fancy dress; the lexia title is also suggestive of leisure. In Group C, the picture depicts 'depression-era gunsels' in {Shooters}. This is much more specific, describing hoodlums or criminals with guns. In Group B, 'gangster' is chosen and communicates a more organised kind of criminal activity. The lexia title, {Group Shot}, alludes to the photograph, but the use of the compound noun 'group shot' introduces a subtle degree of violence because of the hint towards a gun 'shot'; the lexia title thus introduces the weapon directly.

In Figure 4.8, the beginning of the sequence is shown as {Ring}. However, in other readings, the loop could be entered at another point, so that the sequence begins at an alternative lexia. Importantly, at whichever point the reader enters the loop, the text describes the scene in three different ways in such a way that the reader encounters the different descriptions one after the other. They will be more aware therefore of the changes. The structure of the text does not privilege one description over the other once the sequence has been entered. Any privileging that may be associated with the order in which the accounts appear is removed once the lexia paths spiral into a continuous loop; in such a cyclical configuration, none of the three descriptions is prioritised.

In the Actual World, the three scenes in the *Victory Garden* loop are difficult to prioritise between because as a hypertext the lexias are entitled rather than numbered and therefore not ordered according to a numerical hierarchy. Perhaps more importantly, although the changes to the scene are slight and the language used synonymous, the different representations are connotatively significant. In fact it is because the scenes are so similar and occur one after the other that the three different descriptions encourage readers to consider the significance, purpose and status of each.

Similarly, as the lexia titles in Table 4.1 show, the lexia titles simultaneously allude to and differ from each other. The changes to the titles are made either by using synonyms, as in the different terms for a dwelling, such as {Retreat} and {Temple} or by rearranging and modifying some of the same words, as in {Fool's Errand} and {Errant Fool}. Thus, the lexia titles either allude to each other by association or they refer to lexia titles in the loop more directly.

Perhaps it is unlikely that readers would analyse the recurring scenes with the same systematic approach that is adopted for this analysis. It is possible for a reader to see only part of the loop and return to another part at a later stage. In this instance, the allusion to the other descriptions might invoke a feeling akin to déjà vu in that we might remember reading a similar account before. It would be feasible that the reader might think that this is the same scene each time, if he or she is not

Table 4.1   Lexia titles in the lexia loop

		Basic action described			
		Urquhart chased	Tate opens door to Urquhart	Tate and Urquhart converse	Urquhart notices ornaments	Tate tells Urquhart to seek help
Group of Lexias	A	{Ring}	{Fool's Errand}	{Dome}	{Memorabilia}	{Help Mister Wizard}
	B	{Ring Cycle}	{Errant Fool}	{Retreat}	{Group Shot}	{In Need of Help}
	C	{Ring Around}	{Arrant Fool}	{Temple}	{Shooters}	{Helpful}

sensitive to the subtle differences. However, it is because the scenes are so similar that the differences are so revealing. The allusions to other lexias and the changing descriptions of the same scene teach readers that there are various ways in which the Textual Actual World can be represented.

Koskimaa (2000) suggests that the three different descriptions are 'like different drafts, or adjustments, trying to find the exact atmosphere'. This interpretation suggests that the lexia loop is playful, merely exposing the problems encountered in creative writing. However, the lexia loop is more didactic than Koskimaa's view suggests because the different scenes, described by different linguistic labels, expose the rhetoric of representation. By using different synonyms throughout the sequence, the reader's attention is drawn to the way in which small changes to diction can dramatically affect the nature of each scene. The paralleling of the descriptions foregrounds the changes explicitly because, by positioning the many different representations alongside each other, the different choices that are involved in the process of representation are made much more visible.

By placing the different descriptions in a continuous loop, the representational mechanisms that might be otherwise hidden are foregrounded. The paralleling of lexias that the hypertext structure permits means, perhaps uniquely, that once the loop is entered the device is accentuated. However, while the hypertext medium provides a convenient structure for housing this device, the message that it delivers is not exclusive to the hypertext medium. Hutcheon (1996) also observes a similar propensity for representational plurality in historiographic metafiction. She argues that texts that offer contradictory accounts exhibit a 'concern for the multiplicity and dispersion of truth(s)' (477). The implication, she suggests, is that 'there are only truths in the plural, and never one truth; and there is rarely falseness *per se*, just other truths' (479). The alternative descriptions in the *Victory Garden* loop can also be seen to challenge the notion of singularity in favour of multiplicity. They offer a pluralistic account of events so that none are true, but neither are they false.

What is hermeneutically significant about this device in a text such as *Victory Garden* is that the epistemological indeterminism that it presents in the Textual Actual World might also apply to the Actual World. A dichotomous relationship between the Actual World and the Textual Actual World is upheld throughout *Victory Garden* because, as a historical fiction, it is based on Actual World events. Thus, when the text questions its own capacity to represent a definitive version of events it also questions, if only implicitly, the capacity of the Actual World to do the same.

As the analysis has shown, the three descriptions have enough congruity to be analogous with one another but also sufficient differences to be distinct. Hermeneutically, the scenes show the ease with which representations can be altered. Ontologically, the scene is significant, however, because of the impossibility that it represents. Each description of Urquhart and Tate is offered as equally valid and, unlike different World Views that might be offered by different characters, each account is offered by the same third-person narrator, making it impossible to discriminate between them. They create a Textual Actual World in which the Law of the Excluded Middle is broken (see Chapter 3 for a logical account of this law). In *Victory Garden*, the narrator is playful throughout. He or she presents him or herself as potentially unreliable. Readers might see each description as unauthentic or authentic however because they are presented by the *same* narrator with equal conviction or sincerity.

In the *Victory Garden* loop, therefore, establishing the authentic course of events involves making a subjective selection from a set of equally given objective accounts, which some readers might adopt, but that will reveal very little about how the text is working and why. Moreover, the synonymous descriptions and the playful temporal markers within the lexias signal the text's resistance to such a strategy. The point of the device is not to choose between them. Rather, representing another example of the text's self-reflexivity, the narrator's allusion to the loops' multiplicity and the changes in detail are used to draw attention to the Textual Actual World as a premeditated and contrived ontological domain. By being presented with a re-representation of the same scene, the reader is alerted to the artificiality of the domain that the narrator describes so that the boundary between the Textual Actual World and Actual World is, once again, exposed.

Destabilising Ontological and Epistemological Boundaries

The analysis so far has shown that *Victory Garden* exposes its own artificiality using a number of different devices. Even though each works differently, shifting, dissolving and moving ontological structures within the Textual Actual World, each device increases the attention that is drawn to the ontological boundary that surrounds it. As a consequence of the ontological distinction that is enforced between the Textual Actual World and the Actual World, it is with ease that readers can distinguish between entities that originate in the Actual World and those that originate in the Textual Actual World. Even though they must use knowledge from the Actual World, they will probably be aware of when and where the text is adding something to their knowledge and experience of that domain. Some obvious examples of epistemological appendage include the University of Tara – a location that does not exist within the Actual World – and the characters which exist only in the Textual Actual World of *Victory Garden* – Emily, Boris Urquhart, Tate and so on. However, the epistemological congruence of and co-dependence between the Actual World and Textual Actual World that historical fiction enforces is also utilised in *Victory Garden* to show that ontological boundaries are sometimes more difficult to establish.

As was shown at the beginning of this chapter, the principle of minimal departure can be used to explain how readers make sense of references to Actual World counterparts, events and settings in historical fiction. In *Victory Garden* casual references to these entities mean that the epistemological relationship between the Actual World and the Textual Actual World is sometimes tacit. However, it is precisely the epistemological complacency that the text exposes through direct use of the Actual World and the reader's knowledge thereof.

As a relatively obvious manifestation of the text's reliance on the Actual World, a series of quotations are distributed throughout the text. They are taken from a range of sources but examples include political speeches, television shows and radio broadcasts. A selection is given below:

> The war wasn't fought about democracy in Kuwait – George Bush in July, 1991 {By the way …}.
>   The Mother of Battles has just started in the Gulf. The traitors began their attack at 2.30 a.m. on the night of January 16–17. … The thrones of the traitors will soon fall when the will of the Satan of the White House breaks. Palestine and the Golan Heights will be liberated. Mecca will be liberated. The Occupied Territories will be liberated – From Saddam Hussein's radio address, morning of January 17 {The Other Side}.
>   Don't ever go on television out of breath – John Holliman to Bernard Shaw, CNN {Breathless}.

As the samples show, each quotation is accompanied by information about its author and some also have additional contextual information such as the time and/or date on which it was published – verbally or textually – in the Actual World. In the Actual World, at the time of the first Gulf War, Saddam Hussein was the president of Iraq, George Bush was the president of the USA, and John Holliman and Bernard Shaw were television presenters on the CNN television channel. Since *Victory Garden* uses the Actual World as an epistemological template, we also assume that these facts apply to its Textual Actual World.

Structurally, each lexia can be reached via a number of reading routes but, irrespective of that context, each offers a particular perspective on the historical events that are relevant to the narrative of *Victory Garden*. To take one example, while the quotation in {By the way ...} originates in the Actual World, Bush's speech is also epistemologically relevant to the Textual Actual World. It offers an interpretation of and provides context to the conflict that the novel also describes. Epistemologically, therefore, the quotation is relevant to both the Actual World and the Textual Actual World. However, unlike the more casual invocation of Actual World figures or events that readers experience elsewhere in the text – in lexias such as {Cyclops}, for example – the use of the Actual World in this case is much more explicit. The quotation is accompanied by a formal author–date reference which cites a secondary source unequivocally and this makes it apparent that information has been taken from another text – something that originates beyond the ontological boundaries of the Textual Actual World described in *Victory Garden*.

The use of quotations in *Victory Garden* literalises the principle of minimal departure, therefore, by making it explicit that information from the Actual World is being used within the Textual Actual World. Thus, lexias such as {By the way ...}, {The Other Side} and {Breathless} highlight the process that readers must go through when they read a historical novel because they import information very overtly. They make what might otherwise be an implicit process very explicit. The ontological boundary between the two domains is foregrounded by the quotations because the formal references make it clear that the quotations originate from elsewhere. The quotations are used to point to another text – one that belongs outside the boundaries of the Textual Actual World. Further, since the speakers are likely to be known to the reader, their Actual World origin is even more explicit. Moreover, the ontological separateness of the quotations in *Victory Garden* is even more pronounced because of the physical structure of the novel as hypertext. The quotation is placed in its own lexia, quite separate from the events to which it provides context. Its structural separateness further highlights its ontological peculiarity.

Yet while ontologically the quotations originate in and ultimately belong to the Actual World, because they are also used to build the Textual Actual World of *Victory Garden*, their status is relative. Like Actual World counterparts, they are epistemologically relevant to both contexts so that the quotations belong both to the Actual World and the Textual Actual World and, as such, the ontology becomes mixed, indeterminate and volatile. Rather than the Actual World/Textual Actual World dichotomy that many of the other devices in the text enforce, the ontological landscape here is more flexible. It depends on where readers perceive the quotations as being from as to where they locate them and where they have their impact. They make sense in relation to the Textual Actual World because they contextualise the action depicted in *Victory Garden*. Similarly, they are taken from the Actual World and so readers also recognise them as being valid in their system of reality.

In spite of the ontological foregrounding that Actual World quotations such as {By the way ...} achieve, therefore, it is with relative ease that readers can make an indexical switch between the Actual World and Textual Actual World. That is, while, ontologically, the quotations originate in the Actual World, because they are epistemologically relevant to both Actual World and Textual Actual World, readers can use the quotations in either domain. The structural separateness of the quotations in *Victory Garden* accentuates the ontological boundary between the two domains, but the epistemological relevance of the quotations to the Textual Actual World also emphasises the inherent relationship between the two. Thus not only does a fictional background offer a new environment in which to interpret historical documents or events, it also shows the reader just how closely the two contexts are related.

Problematising the Ontological Dichotomy

As a means of exposing the inherent relationship between fact and fiction that the quotations epitomise, the novel contains elements that are more difficult to categorise as belonging to one domain or the other and, ultimately, ask the reader to question whether, in some cases at least, a boundary can be definitively drawn. Like the Actual World quotations in {By the way ...}, {The Other Side} and {Breathless}, a quotation in {Do It Now} offers a commentary about military conflict. It reads:

I'd rather have my husband over there now than have my daughter over there twenty years from now – Wife of Airborne Trooper, South Carolina.

Epistemologically, the quotation in {Do It Now} is relevant to the Textual Actual World as well as the Actual World because of the pertinent issues that it raises about the human impact of a military conflict – something that is relevant to both contexts. The citation that accompanies the quote indicates that it belongs to another text – something that seems, like the other quotations, to originate in the Actual World. However, while the implied ontological *origin* of the quotations in {By the way ...}, {The Other Side} and {Breathless} are easily identifiable, the quotation in {Do It Now} is more ontologically problematic. Unlike the Actual World figures in the other quotations, whose notoriety in the Actual World can be utilised, the author of this quotation is unnamed, unknown and untraceable. She is referred to anonymously as a 'wife of airborne trooper'. Consequently, readers are unable to establish whether the quotation in {Do It Now} originates, like the other quotations, in the Actual World or whether it has been fabricated for the purpose of *Victory Garden*. Consequently, the Actual or Textual Actual *origin* of the quotation and therefore its fictive or factual status is absolutely undeterminable. Rather than being borrowed or copied from the Actual World, the quotation can be categorised as being shared between the two domains because, while it definitely belongs to the Textual Actual World, it may or may not also belong to the Actual World.

Irrespective of the ontological origin of the {Do It Now} quotation, it is, like the other quotations in the text, indexical. Whether or not its Actual World status is authentic, it can be used within the context of either the Textual Actual World or the Actual World. Crucially, however, if the wife's statement is fictitious, then it is possible to mistake fiction as fact and if the wife's statement is authentic, then it is possible to see as fiction, what is, in truth, a fact. While the reader may never know its ontological status, its inclusion shows the ease with which an apparently authentic historical document could be forged. The eventual consequence of this lesson is that the ontological status of all the other quotations is undermined because the reader can infer that what can be done to one quotation can be done to the others. Fact and fiction can be very easily exchanged.

Victory Garden as Historiographic Metafiction

Returning to Hutcheon's definition of historiographic metafiction, we can see how *Victory Garden* might fulfil the same criteria. Hutcheon (1996) uses the term to describe 'novels that are intensely self-reflexive but that also reintroduce historical context into metafiction and problematize the entire question of historical knowledge' (474). The analysis of *Victory Garden* shows that it is a text which, as a historical novel, has a complex epistemological and ontological landscape. It is situated against a real historical event, the first Gulf War, and therefore represents a narration of history itself. The Actual World becomes a Textual Actual World because while the two domains are ontologically separate, they also have an integral epistemological link. Ultimately, therefore, it relies on the Actual World to act as its epistemological template. In order to do this, however, it relies upon mechanisms, such as the principle of minimal departure, which affirm the autonomy of its Textual Actual World. The casual invocation of Actual World figures within the narrative as well as the explicit reference to Actual World quotations mean that the two domains start to become epistemologically comparable and show how historical documents can be categorised as either fact or fiction.

Simultaneously, as a playful text, numerous devices are used to draw attention to its inherent artificiality so that while it depends upon historical fact it is also very obviously fiction. The analysis of the entrance map, the interruptions to the narrative and the re-representation of events are just three examples. These devices cleave a sharp boundary between the Actual World and the Textual Actual World so that while it relies on the Actual World, epistemologically, it also announces its ontological separation from it.

Conclusion

The switch between a hidden and a visible ontological seam epitomises the ontological trickery at work throughout *Victory Garden*. The use of quotations, which could belong equally to either domain, is perhaps the most pertinent expression of indexical ontology because events, locations, people and documents can be deemed either as factual or fictional depending on where and when they are presented or perceived. Such epistemological duality and associated ontological ambiguity is crucial to the thematic concerns of *Victory Garden* because, by exposing the means by which fact and fiction are conflated in this context, it shows the ease with which such a process might also operate elsewhere. In so doing, like historiographic metafiction, it undermines the authenticity, legitimacy and validity of testimonies and representations within the Actual World on which it is based so that through the separation of these domains, the significance of their slippery boundaries is also exposed.

The correlations that can be drawn between *Victory Garden* and Hutcheon's description of historiographic metafiction show that a concern with the ontological status of historical discourse is not exclusive to hypertext fiction. However, the ontological self-consciousness of the novel is partly due to the hypertext form; readers are aware throughout that what they are reading is artificial because they are physically involved in its construction. Thus, hypertext provides an additional means of hermeneutic expression. Indeed, it is precisely because *Victory Garden* houses an ontological landscape that is complex, diverse and malleable but which readers are responsible for constructing that the correlation between Textual Actual and Actual or between fiction and reality is so neatly achieved.

5
Is there a Mary/Shelley in this World? Rewrites and Counterparts in Shelley Jackson's (1995) *Patchwork Girl*

Shelley Jackson's *Patchwork Girl; Or, a Modern Monster* (1995) is a gothic novel in which the protagonist, the patchwork girl of the title, is a supernatural being comprised of a collection of human body parts donated, willingly, from the dead. The narrative documents her adventures in nineteenth-century England and modern-day urban America as she transforms from a solitary figure to a confident and independent member of contemporary society.

Structurally, *Patchwork Girl* is rather different to the texts discussed in the preceding chapters. Unlike the hidden links of *afternoon* (see Chapter 3) or the intricate structure evidenced by the map in *Victory Garden* (see Chapter 4), *Patchwork Girl* has a relatively straightforward configuration comprised of five different sections. The text does not instruct readers to start at 'graveyard' and progress to 'broken accents', but, as Figure 5.1 shows, the visual concatenation of the sections on the title page does at least suggest that each section should be seen as part of the larger whole.

While, visually, the title page suggests a particular reading sequence, the order in which each section is read is largely inconsequential for the overall narrative experience. This is because while they contain thematic similarities, each of the five sections of *Patchwork Girl* addresses a different facet of the novel: 'a graveyard' offers details of the donors of the patchwork girl's body parts; 'a journal' is narrated by the patchwork girl's creator and describes the relationship between her and the patchwork girl; predominantly narrated from the creator's perspective but also containing extracts from other fictional texts, 'a quilt' details the process of the patchwork girl's construction; 'a story' is narrated by the patchwork girl and offers her own perspective on

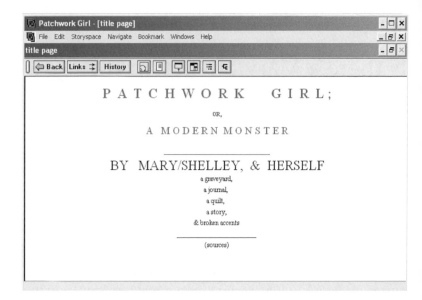

Figure 5.1   Screenshot of {title page}

her life; 'broken accents' offers reflections on the process of hypertext fiction writing.

Readers might choose to explore the text in a sequential fashion but this is not essential for an overall comprehension of the text. Similarly, while in *afternoon* and *Victory Garden* different reading paths depict different narratives, in *Patchwork Girl* fewer choices are offered. The structure allows readers to explore each section by following hyperlinks but with few narrative consequences tied to their selections. Each reading will inevitably result in a slightly different configuration of lexias but, because there are fewer hyperlinks and therefore fewer options, incongruent narratives are few in number. In this respect, the text makes relatively conservative use of the hypertext form. However, the overall interrelated configuration of the narrative is anything but simple.

Of the texts analysed in this book, *Patchwork Girl* has perhaps received the most critical attention, including an extensive analysis by the author herself (e.g. Joyce, 1997, 2003; Landow, 1997; Amerika, 1998; Jackson, 1998; Page, 1999; Hayles, 2000; Bolter, 2001). Most readings emphasise the influence of secondary sources within the novel. Hayles (2000) notes, for example, that *Patchwork Girl* is 'intensely parasitic on its print predecessors' (paragraph 15), an interpretation that acknowledges the importance of intertextual sources. Joyce (2003) also notes the relevance of secondary material in *Patchwork Girl* and argues that the inclusion of other texts forces our attention beyond the world offered in *Patchwork Girl*. She describes *Patchwork Girl* as a collection of 'random interlocking fragments' (39) and sees the constituents of the novel both inside and outside the text as causing a fractured reading.

This chapter will show how the textual interdependency that other critics have identified can be most accurately examined using Possible Worlds Theory. It will begin by showing how some sections of *Patchwork Girl* acknowledge a clear and apparent distinction between the Actual World and the Textual Actual World so that the reader is acutely aware of the artificiality of the novel and also its status as an *autonomous* fictional domain. The analysis will then show how this onto-logical distinction is problematised by the attention Jackson's hypertext continually draws to the intertextual relationships. Finally, focusing on the relationship that the text presents between text and author or between creator and invention, this chapter will show how the novel presents an elusive and changeable ontological landscape. The chapter concludes by showing that the novel is self-conscious about its own processes of world construction but that this is ultimately utilised in order to explore the relationship between reality and fiction, creator and created.

Piecing Together the Protagonist

If, as the title page encourages, *Patchwork Girl* is entered through the first section of the implied sequence, 'a graveyard', the protagonist introduces herself in the first person. She states:

> I am buried here. You can resurrect me, but only in piecemeal. If you want to see the whole you will have to sew me together yourself {graveyard}.

This rather elusive if not foreboding declaration leads to a {headstone} lexia in which various body parts are listed. As Figure 5.2 shows the graphology, lexia title and punning eulogy collectively allude to a grave-yard headstone.

Clicking on the various body parts leads to a description of the person to whom the part originally belonged. The collection of options in the {headstone} lexia provides an opportunity for readers to choose from a number of different options. They are encouraged to interact with

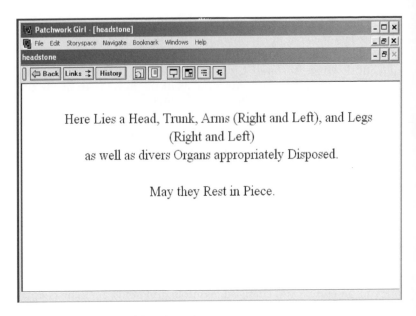

Figure 5.2   Screenshot of {headstone}

the text in order to gain information about the protagonist and her origins.

Within each of the resulting lexias, numerous voices emerge from the gravestone to detail the history of the monster's limbs and organs, with constituents seemingly selected for their desirable or valuable attributes. The 'Arms (Right)' link, for example, leads to a lexia in which the monster details the background to the donors of this limb. She tells us, 'my right arm has two parts: the upper belonged to Tristessa, a woman known in the ship-yards for her deadly aim with a bottle. ... The lower part was Eleanor's, a lady very dexterous with the accoutrements of femininity' {right arm}. In addition to their physical proficiencies, the body parts also offer details about the donor's psychological or emotional temperament. The patchwork girl informs us that 'my body is both insinuating and naïve' {trunk} and that her 'liver is modest, efficient, shapely and affectionate' {liver}. The constituent body parts do not just provide the physical shell of the protagonist therefore; they also influence her emotional qualities and behaviour.

In her analysis of *Patchwork Girl*, Hayles (2000) emphasises the association between the structure of the text and the patchworked body of the protagonist. She observes that 'like the female monster's body, the body of this hypertext is also seamed and ruptured, comprised of disparate parts with extensive links between them' (paragraph 23). Joyce (2003) also suggests that because the hypertext exists as a 'concatenation of ephemera' (43), it 'replicates the composition of the Girl's body' (43). While the protagonist is flesh and sutures and the text is lexias and links, both Joyce and Hayles note the association between monster and text in structural terms. Using Possible Worlds Theory, however, the ontological mechanisms that cause the reader to be alienated in this part of the text can be identified.

As the critics note, the 'a graveyard' section exploits the structural capacity of the hypertext medium as a means of constructing its protagonist. Using the metaphor of the patchwork, it asks the reader in the Actual World to stitch together the text, cohering pieces of information about the protagonist from a host of female contributors. These lexias construct the patchwork girl within the Textual Actual World so that, in this context, the fragments of text introduce the supernatural protagonist to the reader and establish her existence within the fictional domain. Her composition is ontologically significant, however, because it draws attention to the artificiality of the domain to which she belongs. Since the building of a character, lexia by lexia, is the responsibility of the reader, his or her role as picker and chooser of the various body parts does, as the critics above point out, parallel the way in which the entire text is constructed: as a collection of individual lexias and links which must be joined together. In addition, the literary convention by which a character is traditionally created – as a collection of individual stories or examples of their behaviours, relationships or contexts – is parodied. That is, the figurative convention of 'constructing' a fictional entity is literalised because the reader must physically join together the pieces of the protagonist. The reader is invited to take part in the process of world construction and to some extent this endows her or him with some degree of responsibility. The protagonist also allows the reader to explore her body – something which constitutes a relatively intrusive and therefore potentially intimate act. Yet the piecing together of the protagonist, via the piecing together of the text, is something that must be undertaken by the reader in the Actual World – a position which is *exterior* to the Textual Actual World. The ontological boundary between the Textual Universe of *Patchwork Girl* and the Actual World is foregrounded and the artificiality of the text exposed because readers are alerted to their role in the fiction-making process. The patchwork girl is a fictional entity and the world to which she belongs is ontologically alien to us.

Patchwork Girl and the Style of *Frankenstein*

While 'a graveyard' highlights the autonomy of *Patchwork Girl*'s Textual Actual World by drawing attention to the ontological boundary that surrounds it, the text also continually signals its reliance on and inter-dependence with other texts. The most obvious manifestation of this is the hypertext's reference to Mary Shelley's *Frankenstein*. Originally published in 1818, it is within this gothic novel that the protagonist of *Patchwork Girl* can be seen to originate. Shelley's text describes Dr Frankenstein's project in which he creates a male monster through the stitching together of human remains. Crucially, at the monster's request, Frankenstein also creates a second, female creature which, like the patchwork girl in 'a graveyard', is stitched together from a collection of human body parts. On reconsidering the potential consequences of his actions, Frankenstein destroys the female creature but various clues within *Patchwork Girl* suggest that the female protagonist is a manifesta-tion of Shelley's ill fated character.

The connection between *Frankenstein* and *Patchwork Girl* undoubtedly relies on the protagonist and the text tries to ensure that this vital piece of information is recognised by the reader. An extract from *Frankenstein* in which the female monster is built is even included within *Patchwork Girl*. It is perhaps for this reason that Hayles (2000) suggests that the affiliation between the two texts 'begins with the main character, who is reassembled from the female monster in Mary Shelley's *Frankenstein*' (paragraph 23) and thus attributes the characters as being the ultimate site of the intertextual relation. However, readers are given references to Shelley's novel well before they enter the hypertextual narrative in which she appears and it is precisely because of the existence of numerous intertextual devices that none can be seen as *solely* responsible for sig-nalling the connection between the two texts.

To begin with, the title, *Patchwork Girl; Or, a Modern Monster*, echoes Mary Shelley's *Frankenstein; Or, the Modern Prometheus*. Stylistically, the clause construction is the same in each title: proper noun, semi-colon, conjunction, and noun-phrase. The noun phrase in both titles also uses the modifier 'modern'. The juxtaposition of one title with the other exposes the idiosyncrasies of each. For example, 'the Modern Prometheus' of Shelley's title becomes 'a Modern Monster' in Jackson's. The substitution of the definite article in Shelley's original for an indefi-nite article in Jackson's highlights that the male monster of the canoni-cal text is familiar, but that the patchwork girl of this hypertext is, as yet, unknown.

Other changes also highlight a relationship of both reliance and independence. The doctor, 'Frankenstein', in Shelley's title is replaced by the 'Patchwork Girl' in Jackson's, so that the creator as subject is replaced by monster as subject. More importantly, the male as subject is replaced by the female as subject so that Shelley's choice of male protagonist is challenged with a female alternative. Finally, the male doctor as 'Prometheus' is replaced by patchwork girl as 'monster', so that while the male is assigned Greek mythological status, the female patchwork girl is demonised. In each case, the invocation and refashioning of the title shows how Jackson's title is similar but also different to Shelley's original.

In addition to displaying the title of the novel, the title page also heralds a paralleling of Jackson and Shelley. Authorship is attributed to 'Mary/Shelley, & Herself' (see Figure 5.1) and the graphology with which it is presented invites a number of different interpretations. 'Mary' and 'Shelley' can be merged to make one name – Mary Shelley – or 'Mary' and 'Shelley' can be split by the punctuation to make two names. Merging the two names to make 'Mary Shelley' highlights the influence of the Actual World author of *Frankenstein*, further drawing attention to the interconnectedness of *Frankenstein* and *Patchwork Girl*. The autonomy of each text is also acknowledged by the forward-slash which can be used to separate Mary (Shelley) and *Frankenstein* from Shelley (Jackson) and *Patchwork Girl*.

In addition to the invocation of two Actual World authors, both separate and connected, the use of 'herself' as a third author is also significant. As a reflexive pronoun, 'herself' is used to refer back to the preceding subject. However, because multiple females are listed, the anaphoric reference could refer to Mary Shelley, Shelley Jackson or the monster. The ambiguity with which the authorship is presented means that the three women are textually united but also granted independence as individual subjects.

Hayles (2000) argues that the linking of authors on the title page represents an 'attack on the "originality" of the work' (paragraph 38) by showing the way in which the authors and, by implication, their texts are related. In addition, however, the united authorship in Jackson's novel also implies that the author of *Patchwork Girl* has a different sort of relationship with her work than the author of *Frankenstein*. Mary Shelley stands apart from the protagonist of her title, but Shelley Jackson and her fictional companions are presented as united. Thus while the attributed authorship does signal the importance of Mary Shelley for the text, the tripartite authorship of *Patchwork Girl* also portrays a sense of female solidarity.

Stylistic Imitation Inside the Text

As the analysis of the title page has shown, a number of implicit references to Mary Shelley and her novel, *Frankenstein*, are made before the reader enters the text. It therefore signals that Shelley's novel may be epistemologically if not hermeneutically influential. While the amount of knowledge a reader has about the Textual Actual World of *Frankenstein* will vary, *any* recognition of the parallel between the two will lead to an association being drawn. The parallel that the title establishes is therefore epistemologically crucial for heralding some of the more subtle forms of reference that the novel contains within.

Indeed, a similar form of stylistic mimicry to that shown in the title is also evident within some lengthier sections of the novel. In particular, if readers follow the sequence that is implied by the title page and proceed from 'a graveyard' to 'a journal' they will encounter a first-person narrative that reflects the formalised and, in a contemporary context, rather archaic prose style of Shelley's gothic novel. The first two lexias in 'a journal' contain the following text:

> Yesterday I went for a walk down the lane that branches off at the holly tree from the main road. The day was gray, and the constant moisture hung in the air, agitating occasionally into the light rain. The sun, if I may give that name to a light so stripped of warmth, so pale and abstract that it seemed more a passing and careless allusion to the possibility of light than its manifestation, played fitfully in the upper reaches of the cloudbank overhead. ... I was as far as the little stone bridge and debating whether to turn back or cross and continue on the small perhaps firmer trail to the crossroads, where with luck I might beseech a ride of a farmer returning from town, when I saw on the far side of the span a sight that made me stop ankle-deep in mud and stare {my walk}.
>
> It was my monster, stark naked, standing still as if I had not yet breathed life into her massive frame, and waiting for me. She held in one hand a scrap of cloth I recognized, all that was left of the clothes I had thrust upon her when she fled me shortly after her conception. ... I could not help but quail before the strangeness of this figure, from which, I fancifully imagined the very blades of grass seemed to shrink, but curiosity, and a kind of fellow feeling was the stronger impulse, and I forced myself to continue {sight}.

The reflective style of the narrative in *Patchwork Girl* imitates the affectation and formality of a comparable scene in *Frankenstein*:

> I looked on the valley beneath; vast mists were rising from the rivers which ran through it, and curling in thick wreaths around the opposite mountains, whose summits were hid in the uniform clouds, while rain poured from the dark sky, and added to the melancholy impression I received from the objects around me. ... I suddenly beheld the figure of a man, at some distance, advancing towards me with superhuman speed. He bounded over crevices in the ice, among which I had walked with caution; his stature also, as he approached, seemed to exceed that of man. I was troubled: a mist came over my eye and I felt a faintness seize me, but I was quickly restored by the cold gale of the mountains. I perceived, as the shape came nearer (sight tremendous and abhorred!) that it was the wretch whom I had created. I trembled with rage and horror, resolving to wait his approach, and then close with him in mortal combat. He approached; his countenance bespoke bitter anguish, combined with disdain and malignity, while its unearthly ugliness rendered it almost too horrible for human eyes (Shelley, 1998 [1818]: 97–9).

In terms of the narrative, similar concerns can be detected in both extracts. Each creator roams the valley, oblivious of the meeting that is about to ensue. Both narrators display a typical Romantic preoccupation with the landscape and natural surroundings before their contemplations are interrupted by the appearance of a supernatural being. Each narrator also details the setting of their encounter, paying particular attention to the visual context. However, despite an evident preoccupation with the surrounding landscape, neither is fully satisfying to the observer because the beauty of nature is blighted by an impending doom. The light in both scenes is low; in *Patchwork Girl*, it is 'gray', in *Frankenstein*, the sky is 'dark'. These corresponding images are also indicative of the way that nature is personified in each piece. In *Frankenstein*, the absence of light contributes to the 'melancholy impression' given by the landscape. In *Patchwork Girl*, similar solemnity is indicated by the sun that has been 'stripped of warmth'; the description in this case suggests that the sun's personal space has been breached so that the landscape seems to somehow anticipate the appearance of the figure.

On meeting their protégés, both creators are incredibly fearful, and this eventually results in a physical reaction. In *Patchwork Girl*, she 'could not help but quail' and in *Frankenstein* he 'trembled' and there is again a similar connection between the creator, monster and the natural surroundings; the earth seems to mirror their fear. In *Patchwork Girl*, the earth appears scared of the figure, as if aware of its capabilities: 'the very blades of grass seemed to shrink'. In *Frankenstein* too, the monster is 'unearthly' as if disconnected or inherently separate from nature. The creators also imply a familial relationship between themselves and the monsters, using definite proximal reference and possessive pronouns. It is either 'my monster' and 'this figure' or 'the wretch'; the unnamed monster, denied natural status, is also denied the personal qualities associated with the human race.

Some shared linguistic structures provide a further source of compatibility. Syntactically, the multi-clausal sentences used in *Frankenstein* are replicated in *Patchwork Girl*. The third sentence in the second part of the {my walk} quotation, for example, is a 46 word sentence, comprising multiple clauses. An equally complex multi-clausal construction appears in the first sentence of the *Frankenstein* extract, which is 54 words in length. Both texts are written in the simple past and active voice and both are heavily reporting with regular use of verb phrases. The eloquent narration and learned diction utilised in *Patchwork Girl* is inescapably suggestive of the style of *Frankenstein*. The verbs used to describe the natural surroundings generally denote movement and a degree of nervousness. In *Frankenstein*, the mists are 'rising' and 'curling', the rivers 'ran' and rain 'poured'. Showing a similar kinetic energy, the moisture in the air is 'agitating' and the sun 'played fitfully' in *Patchwork Girl*. Nature appears to be roused in expectancy in both texts and in each case the appearance of the monster changes this dynamism.

Although the scenes are stylistically and structurally similar, however, the actions of the characters are significantly different in each text. Where Frankenstein's monster actively 'advanced', 'bounded' and 'approached' his maker, the monster in *Patchwork Girl* appears much more passive. She is 'standing still' and 'waiting' for her creator to approach. In this case, the male couple show antagonism whereas the female duo shows less ill feeling. Hayles (2000) acknowledges that 'the relation between creature and creator in *Patchwork Girl* stands in implicit contrast to the relation between the male monster and Victor Frankenstein. ... [The creator] feels attraction and sympathy rather than horror and denial' (paragraph 34). In Hayles's analysis she observes animosity in the Frankenstein–monster relationship which can be juxtaposed with the affection and compassion in the equivalent female relationship and the close reading of the two extracts above supports this view. In *Patchwork Girl*, the creator has a 'fellow feeling' for the monster, in Shelley's text the creature is 'abhorred'; where the male displays antagonism, the female shows maternal instincts.

The Consequences of Stylistic Imitation

The stylistic imitation, while hermeneutically revealing, however, also has ontological consequences. In her analysis of literary pastiche, Ryan (1991) notes that stylistic imitation prevents readers from becoming immersed in another ontological domain because the device is reliant on an ontological distinction being acknowledged. She suggest that in 'literary pastiche ... authors publish under their own names a text ostentatiously written in the style of another ... [so that] the author ... select[s] as narrator the counterpart of a real writer, and tr[ies] to reproduce the style and identity of the author being imitated' (89). Crucially, she suggests that 'the author of a parody of Proust does not tell readers: "Pretend that I am Proust," but rather: "I am myself but I can write like Proust". ... In distancing themselves from the parodee, parodists prevent their real-world addressee from relocating into TAW and engaging in make-believe' (89). As Ryan suggests, for stylistic imitation to be successful, readers must recognise the rhetorical game to which they are witness and, in order to acknowledge the game, they must remain at a critical distance from the Textual Actual World that is described. Thus, when a style is parodied and another narrative invoked, readers are simultaneously engaged in two different forms of communication. The ontological landscape that the stylistic imitation creates is shown in Figure 5.3.

As Figure 5.3 shows, the narrator in the {my walk} and {sight} lexias communicates information about the scene to the narratee. As Ryan's analysis of pastiche shows, in order that the reader can recognise the stylistic imitation of Mary Shelley that the narrator is responsible for delivering, the reader must also acknowledge the intentions of the author. Thus, a more explicit but also mediated form of communication between author and reader also takes place within the Actual World. As Ryan's observations suggest, this dual form of communication is ontologically significant because it foregrounds the artificiality of the Textual Actual World. Readers are assigned an interpretative role by pastiche because they must listen to two voices – one Actual and one Textual Actual – but, in order to perform that function, they must be located outside of the Textual Actual World. Accordingly, the boundary

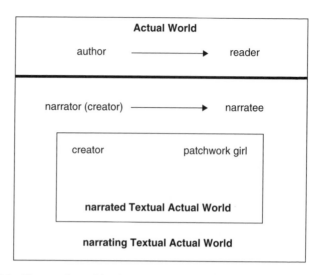

Figure 5.3   The ontological landscape created by stylistic imitation

between the Actual World and Textual Actual World is foregrounded on the diagram. As Ryan's analysis confirms, the literary pastiche in *Patchwork Girl* is fundamentally self-conscious because it relies on the visibility of its source.

Patchwork Girl as Postmodern Rewrite

The stylistic comparison of *Patchwork Girl* and *Frankenstein* reveals a number of linguistic, thematic and narrative similarities between the two texts. These features help to establish a connection between the two novels by providing formal points of comparison. In addition, as Hayles's and my own observations also show, the entities that populate each Textual Actual World are also important in the formation of the intertextual link. Thus while the relationship between the style of the original text and the style of the rewrite is essential for locating linguistic imitation, other factors such as the characters and the setting in which they appear are also essential for creating and sustaining the motif.

Doležel (1998a) isolates a tendency within particular types of contemporary writing to rework classic literary texts which he defines as 'postmodernist rewrites of classical works' (206). According to his definition, 'the rewrite appropriates the classic work's well-spun story, its popular characters, and, in some cases, its familiar setting' (206) but modifies it so as to 'redesign, relocate, reevaluate the classic protoworld' (206). Doležel's conceptualisation of a rewrite emphasises that a relationship is formed between two *ontological* domains: the original Textual Actual World – what he calls a 'classical protoworld' – and the newfangled Textual Actual World – what he calls the postmodern rewrite. Importantly, his use of verbs, each prefixed with 're', emphasises the importance of retrospection and repetition as well as revision in a postmodernist rewrite. The terminology implies that the original text is as important to the rewrite as its new incarnation.

As Doležel's definition shows, the consequences of rewrites are epistemological – in that one text illuminates the idiosyncrasies of the other – and also ontological – in terms of the autonomy of each Textual Actual World that it illuminates. Indeed, as Doležel notes in his development of the category, 'the complexity of the rewrite's meaning and its challenge to semantic interpretation is due precisely to the fact that it refers not only to its fictional world but also, in various ways and degrees, to its source' (222). Doležel acknowledges that the effect of a rewrite is due to the simultaneous paralleling that it enforces. When the reader of a work recognises that the text is drawing on another, they inevitably invoke their knowledge of that other Textual Actual World. Such knowledge is what Doležel calls the 'fictional encyclopaedia' (177) of another text (see Chapter 6 for further discussion of encyclopaedic knowledge). He suggests that when a reader recognises a text as a rewrite of another, the texts become 'bound in a relationship of mutual semantic illumination' (201). Doležel's interpretation of the effects of a rewrite predominantly acknowledges the epistemological consequences of the two-way relationship. Yet while the parallel is activated epistemologically, as Doležel acknowledges and the analysis of *Patchwork Girl* shows so far, its effect is also ontological because it requires that readers retain a critical distance from the fictional domain that the imitating text describes. Importantly, both processes happen simultaneously and are equally dependent on each other: the juxtaposition enforces an ontological paralleling and the ontological paralleling enforces a critical juxtaposition. Thus, for the incongruities to be recognised, the Textual Actual Worlds must be sufficiently epistemologically linked but also remain ontologically separate. In the context of *Patchwork Girl*, by alluding to another text – that of *Frankenstein* – it also invokes information about another Textual Actual World. That is, the stylistic, narrative and character parallels are not just aesthetic tricks; rather they are also important for importing information about the Textual Actual Worlds to which they are attached.

The Principal of Minimal Departure and Intertextuality

Since *Patchwork Girl* relies, if only partially, on *Frankenstein* for the construction of its Textual Actual World, it can be seen to use similar mechanisms to that of a historical novel. In both cases, the epistemological origins of at least some of a Textual Universe's constituents are located in another system of reality. As has been shown in previous chapters, the principle of minimal departure can be used to explain how readers utilise their own knowledge of the Actual World to make inferences about the domains constructed by a fictional text. The principle explains that readers assume that a Textual Actual World contains the same inventory of inhabitants, logical laws and behaviours as the Actual World unless the text specifies otherwise.

Yet while the Actual World is inevitably available as an epistemological template, a text such as *Patchwork Girl*, which is thematically linked to another text, also relies on another ontological domain as an additional source of information. As Ryan (1991) notes, 'texts also exist as potential objects of knowledge, and this knowledge may be singled out as relevant material for the construction of a textual universe. The principle of minimal departure permits the choice, not only of the real world but also a textual universe as a frame of reference' (54). Ryan's principle of minimal departure is sufficiently flexible to explain that while a reader has access to their knowledge of the Actual World they also possess knowledge of other Textual Actual Worlds. Both sources of knowledge can be utilised when reading. This, as Doležel's definition of a 'postmodern rewrite' acknowledges, is especially true of canonical fiction because of the reputation that comes with that kind of cultural status. In the case of *Patchwork Girl*, even if readers have not read *Frankenstein*, because it currently belongs to the canon of English literature, it is likely that they will know at least something about the novel, its characters, its author and its plot, and this is all information that *Patchwork Girl* can utilise.

In his analysis of parody and literary pastiche, Doležel (1998a), like Ryan, makes an explicit association between texts which draw on historical events or persons – historical fiction – and those that draw on other well-known tales – parodies or rewrites. His focus, however, lies on the significance of counterparts in both types of text. He notes that 'just as the actual Napoleon can be transformed into an unlimited number of fictional Napoleons ... so can the fictional Edward Rochester appear in an unlimited number of alternative incarnations' (225). Doležel's comparison might imply that the utilisation of a character from another

Textual Actual World relies on the same mechanism as the utilisation of an individual from the Actual World. Yet while historical fictions and rewrites each utilise entities from other domains, the ontological mechanics are slightly different. When a character is based on a figure in the Actual World, the ontological composition of each domain is different: one is the Actual World and one is a Textual Actual World which, according to Possible Worlds Theory is a particular type of possible world. Conversely, when a character from one text is used in another, both the original and the copy belong to the same kind of world: a Textual Actual World. Thus, while initially the process might appear to be the same, in Possible Worlds Theory at least, there is a fundamental difference.

Similarly, while he does not make an explicit commitment to any particular philosophical position, because Doležel describes Edward Rochester in terms of 'alternative incarnations', his terminology suggests that each version is a new manifestation of the original. In Possible Worlds Theory, this would translate as a character appearing as a counterpart of the other. However, as was seen in the analysis of historical fiction in Chapter 4, different factions of Possible Worlds Theory conceptualise the relationship between worlds and their constituents in different ways. Thus, if the theory is to be utilised, the ontological mechanics need to be clarified.

Transworld Identity, Counterpart Theory and Intertextuality

As was shown to be the case in the discussion of historical fiction, Possible Worlds Theory in literary studies has inherited the unresolved debate with different theorists allying with different positions from philosophical logic. Making an explicit commitment to the Concretist perspective, Margolin (1990) states that: 'following David Lewis (1986) … I hold that it makes little sense to speak of an identity relation between INDS [non-actual individual] in different, disjointed possible worlds. INDS are world-bound. Instead, we can say that each surrogate stands in a relation of *counterparthood* to its prototype' (865). Margolin stresses that a fictional entity is created *within* a particular ontological domain – that is, within a particular Textual Actual World. According to this premise, fictional characters are ontologically fixed to the domain in which they are originally constructed and cannot be taken and utilised elsewhere. Consequently, even if similarities can be indentified between characters, each is seen as being created as a separate entity within their respective Textual Actual Worlds. Margolin, like other Concretist theorists, regards apparent occurrences of the same character in different texts as constituting entirely different characters or – to use possible-worlds terminology – different *counterparts*.

Conversely, Pavel (1979) invokes and aligns himself with an Abstractionist perspective. He argues that 'in the world where Hamlet marries Ophelia and lives happily ever after, he is still Hamlet and she is still Ophelia, in the same way in Kripke's arguments, a Napoleon who spent his whole life in Corsica, would still have been *himself* (181–2). In his explanation of duplicated characters, Pavel also utilises possible-worlds logic in order to substantiate his alliances but from an opposing position to that of Margolin. Since from an Abstractionist perspective, possible worlds are regarded as mental conceptions rather than concrete domains, constituent entities are seen as possessing transworld identity rather than existing as counterparts in each different possible world. Since a Textual Actual World is a specific type of possible world, from an Abstractionist perspective a character is also seen as possessing transworld identity rather than appearing as a different counterpart in each Textual Actual World. Anticipating the Concretist counterargument, Pavel continues, 'although some aestheticians would probably want to claim ... [that Shakespeare's Cordelia is an entirely different character from Nahum Tate's Cordelia], the common intuition is rather that Nahum Tate has not created a second Cordelia, but simply has provided Cordelia with a happier destiny' (182). Pavel stresses that, irrespective of the laws of possible-worlds logic, when a character appears in more than one text, readers regard them as the *same* character whose circumstances have changed – as a character with transworld identity – rather than a completely different character or counterpart.

As the theoretical conflict between Margolin and Pavel shows, both factions of possible-worlds logic can be used, independently, to explain the process by which a fictional character can occur in more than one text. When the ontological autonomy of a character is emphasised, they are deemed to be a counterpart and when the ontological congruities are emphasised they are seen to possess transworld identity. While strictly logically incompatible, each perspective holds claims about the status of duplicated characters that can aid a literary analysis of the device. In order to recognise that a character originates in and is therefore taken from another text, characters must be seen, as Pavel advocates from an Abstractionist perspective, to possess transworld identity. In addition, in order that readers can recognise changes to the character's original circumstances, they must, as Margolin maintains from a Concretist perspective, remain connected to their original Textual Actual World. Thus, both theoretical positions can contribute something to this analysis of a rewrite.

Since concepts from both Abstractionism and Concretism are useful for this study in particular, both will be used. Thus, the Abstractionist term, 'transworld identity', will be retained to describe the process through which a Textual Actual World counterpart is transferred across ontological domains. The Concretist term, 'counterpart', will be used to describe the apparently different versions of a character that are found within a number of different texts. This will be prefixed with 'Textual Actual World' in order to distinguish it from the Actual World counterparts found in historical fiction. While the logical implications of conflating terminology are severe within the context of possible-worlds logic, as long as definitions are provided, they are less important to some analyses of fiction. As Pavel (1979) stresses 'some disciplinary tactics of the philosophers interested primarily in more fundamental problems than the aesthetic ones may render rational talk difficult or impossible in a field where a more tolerant, descriptively oriented stand may be needed' (186). Pavel's solution to the potential hindrances that possible-worlds logic can cause literary studies is to adopt a more 'flexible ontology' (179) – an approach that embraces the fundamental principles and efficacy of Possible Worlds Theory while also maintaining loyalty to the concerns of a literary critical context.

Indeed while terminology and conceptual boundaries are important to establish, the evidence on which associations are based are equally if not more pressing for a literary critical agenda. As Margolin (1990) notes, 'questions immediately arise about whether there is a minimum degree of similarity required for counterparthood and what it may be' (866). As was discussed in Chapter 4, historical fictions can signal their use of Actual World counterparts by using proper names as a form of rigid designation. Pavel (1979) suggests that the same process can also be applied when analysing fictional worlds, arguing that 'names in fiction work like usual proper names, that is as rigid designators attached to individuated objects, independent of the objects' properties' (185). According to Pavel's proposal, proper names can always be used to identify a character from another text. Implicitly, this form of reference holds true whether or not the Textual Actual World counterpart has identical properties to the original.

Using a proper name as a form of rigid designation is attractive because it allows a particular individual to be invoked while also allowing changes to be made to that individual's properties. However, while Pavel's approach might prove useful in some cases, it is not entirely appropriate in all contexts because characters are not always named in either the original or the rewrite. The female monster in *Frankenstein*, for example, is unnamed so that a proper name as a form of rigid designation is unavailable to readers of *Patchwork Girl*. In addition, some texts are not necessarily explicit about the characters that they utilise. As the analysis has shown so far, *Patchwork Girl* uses some relatively subtle means of allusion to signal its connection to its most influential source.

Indeed Doležel (1998a) notes that 'postmodern rewrites do not always obey the semantics of rigid designation' (226) and thus insists that numerous texts are, like *Patchwork Girl*, more coy or playful in their appropriation of other fictional characters. In cases of less explicit forms of reference, he suggests that alternative means of cross-identification must be applied. In particular, he suggests 'aligning the protowork and its presumed rewrite on the basis of some strong textual and structural evidence – the title, quotations, the intertextual allusions, the similarity of the fictional world's structure, the homology of agential constellations, the parallelism of the story lines, the like setting. Only when we have strong enough evidence for the rewrite hypothesis will we draw the transworld identity lines' (226). Doležel suggests that sufficient evidence must be gathered in order to substantiate apparent connections between characters in different worlds. His approach is appealing because it requires that sufficient substantiation is made in support of counterparthood but it is also sufficiently flexible to allow for any changes that the new text might add to the original character.

Returning to the analysis of *Patchwork Girl*, while a proper name as a form of rigid designation is unavailable, strong textual evidence can be used to categorise the patchwork girl as a Textual Actual World counterpart of the female monster in *Frankenstein*. As the stylistic analyses have shown, the full title is comparable to that of *Frankenstein* and some parts of the text are written in a style that emulates Shelley's prose. Scenes such as those described in {my walk} and {sight} in *Patchwork Girl* provide further evidence for the cross-identification because of the narrative structures that they share with sections of *Frankenstein*. Finally, as the analysis of the {a graveyard} section shows at the beginning of the chapter, like Frankenstein's monster the patchwork girl is built from a collection of human body parts. Thus there is an immediate physiological connection between the two creatures.

Making more explicit use of Shelley's text, a number of lexias in 'a journal' – namely {plea}, {a promise filthy work} and {treachery} – quote entire sections from Shelley's text. Here the reader is shown how

Frankenstein's monster pleads for Victor to build a mate for him to live with in isolation. Victor reluctantly builds a female monster but subsequently destroys it, an action that leads the monster to 'howl with a devilish despair and revenge' ({treachery} and Shelley (1998: 166). In addition to direct quotations, the protagonist of *Patchwork Girl* also alludes to her literary ancestry. In 'a story', a section which is narrated by the patchwork girl, she refers to her 'unfortunate and famous brother' {I am}. The adjective, 'famous', acknowledges the monster's notoriety as a canonical fictional character and 'unfortunate' implies her brother was ill-fated in a way that she was not. The use of the noun, 'brother', is potentially ambiguous because it can denote either a familial or social kinship. However, either way, an association is asserted.

The Consequences of the Textual Actual World Counterpart

As these examples show, even if readers are unfamiliar with the themes, plot and characters from Shelley's text, the text supplies them with information so as to ensure – as far as possible – that they recognise that a connection is being drawn between one text and the other, with the protagonist in particular used as a significant carrier of intertextuality. Since the hypertext provides an alternative history for the female monster, Shelley's novel can be seen as acting as its prescript providing contextual information regarding the protagonist's origins and heritage. *Frankenstein* therefore has an important epistemological role for the reader's interpretation of *Patchwork Girl*.

In addition, in her original context of the Textual Actual World of *Frankenstein*, the female monster is destroyed. In *Patchwork Girl*, she is alive. Thus while *Patchwork Girl* does utilise the Textual Actual World of *Frankenstein* to provide context, it also invokes an associated Textual Possible World – one in which the female monster survives. Figure 5.4 provides a graphical representation of the ontological landscape constructed by the use of the Textual Actual World counterpart in *Patchwork Girl*.

Figure 5.4 depicts two Textual Actual Worlds: one constructed by *Patchwork Girl* and one constructed by *Frankenstein*. The Textual Actual World of *Frankenstein* resides in the Actual World and is surrounded by satellites of possible worlds. These represent alternatives to the Textual Actual World that is depicted in Shelley's novel as might be imagined by readers. The examples shown on the diagram include a possible world in which the female monster survives and also an additional hypothetical possible world in which the female monster is not constructed at all.

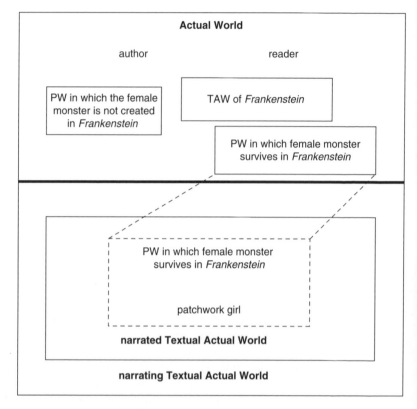

Figure 5.4 The ontological landscape created by the use of the Textual Actual World counterpart

While the diagram shows only two alternative possibilities, theoretically at least, an infinite number of possible worlds exist and are imagined by readers in the Actual World. The possible world in which the female monster survives is affiliated to the Textual Actual World of *Frankenstein* in the Actual World. This possible world is also shown within the Textual Actual World of *Patchwork Girl* because it is here that this possibility is realised.

Importantly, the possible world associated with *Frankenstein* appears as a dotted line within the Textual Actual World of *Patchwork Girl*. This is to indicate that its presence is optional. Ontologically, neither the construction of the Textual Actual World nor the construction of the patchwork girl depends on the possible world which is affiliated with *Frankenstein*; both exist whether or not readers recognise the connection to Shelley's novel. Some readers will have no or limited knowledge of Shelley's *Frankenstein* and thus may overlook or be ignorant of the epistemological relation between the two texts. In such cases, the patchwork girl still exists within the Textual Actual World of *Patchwork Girl* but the significance of her origins will be absent.

Yet while the ontological construction of the Textual Actual World is unaffected by the parallel between the two texts, the use of a Textual Actual World counterpart can have significant epistemological and hermeneutic consequences. As the discussion above has shown, since characters are associated with a particular text, their invocation also brings information about their host ontological domain. In *Patchwork Girl*, the female monster is shown as relevant through a number of implicit references. This character is then used within the new context of the Textual Actual World of *Patchwork Girl*. However, since the text suggests that we acknowledge her original context, the two Textual Actual Worlds, although ontologically distinct, become bound in an inextricable epistemic relationship in which the idiosyncrasies of each are illuminated.

It is important to emphasise at this point that while the device requires readers to look to another ontological domain, the use of a Textual Actual World counterpart is not necessarily ontologically disruptive. McHale (1987) gives the example of '*retour de personage*, when identical characters recur in different texts by the same author' (57) as an archetypical unmarked form of transworld identity. However, as McHale also notes, some texts foreground the very device that they deploy. In this case, he suggests that *retour de personage* and transworld identity can be 'parodied in such a way as to spectacularly violate, and thereby foreground, the ontological boundaries between fictional worlds' (58). McHale suggests that there are numerous ways in which ontological foregrounding can be instigated, but he notes that when a character seems to be aware of his or her status as a fictional entity, they 'destabiliz[e] rather than consolidate[e] fictional ontology' (57). This is because, he suggests, such a device 'foreground[s] the intertextual dimension of th[e] text for the reader' (58) so that the reader is alerted to the character's role as a marker of intertextuality. As has been shown in the analysis so far, *Patchwork Girl* contains numerous elements that foreground the ontological status of the protagonist. In {a graveyard} she is aware that she must be pieced together; in her first-person narratives, she makes reference to the male monster from *Frankenstein*. Thus, the protagonist certainly helps to alert the reader to the intertextual device in which she plays a significant role.

Yet while the protagonist's self-consciousness does contribute to the ontological foregrounding, this is not the only device which is responsible for such an effect. The context in which the patchwork girl is presented also provides quite striking juxtapositions. Indeed, while McHale locates the site of self-reflexivity with the character, Margolin (1990) suggests that the context in which a counterpart appears can also draw attention to their extra-textual status. He suggests that 'if the properties associated with the home world of the guest are very different from those of the host world, they become highly marked through this procedure [of counterpart creation]' (867). According to Margolin, the parallel between two ontological domains that counterpart creation creates can be utilised as a way of foregrounding the very process on which it relies. That is, the ontological appropriation can be highlighted by inserting a counterpart into a Textual Actual World that is noticeably incongruous with their original environment.

In the context of *Patchwork Girl*, Margolin's hypothesis is validated in the extreme, primarily because the modern characteristics that the patchwork girl possesses sharply contrast with the temporal, spatial and also generic context from which she is taken. Contrasting with the male monster in *Frankenstein* who is forced to hide from society because of his grotesque appearance and antisocial behaviour, the patchwork girl is outgoing and sociable. She is also able to form intimate relationships with others and she emulates human domesticity by keeping a pet, albeit a rather unusual and therefore additionally marked choice of an armadillo {stretched out}. The text also documents some rather extraordinary events which highlight her unlikely existence. In one of the most absurd parts of the narrative, the patchwork girl loses a leg in a car accident, barters for a prosthetic replacement with an unlikely 'congenial tramp' {an accident} and arranges a public funeral for her amputated foot {funeral}. The patchwork girl also develops 'noticeable signs of Tourette's Syndrome' {tourette's} – a medical condition associated with humans as opposed to supernatural beings. While the activities are not fundamentally remarkable, because they are completely incongruous with the context from which she has been taken, they are notable. The text implies that the patchwork girl is brought from a nineteenth century, gothic setting to what appears to be modern day domesticity and her adventures are therefore rather different to what we might have expected from her counterpart had she survived. Each detail contributes to the construction of a highly unlikely and therefore artificial ontological domain.

Piecing Together the Text

So far, the analysis has shown how *Patchwork Girl* utilises implicit allusions which alert the readers to its reliance on *Frankenstein*. Other parts of the text also consider the importance of other texts but deploy a more explicit form of intertextual reference. In addition to the large chunks of Shelley's text, which appear unacknowledged in 'a journal' to document relevant information, the entire 'a quilt' section is comprised of quotations from other texts. The first lexia from this section, entitled {scrap bag}, is shown in Figure 5.5.

Read as a narrative the 'a quilt' section documents the construction of the patchwork girl from the creator's perspective. In {scrap bag}, the narrator describes the gathering of constituent materials. In addition to the narrative discourse, however, the structure of the lexias adds an additional dimension to the text. As Figure 5.5 shows, the text is comprised entirely of textual fragments and the mismatched typefaces along with the associated reference key underneath can be used to determine the source of each.

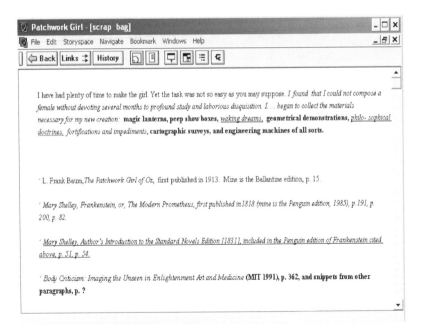

Figure 5.5   Screenshot of {scrap bag}

As the screenshot shows, {scrap bag} contains extracts from Mary Shelley's gothic novel, *Frankenstein*, L. Frank Baum's (1990 [1913]) children's story *The Patchwork Girl of Oz* and Barbara Stafford's (1991) monograph, *Body Criticism*. The rest of the 'a quilt' section is also presented in a similar format. Extracts from Cixous' (1991) *Coming to Writing and Other Essays*, Deleuze and Guatarri's (1988) *A Thousand Plateaus* and *Elle* Magazine appear alongside quotations from the *Storyspace* software instruction manual. While each quotation contributes to the creation of the Textual Actual World in *Patchwork Girl*, therefore, because each piece is taken from another text, textual influences are made very explicit.

Paralleling the structure of the patchwork girl in 'a graveyard' as well as the hypertext itself, 'a quilt' exists as a collection of individual fragments which are combined to make a coherent whole. However, the fragments provide more than just typography because each source text can be seen to have some relevance to the novel so that the external influences are as important to our understanding of a novel as the individual words on the page. Crucially, each quotation is taken from a text which appeals to a particular type of audience and they each exist on a scale of relative notoriety and accessibility. *Elle* magazine represents popular culture but it is also indicative of a genre which places aesthetic value on particular types of female body; *A Thousand Plateaus* is an essay in which Deleuze and Guattari describe a rhizome text and, as was shown in Chapter 2, has been used by some hypertext theorists as a way of envisaging hypertext; *Frankenstein* is a canonical literary text but it is also the text against which *Patchwork Girl* can be compared; the *Storyspace* manual represents a technical guide which is associated with a very specific type of text but it also draws attention to the technological means by which the text in which it now appears was created.

In {scrap bag}, the extract from Baum's novel highlights the fact that *The Patchwork Girl of Oz* contains, like Jackson's novel, a protagonist comprised of patches, albeit cloth as opposed to flesh. Similarly, the quotation from *Frankenstein* reiterates the fact that a female monster was also the product of Frankenstein's labours in Shelley's nineteenth-century novel. In this respect, therefore, each fragment provides an epistemological perspective from which the novel can be viewed, influencing the reader's interpretation of the novel.

The Consequences of the Patchwork Text

The invocation of texts is important in the overall context of the novel because the lexias in 'a quilt' act as a literal embodiment of an intertextual network, bringing an evident self-consciousness to the conception and potential reception of the text in which they are housed. In addition while the significance of each quotation can be assessed individually, the juxtaposition of sources, genres and registers is also important. As Joyce (2003) notes in her analysis of 'a quilt', 'by forcing ... comparisons between them [the quotations], the text heightens awareness of the disjunctiveness of appropriation' (45) so that the textual medley emphasises the disparity and variety of influence to which each text is attached. The comparison is immediate because the quotations are placed alongside one another and consequently the clashes that they create are more visible.

In addition to their epistemological influence, the quotations are also responsible for creating ontological disjunctures. Joyce observes that 'the continual reference to the previous existence of the quotations forces a discontinuous reading, a narration that fractures under the weight of voices from the past' (44). Yet while the temporal incongruity between *Patchwork Girl* and its secondary influences in 'a quilt' is significant, it is the ontological incongruity that creates the resulting self-reflexivity. First, the formal referencing conventions in which they are presented foreground the fact that each source is taken from a text in another ontological domain – the Actual World. This highlights the ontological peculiarity of *Patchwork Girl* by showing that it is also a product of that domain. The fictional sources, such as *Frankenstein* and *The Patchwork Girl of Oz*, are particularly significant in that respect because they also construct Textual Actual Worlds. These are ontologically congruous with the domain constructed by *Patchwork Girl* but are also shown as autonomous and therefore ultimately artificial. Thus, the autonomy and artificiality of the Textual Actual World of *Patchwork Girl* is exposed by implication to ontologically congruous domains. Finally, the artificiality of the novel's Textual Actual World is accentuated because the narrative is presented in a format that is usually associated with factual as opposed to fictional discourse. The incongruity of style and function therefore draws further attention to the ontological peculiarity of the text and the Textual Actual World that it describes.

As the preceding analysis shows, the collage of quotations in 'a quilt' makes the relationship between *Patchwork Girl* and other texts very explicit by exposing its network of literary, theoretical and cultural influence forthrightly. However, this section also contains an additional warning. While the extra-textual sources of each quotation are immediately obvious to readers who access this section, each lexia can also be displayed in an alternative format. If readers click on any part of the text, a dramatically different structure emerges. Figure 5.6 shows the alternative structure of {scrap bag}.

A dotted line sits in place of the references and a uniform font is used to display the narrative. In the alternative format, therefore, the influence of extra-textual sources is hidden and the autonomy of the Textual Actual World of *Patchwork Girl* takes precedence. Significantly, while readers can switch between two versions of the same lexia, they can only move on to the next lexia when the text is displayed without its references. So, in order to proceed through the text, readers must access the narrative in its covert form.

While visually playful, the movement between the two formats in 'a quilt' is also thematically significant because the paralleling of formats teaches readers about the significance of secondary sources in *Patchwork Girl* as well as, potentially, in all other texts. In one format, the lexias provide information about the novel's influences and in so doing offer a range of contexts against which the novel can be read. In the other format, the influences are hidden so that the framework is unavailable and it is up to the reader to identify the sources that have been more overtly plagiarised elsewhere. Readers are shown that *Patchwork Girl* is a novel that is anything but autonomous but that it is open about its

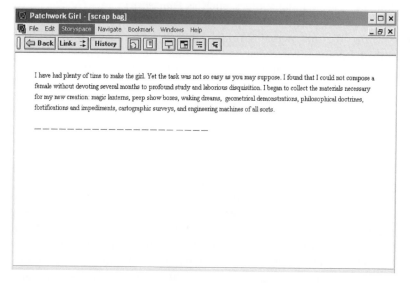

Figure 5.6   Screenshot of {scrap bag} without citations

literary heritage and influence. The covert formats displayed in 'a quilt' show the ease with which this can be hidden or erased.

Ambiguous Ontological Structures

The analysis so far has shown how *Patchwork Girl* utilises other texts and their constituents to populate and narrate its Textual Actual World. The result is a rather humorous and self-reflexive novel which foregrounds the thematic and narrative peculiarities of other texts while also acknowledging its fundamental reliance on and influence from those works. While the use of a Textual Actual World counterpart and the patchwork of quotations are both ontologically and epistemologically revealing, however, they do not necessarily represent a challenge for readers of the novel. That is, while the patchwork girl originates in another ontological domain, her reflections in 'a journal' and 'a graveyard' allow readers to place her within the Textual Actual World of *Patchwork Girl*. Similarly, while the narrative in 'a quilt' is comprised of fragments from other sources, it still presents a coherent narrative that readers can use in order to construct the Textual Actual World. Other parts of the text, which continue the theme of appropriation, represent more of an interpretative challenge however.

The 'a journal' section of *Patchwork Girl* is narrated by the patchwork girl's maker. It describes her intentions for and love of her creation. It also documents the construction of the patchwork girl from conception to birth and beyond. In this section, however, significant ontological ambiguities are introduced because readers are presented with two contrary scenarios: one in which the patchwork girl belongs to the same ontological domain as her maker and one in which she does not.

The ambiguity is achieved as a consequence of a fork in the text. Here the sequence of lexias splits into two alternative reading paths before converging back to the same point. The structure of 'a journal' is depicted in Figure 5.7.

The first lexia of the 'a journal' section does not contain any hyperlinks. Therefore, as Figure 5.7 shows, unless the reader terminates his or her reading, the {my walk} lexia always leads to {sight}. After reading the {sight} lexia, readers must then choose from one of two links which lead to either {sewn} or {written}. Both lexias then lead back to the same lexia, entitled {she stood}, and the path continues with lexias that contain more hyperlinks and therefore more reading choices.

In terms of the narrative, in the first two lexias, {my walk} and {sight}, the narrator recollects a meeting with the patchwork girl in an outdoor

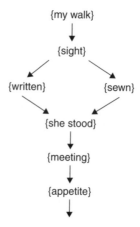

Figure 5.7   The two reading paths at the beginning of 'a journal'

rural setting. The next part of the narrative then depends on whether the reader chooses the {sewn} or {written} route. In the {sewn} lexia, the narrator asserts: 'I had *sewn* her, *stitching* deep into the night by candlelight, until the tiny black *stitches* wavered into script and I began to feel that I was writing' {sewn, my italics}. Conversely, in the {written} lexia the narrator proclaims: 'I made her, *writing* deep into the night by candlelight, until the tiny black *letters* blurred into stitches and I began to feel that I was sewing a great quilt' {written, my italics}. Therefore, whereas in {sewn}, the narrator recalls stitching a patchwork of flesh to create an animate being, in {written} the patchwork girl is a fictional construct. In both cases the creator describes her creation in figurative terms, using the same trope: in {sewn}, needlework is likened to the creativity of writing and in {written} the process of writing is likened to sewing with the concept of creativity providing the conceptual link.

Since both reading paths are narrated by the same first-person narrator and each account is offered with equal conviction, readers are not necessarily able or encouraged to choose between the two alternative Textual Actual Worlds. Compounding the ambiguity, many of the other lexias in the 'a journal' describe qualities that could apply to the patchwork girl in either context. For example, the creator recounts that the patchwork girl 'is moody and quieter than I' {appetite}; 'wants to learn' {learn}; and 'is exuberant, ferocious, loving, unhinged' {infant}. These descriptions could apply to either a real or an imaginary entity because, as personal attributes, they could belong to a human being or a fictional character.

The ambiguity that is achieved in the 'a journal' section is also reflected in other areas of the novel. In 'a story', the patchwork girl obscures her status and collaborates in the textual game by proclaiming that her 'birth takes place more than once. In the plea of a bygone monster, from a muddy hole by corpse-light; under the needle, and under the pen. Or it took place not at all' {birth}. In this case, the patchwork girl suggests that she may be real, imaginary, both or neither and consequently readers are faced with a number of irresolvable incongruities.

In other lexias, the descriptions seem to imply one state or another more categorically so as to compound the contradiction. In some sections, the creator describes intimate encounters with a female which suggest that bodily contact has taken place: 'last night I lay in her arms, my monster, and for the first time laid my hand on her skin' {I lay}; 'in bed she was curiously shy' {shy}; 'I pressed myself against her with a ravenous heart' {her, me}. In these depictions, the two figures appear to belong to the same space. They can touch one another and interact physically. Conversely, in other lexias, the narration implies that the patchwork girl is a fictional character constructed only in the imagination of her creator. She gushes: 'I crave her company. I crave even the danger. Do I yearn for the easement of my own company? Do I resent the fierce mad engine that is throbbing inside my serene life, staining my underclothes, making me jump up ... to go to my writing desk?' {crave}. While the passion that the narrator describes in {crave} could apply to a physical relationship with another, the latter part of the lexia implies that her fervour is for writing. She speaks of it as an escape from her own life, as an addiction. In these scenes, the female monster is brought to life but only figuratively through creative writing.

The Consequences of Ambiguous Ontological Structures

Whether real or fictional, the ambiguity regarding the ontological status of the patchwork girl results in the construction of two different ontological landscapes. If, as the {sewn} lexia suggests, the monster is an animate being that belongs to the same Textual Actual World as Mary Shelley, then the ontological landscape is as in the rest of the novel. Conversely, if, as the {written} lexia suggests, the patchwork girl is a character within Mary's novel, then she belongs to a separate Textual Universe to Mary.

While significantly different, both ontological configurations are equally constructed because the text presents two contradictory ontological landscapes neither of which are confirmed. In the {sewn} lexia, the text implies

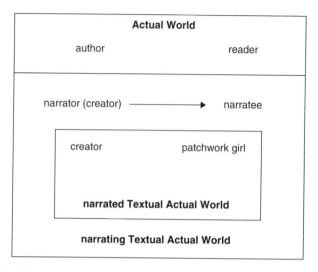

Figure 5.8   The ontological landscape created by {sewn}

that the patchwork girl is real and exists as her creator's lover. This results in the dichotomous ontological landscape as shown in Figure 5.8.

In the {written} lexia, it is implied that the patchwork girl is a product of her creator's imagination and writing. In this case, as shown in Figure 5.9, an additional Textual Universe is constructed and this is embedded within the other. The extra embedded Textual Universe will contain the patchwork girl's narrative in 'a story' and 'a graveyard'. These two sections describe what the reader believed to be the Textual Actual World to which the creator also belongs.

Each scenario is incompatible with the other and consequently the Law of Non-Contradiction is broken. However, in this case, the logical impossibility results in an extremely unstable and fickle ontological landscape in which Mary Shelley and the female monster appear to jump in-between ontological domains. The reader initially believes them to be ontologically congruous and indeed {sewn} implies they are. However, their ontological incongruity is also posited by {written}. It is precisely this type of indeterminacy and inconclusiveness that the novel utilises in projecting an ontological landscape that evolves and changes, forcing continual renegotiation and causing a constant feeling of disorientation for the reader.

Yet while the ontological landscape can be destabilising, the overriding message is positive. In each case, the relationship between the women

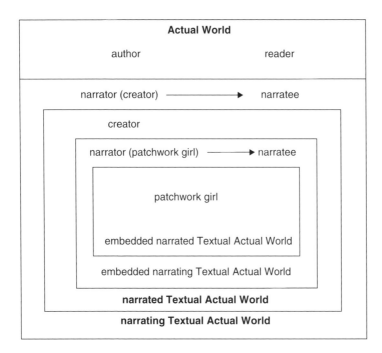

Figure 5.9   The ontological landscape created by {written}

is genuine, intimate and passionate. Unlike their male counterparts in *Frankenstein*, they are able to coexist. Their relationship is documented in 'a journal' as passionate and sometimes volatile, but it ultimately brings joy to both. The women are empowered by female relationships and creativity in a way that their male equivalents are not.

Mary Shelley and *Patchwork Girl*

The relationship between creature and created or between author and text that is explored in 'a journal' invites the reader to compare the passion associated with love with the passion associated with writing. The relationship between author and work is complicated, however, because a number of implicit references throughout this section imply that the author of the 'a journal' section and therefore the creator of the patchwork girl is Mary Shelley, author of *Frankenstein*. Jackson therefore brings her influences into her work both figuratively and literally. Invoked rather subtly, just as the connection between the patchwork girl and the female monster from *Frankenstein* must be established using strong textual evidence, so too must the connection between the creator-figure and Mary Shelley. As is the case with the female monster, a full proper name is unavailable as a form of rigid designation and instead recurrent references to 'Mary' are coupled with activities and situations which link the character in the Textual Actual World of *Patchwork Girl* to Mary Shelley in the Actual World.

In a lexia fittingly entitled {Mary}, the patchwork girl recalls that she 'jumped up again and again from Mary's tiny writing table' while 'Mary checked the clock, for it would not do for Percy to come home in the middle of what was next'. While 'Mary' and 'Percy', do not provide complete forms of rigid designation because their surnames are missing, additional contextual information provides sufficient detail with which readers can connect the names with 'Mary Shelley' and 'Percy Bysshe Shelley'. In the Actual World, Mary was married to Percy (Shelley) and in the Textual Actual World of *Patchwork Girl*, 'Mary', at the very least, cohabits with someone called 'Percy'. As author of a canonical text in the Actual World, Mary Shelley is associated with writing; the 'writing desk' from which the patchwork girl jumps up implies that is also a preoccupation of Mary in *Patchwork Girl*. In addition, the partial authorship that is attributed to 'Mary/Shelley' on the title page serves to further secure an affiliation between 'Mary' in the Textual Actual World and the author of *Frankenstein*.

Methodologically, Possible Worlds Theory provides tools with which this epistemological connection can be established. As was shown in the analysis of historical fiction in Chapter 4, the association between Mary Shelley in the Actual World and Mary Shelley in the Textual Actual World can be explained using counterpart theory and transworld identity. More specifically, 'Mary' in *Patchwork Girl* is deemed to be an Actual World counterpart of Mary Shelley.

It is important to note that the use of the Actual World counterpart of Mary Shelley as a character in the novel represents a different epistemological and ontological mechanism to the stylistic imitation of *Frankenstein* in 'a journal'. The stylistic imitation mimics Mary Shelley's style in the novel *Frankenstein* and, to be successful, it requires that readers are acquainted with Shelley's writing. Conversely, using Mary Shelley as a character provides the author of 'the journal' section with a more precise identity and, to be acknowledged, it requires that readers have some specific knowledge of Shelley's life. Inevitably, recognising the association between Mary Shelley in the Actual World and the counterpart in *Patchwork Girl* partially relies on Shelley's association to her novel *Frankenstein*. However, the stylistic imitation and the use of an Actual World counterpart each rely on a slightly different kind of knowledge. As a novel, *Frankenstein* exists as a stable document, the contents of which will not usually change over time. Conversely, details about Shelley's biography are not necessarily uniform because they are constructed according to multiple accounts and different interpretations of her life. Thus, there is an inevitable subjectivity associated with biographical information.

Margolin's (1996) examination of counterparts reveals the epistemological conditions associated with transworld identity. He notes that 'in the vast majority of cases ... the author's knowledge and image of the historical original underlying his work is based on verbal records contained in various certifying discourses of his culture, that is, discourses with institutionalized truth or fact claim, such as newspapers and history books' (128). The consequence is that authors can construct counterparts in texts by drawing on particular types of information about a public figure. This, Margolin defines as 'institutionalized truth'. While he recognises that 'any such factual source is partial ... and none of these sources can provide absolutely certain knowledge about, say, the inner states of this individual' (128), he suggests that culturally certified knowledge carries legitimacy because of the authority that it is granted by institutionally authoritative discourses.

As the above analysis of 'a journal' shows, institutionalised truth and cultural knowledge from the Actual World can be utilised in order to construct a character within a Textual Actual World. Yet for an association to be made between a figure in the Actual World and a character in a Textual Actual World, the reader must have access to the same 'institutionalized truth' that the author has drawn upon. Thus, the use of an Actual World counterpart depends on a shared knowledge but this is something which is always culturally specific.

As a Western canonical novel, Shelley's *Frankenstein* is likely to be widely recognised by a Western audience at least. Details about Mary Shelley's life, however, are not necessarily universally accessible because they depend upon readers having access to a particular cultural discourse. Acknowledging the socio-cultural specificity of institutionalised truth, Margolin notes that 'the cultural stereotype of generic images of most prominent historical figures vary enormously according to the nation, period, race, or ideology that constructs historical images in its certifying discourses. The upshot ... is that the image of the actual individual, serving as original for the creative writer, is a complex *textual* construct or entity' (128–9, my italics). Margolin's claim about the 'textual' nature of an Actual World counterpart is useful because it emphasises that knowledge about famous or notorious individuals is constructed discursively. Importantly, however, as something that is assembled, a cultural identity can change in light of new discoveries or shifting socio-cultural perspectives. The effect of incorporating an Actual World counterpart is therefore vulnerable to unpredictable and uncontrollable alterations precisely because the device relies on *extra-textual* sources of information and knowledge.

Returning to *Patchwork Girl*, recognising that 'Mary' in *Patchwork Girl* is a counterpart of Mary Shelley in the Actual World depends on the reader having access to the 'institutionalized truth' or, more specifically, literary historical knowledge about Mary Shelley. However, it also depends on the 'textual' construction of Mary Shelley inside the text being compatible with the 'textual' construction of Mary Shelley outside the text. As the analysis above shows, *Patchwork Girl* invokes personal details about her marital relationship with Percy (Bysshe Shelley) and her professional credentials as a novelist – information which is related to both the Actual World figure, Mary Shelley, as well as her novel, *Frankenstein*. Yet since the 'text' of an Actual World figure is built on a particular type of knowledge, some readers of *Patchwork Girl* may have little or no knowledge of Mary Shelley. Consequently, they might miss the clues upon which the connection relies and the construction of the character as a *counterpart* of Mary Shelley will not be achieved. Ontologically, the character will still exist in the Textual Actual World, but the epistemological connection between Mary in *Patchwork Girl* and Mary Shelley in the Actual World will be absent.

The Consequences of Mary Shelley in *Patchwork Girl*

Despite the risk associated with devices that rely on extra-textual knowledge, since Mary Shelley and her novel, *Frankenstein*, are currently relatively well known to a Western audience, it is likely that the majority of readers of *Patchwork Girl* will recognise the intended allusion. An acknowledgment of her status is important in *Patchwork Girl* because of the self-reflexive function that she plays. As discussed in Chapter 4, Actual World counterparts are not uncommon in fiction and need not be ontologically significant. However, the use of Mary Shelley in *Patchwork Girl* is particularly marked because of the extreme changes that are made to her 'text' in the novel. As the analysis of 'a journal' shows, Mary is presented as either a feisty, passionate writer who is so preoccupied with her writing that she pays her husband, Percy, little attention, or as a closet homosexual whose disinterest with Percy can be explained by her intimate relationship with a supernatural being. In either scenario, details about her life are dramatically changed and the difference between Mary Shelley in the Textual Actual World and the 'text' of Mary Shelley in the Actual World draw attention to the artificiality of her counterpart.

Shelley Jackson and *Patchwork Girl*

As the analyses of four sections of *Patchwork Girl* have shown, the text presents reading as an organic and unpredictable process which can be dramatically enriched by knowledge of other sources. Similarly, the narrative shows writing to be an intense and profound experience which results in a product from which the writer can never be entirely divorced. In 'a journal', the artist and her work are portrayed within a passionate relationship, with the encroaching ontological levels providing an appropriate metaphor for the intrusiveness of the artist's work within her life. The final section of the novel, entitled 'broken accents', examines these key issues further by exploring a rewarding but also frustrating relationship between an author figure and her hypertext fiction.

As Figure 5.10 shows, the first lexia of this section contains a profile image of a human head depicted as a phrenology diagram. Some sections of the head are labelled with a word, such as 'fog' and 'embryo' and others with symbols, such as '&' or '+'. Navigation in this section is enabled by hyperlinks which appear in the constituent parts of the diagram. However, most links lead to the same destination which is a lexia entitled {this writing}. It begins:

> assembling these patched words in an electronic space, I feel half blind, as if the entire text is within my reach, but because of some myopic condition, I am only familiar with from dreams, I can only see that part most immediately before me and have no sense of how that part relates to the rest.

The lexia describes the frustration felt by a writer, struggling against a creative block and it serves as the beginning of an entire sequence in which an author contemplates the balance between frustration and emotional reward that she experiences during creative writing, in particular the process of writing a hypertext fiction novel. Importantly, throughout the 'broken accents' section, occasional links lead to other sections of *Patchwork Girl*. Thus, the musings of the writer intersect with material from the novel which she has apparently produced. For example,

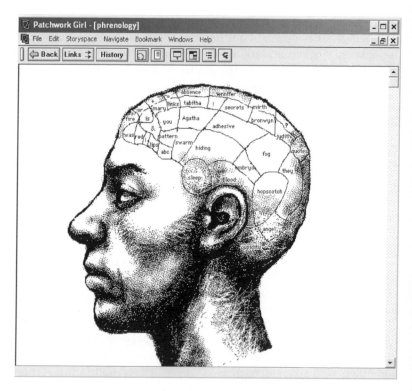

Figure 5.10   Screenshot of {phrenology}

the 'jennifer' and 'Agatha' sections of the phrenology diagram link to the 'a graveyard' lexias in which the patchwork girl's body parts detail their heritage. Similarly, from the {this writing} lexia some reading paths also lead to lexias in which the patchwork girl takes over as narrator.

The apparent appearance of the author within 'broken accents' is fundamental to the puzzling and conceptually difficult ontological landscape that is presented throughout the novel. Indeed, while 'broken accents' represents the most sustained characterisation of an author, it is not the only part of the novel in which traces of this figure can be found. In some of the references in 'a quilt', an authorial presence is apparent. The reference for *The Patchwork Girl of Oz* in the {scrap bag} lexia, for example, is given as:

L. Frank Baum, *The Patchwork Girl of Oz*, first published in 1913. Mine is the Ballantine edition, p. 15.

In this case, the first-person possessive pronoun attributes ownership of the book to the author of the citation. Similarly, there are instances throughout 'broken accents' in which the exact source seems to have been forgotten by the author. One such reference reads:

Body Criticism: Imaging the Unseen in Enlightenment Art and Medicine (MIT 1991), p. 362, and snippets from other paragraphs, p. ?

Here, an accurate reference is sacrificed in favour of an imprecise question mark and the colloquial term, 'snippets', introduces an element of informality into what would otherwise be a formal register.

As the examples show, both 'a quilt' and 'broken accents' contain either narration from or stylistic evidence of an author figure and these often appear alongside descriptions of the Textual Actual World. Collectively, they serve to suggest that the author *in* the novel is the author *of* the novel.

Yet, while readers might equate the author figure in these examples with the author of *Patchwork Girl* – Shelley Jackson – ontologically, they are distinct entities. Joyce (2003) articulates the ambiguity that ensues in her own discussion of this section noting that: 'the narrator (and should I be saying "Jackson" here?) talks to us directly about how she makes the text' (46). Joyce's indecision occurs because she is unable to place the narrator and the author within their appropriate ontological spaces. While she recognises that there is a level of indeterminacy, her questions epitomise the ontological interchange between narrator and author with which the text plays. The narrator of 'broken accents' may correspond to, resemble or characterise the author of *Patchwork Girl*, but this figure is not the same 'Shelley Jackson' that belongs to the Actual World. Primarily this is because we cannot access the Actual World or an Actual World figure directly through a text. Any entities that appear in a text are always fictional.

McHale (1987) ponders a similar ontological ambiguity in his analysis of postmodernist print fiction and enquires: 'does not the mere introduction of the scene of writing into a text involve a ... very large degree of fictionalization? ... "Someone sitting there writing the page" is always ... only a fictional reconstruction' (198). McHale recognises that the author can be introduced into a text and notes the ontological peculiarity of this figure as a 'fictional construction'. However, he also recognises that while their ontological status is strictly fictional, their status in the Actual World is also required for the device to function. Defining the fictionalised author as an 'ontologically amphibious figure' (202) he argues that 's/he functions at two theoretically distinct levels of ontological structure: as the vehicle of autobiographical *fact* within the projected fictional world; and as the *maker* of that world, visibly occupying an ontological level superior to it' (202).

McHale's conceptualisation of the fictionalised author is useful because the ontological duality that he foresees places them in two separate domains: one fictional and one real. His analysis of the author figure and his conceptualisation of the dual ontological status can be seen to parallel the process of Actual World counterpart creation in historical fictions. In both cases, readers must use the Actual World as an epistemological source but simultaneously a fictional entity is created within the Textual Actual World. Ryan (1991) and Doležel (1998a) analyse fictionalised authors in terms of counterpart relation and transworld identity but introduce restrictions. Both suggest that in order for an association between author in the Actual World and narrator in the Textual Actual World to be secured, a proper name is required as a form of rigid designation. Ryan (1991) suggests that 'the counterpart is *only* allowed when the narrator is identified by the name of the actual speaker' (93, my italics). Doležel (1998a) is more lenient in his analysis and talks of 'transworld identity being *ensured* by the rigid designator of the proper name' (167, my italics).

As Doležel and Ryan suggest, a proper name can provide considerable evidence with which to connect the author with his or her fictional incarnation in the text. However, as was discussed above in the analysis of the Mary Shelley counterpart, texts are not always explicit about the individuals that they invoke. Similarly, even if a proper name does rigidly designate the Actual World author, the text can characterise that figure in any number of ways, stretching the lines of transworld identity. Thus using a proper name as a form of rigid designation is not always possible or entirely reliable.

In many ways, it is perhaps easier to draw counterpart correlations between an authorial voice and the author in the Actual World than it is when a historical figure or a fictional character from another Textual Actual World is invoked. A historical figure or character from another text may or may not be known to the audience so that the invocation of an Actual World or Textual Actual World counterpart can be missed by the reader. Conversely, the author of the text will always be recognised by the role that they play in relation to that text. Even if readers have no extra-textual knowledge of the author, they will at least know that they have written the text that they are reading, so that a voice that talks about the process of creating that text can always be attributed to the author.

Returning to the analysis of *Patchwork Girl*, the intrusive author is not named in either 'broken accents' or 'a quilt'. However, since an authorial voice appears within the narration, associations can be drawn between that voice and Shelley Jackson in the Actual World. As has been emphasised above, the 'Shelley Jackson' of the text is ontologically distinct from 'Shelley Jackson' in the Actual World; instead the author figure is a counterpart of Shelley Jackson. However, the essential epistemological relation between the two figures that is enforced by Shelley Jackson's inevitable association to her own text means that a transworld identity relation can be drawn.

The Shelley Jackson counterpart uses a slightly different mechanism to the Mary Shelley counterpart because whereas Mary Shelley is alluded to implicitly in 'a journal', the fictionalised author is characterised very explicitly in 'broken accents' and 'a quilt'. Irrespective of the mechanisms with which they are introduced, both have similar ontological consequences. Like the Mary Shelley counterpart, the appearance of Shelley Jackson ensures that the ontological boundary between Actual World and Textual Actual World is foregrounded because when Shelley Jackson appears as the author of the text, the autonomy of the entire Textual Actual World is exposed. As McHale (1987) observes 'if the fictional world acquires a visible maker … its own status must inevitably change, too; it has become less the mirror of nature, more an *artifact*, visibly a *made* thing' (30). Somewhat paradoxically, therefore, rather than strengthening the authenticity of the Textual Actual World, the appearance of the author – the actual maker of the text – emphasises the artificiality of that domain. This is because in order to recognise that the author figure is based on Shelley Jackson, the reader has to access information from the Actual World. He or she must remain outside of the Textual Actual World, prevented from completely recentering by a device that asks them to acknowledge the text's maker.

The Consequences of Shelley Jackson in *Patchwork Girl*

While transworld identity and counterparthood can help to explain the ontological mechanics by which 'Shelley Jackson' can appear in the Textual Actual World of *Patchwork Girl*, there is more to say about this example. While 'Shelley Jackson's' musings are interwoven with other parts of the narrative, her deliberations are ontologically separate from the space in which the patchwork girl and Mary Shelley exist. 'Shelley Jackson' belongs to the Textual Universe of *Patchwork Girl* but she does not belong to the same Textual Actual World as the characters. Instead, as Figure 5.11 shows, *Patchwork Girl* constructs two Textual Actual Worlds: one in which the patchwork girl exists and one in which the fictionalised author resides.

As Figure 5.11 shows, Textual Actual World 1 is the domain to which the patchwork girl belongs and Textual Actual World 2 is the domain to which the Shelley Jackson counterpart belongs. These worlds are separate and, while the two Textual Actual Worlds are depicted alongside each other in the diagram, the boundary between them is used to show that there is no access between them; Shelley Jackson does not operate in and therefore does not have access to Textual Actual World 1 and the patchwork girl does not operate in and therefore does not have access to Textual Actual World 2. Although the two domains are ontologically independent they are epistemologically linked. When we read sections of the text, such as 'a quilt' and 'broken accents' in which Textual Actual World 2 is constructed, we are simultaneously made aware of Textual Actual World 1. This is because Shelley Jackson is the author who constructs Textual Actual World 1 in the Actual World. Thus, there is a simultaneous epistemological connection and ontological disparity between the three ontological domains.

Irrespective of the ontological mechanics, this part of the text is hermeneutically significant. Thematically, the two instances of counterparthood – Mary Shelley and Shelley Jackson – are connected because they both comment on the nature of the fiction-making process and also, perhaps, on the patriarchal nature of the literary canon. As maker of *Patchwork Girl*, Shelley Jackson is always, implicitly, connected to its

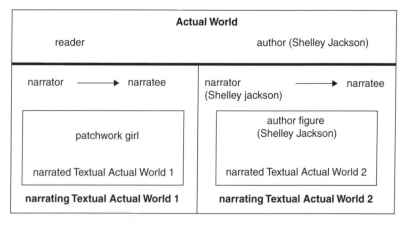

Figure 5.11   The ontological landscape created by the Shelley Jackson counterpart

Textual Universe. Her apparent appearance within parts of the texts emphasises the intimate connection between creator and work. Mary Shelley also, as creator of the patchwork girl, has a similar emotional connection with her creation. More importantly, in both instances both women overtly intrude on their creations and thereby make themselves visible within their works, challenging a patriarchal tradition that has historically erased the female voice.

The Complexity of *Patchwork Girl*

The analysis has shown that *Patchwork Girl* is a rich and complex text with a narrative that creates a multitude of ontological domains which can be configured in various ways. It is for this reason that a definitive or stable ontological landscape is difficult to establish. As a way of reflecting its complexity, Figure 5.12 shows how the various ontological landscapes can be combined.

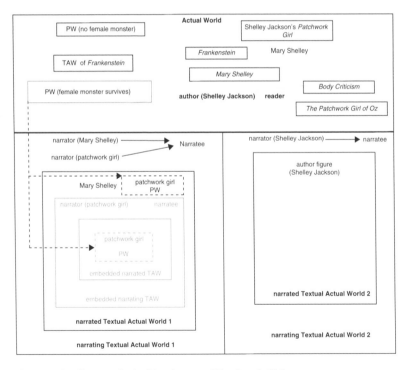

Figure 5.12   The ontological landscape of *Patchwork Girl*

Figure 5.12 shows the two Textual Actual Worlds. In Textual Actual World 1, the patchwork girl and the Mary Shelley counterpart exist. This represents the scenario depicted in 'a journal' in which Mary and the patchwork girl are lovers. The diagram shows that the patchwork girl is also located in an embedded Textual Actual World. This represents the ontological landscape purported in 'a journal' in which the patchwork girl is a fictional construction created by Mary Shelley. Its boundaries are shown in greyscale to show that is it provisional and depends on readers drawing the conclusion that the patchwork girl is Mary's fictional construction. A possible world associated with *Frankenstein* may also be invoked because allusions such as those in 'a story' suggest that the patchwork girl originates in that text. This is dependent on readers' knowledge and, in order to indicate its conditionality, its boundaries are dotted and are shown in greyscale.

As shown on the diagram, various texts such as *Body Criticism* and *The Patchwork Girl of Oz* are invoked in the Actual World because they are quoted from explicitly in 'a quilt'. Since this device foregrounds the autonomy of all texts in the Actual World the novel, *Patchwork Girl*, is also shown in the Actual World. The diagram shows that Mary Shelley and the 'text' of Mary Shelley, both of which exist in the Actual World, are invoked through the use of the Mary Shelley counterpart.

In Textual Actual World 2, a counterpart of Shelley Jackson is shown. The information required to implement this motif means that Shelley Jackson in the Actual World is invoked as well as the hypertext novel that she has created. In both cases, the boundary between the Textual Actual World and the Actual World appears in bold to represent the ontological foregrounding that ensues as a consequence of the multiple intertextual references and resulting interdependencies. As the complexity of the diagram suggests, readers must consult a host of different information sources in the Actual World while also renegotiating the entire ontological structure of the Textual Universe as and when they read or reread each section of the text.

Conclusion

Patchwork Girl is ontologically dynamic and epistemologically rich. Components from different ontological domains are assimilated and its Textual Universe constructed, like its protagonist and its material structure, as a collection of separate components which influence and affect one another. As the analysis has shown, recurrent allusions to *Frankenstein* as well as the more explicit use of secondary sources throughout *Patchwork Girl* show a respect for literary tradition and heritage with the relationship between influence, creativity and product a central trope throughout. Ultimately, its epistemological playfulness and associated thematic concerns are created through ontological mechanisms and it is through a continual ontological negotiation that the novel hopes to find its place amongst the other texts it unremittingly cannibalises. Tools provided by Possible Worlds Theory offer an effective means of unpicking its ontological and epistemological stitches but its foundations are anything but stable.

6
The Colourful Worlds of Richard Holeton's (2001) *Figurski at Findhorn on Acid*

Richard Holeton's (2001) *Figurski at Findhorn on Acid* (henceforth *Figurski*) presents a strange world through juxtaposing mundane episodes with bizarre situations. Of the four texts analysed in this book, it has received the least amount of critical attention and engagements with the text generally comprise reviews as opposed to detailed analyses (e.g. Parker, 2003; Laccetti, 2006; Ensslin, 2007). This is perhaps because, at its time of publication in 2001, Storyspace hypertext was being superseded by more innovative forms of digital narrative production, with sound, image and film being incorporated more holistically into hypertext works on the World Wide Web. Critical attention was somewhat inevitably being concentrated elsewhere.

The narrative documents the antics of three main characters, taking place in three locations and revolving around three objects. The title of the hypertext heralds the organisation of the text insofar as it is structured according to several different configurations which involve at least one character in one location, sometimes with at least one object. The longest combination within the novel is all three characters with all three objects in one of the three locations. Within the text there are 354 lexias which are connected by 2001 links and generate 147 different episodes but the different pathways through the text are relatively tightly controlled or else very apparent. Reading paths tend to be short and sometimes contain just one lexia which might describe a particular scenario involving one or more characters. Even the lengthier reading paths tend to lead back to one of the navigation screens relatively quickly. Similarly, the different choices, although many, are somewhat inconsequential to any sense of narrative progression; readers are presented with different episodes, but each is so different that they are almost entirely disconnected from one another.

In addition to the episodic structure, *Figurski* houses a number of different modes and text types which are used to document the various scenarios and situations in which the characters are engaged. In addition to prose, which is usually associated with narrative fiction, *Figurski* also contains lexias containing dramatic dialogue and poetry as well as non-fictional discourse such as conference abstracts and email exchanges. Similarly, although *Figurski* is predominantly textual in form, it does house a significant number of greyscale and colour diagrams, photographs and drawings.

The sporadic nature of the text is immediately apparent because of the text's navigation methods. Rather than a map in which readers might test different entrances, the {Navigator} lexia is presented in the style of a contents page and lists 'character options', 'place options' and 'artifact options' as well as 'time options' and 'notes'. Following the 'character options', readers can navigate the text by following one of the three protagonists' movements. They choose from: Frank Figurski, who is a failed PhD student on parole for the murder of his supervisor; Nguyen Van Tho, otherwise known as the No-Hands Cup Flipper, who is a circus performer who flips coffee cups in roadside diners; and Fatima Michelle Vieuchanger, who is a French-Moroccan journalist disguised as a man disguised as a woman. Clicking the 'artifact options' readers can choose to navigate the text according to the different artefacts – Spam, LSD and a mechanical pig – and the 'place options' reveals three different locations: Findhorn in Scotland in the UK, Port St. Lucie in Florida in the USA and the Holodeck from *Star Trek*. 'Time options' reveals a timeline which offers a chronological development of the narrative and the 'notes' section largely contains a selection of images.

The text's fragmented structure is used to present a narrative that is comprised of a collection of individual episodes or incidents in a particular Textual Actual World, as opposed to a text that contains a principal or singular narrative. Despite this, however, there are a number of connected events that give the Textual Actual World some degree of coherence. Following his release from prison, Figurski inadvertently comes across a mechanical pig at Findhorn in Scotland. Many of the scenes that are described within the text involve the three characters' pursuit of the automaton(s) – one an authentic 1737 Rosselini and the other a counterfeit 1884 van Gelderschott version. Sometimes Spam figures, either as a central component or as background detail; sometimes Acid/LSD is used, most often influencing the characters' experience of the scene. The pursuit of the pig(s) culminates with the three characters fighting on the Findhorn beach until they decide to split the mechanical components between them and abandon their mission.

Figurski and Hypertext

The experience of writing *Figurski* has been well documented by Holeton. Speaking of the structure of the novel, Holeton (1998) reflects that he was compelled to write an episodic novel because he 'just can't stick with one topic or one genre relentlessly page after page' (Holeton 1998). He suggests that the hypertext medium provided a forum for that because 'the "combinatorial"… structure of *Figurski* – scenes generated from all the permutations of three characters, three places, and three artifacts – seemed … natural for Storyspace's nested writing spaces. Plus, if you want to highlight that structure for the reader, and you have a tool that generates graphical maps of the structure, well, that's a pretty good match' (Holeton quoted in Bennett, 2001). Holeton's reflections suggest that the hypertext structure was selected because of its distinctive structuring facilities as well as Storyspace's capacity for displaying that structure visually. His desire to 'highlight' the arrangement of the narrative for the reader is notable because it suggests structural transparency was a factor in his design.

A brief analysis of the text's physical structure reveals the kind of effects that Holeton describes. The starkness with which the different combinations are offered reinforces the reader's role in the construction of the text and consequently highlights the artificiality of the reading experience. As in the other three hypertexts, the structuring means that readers are acutely aware of their ontological position in relation to the Textual Actual World. In many ways, however, the structuring in *Figurski* is the most transparent of the four novels analysed in this book. In the different linking options, no attempt is made to hide the game in which the reader is engaged. In the Actual World, readers are alerted to the multi-linearity, but also temporariness of the text; whichever configuration is chosen, the alternatives are still available. The reader's position in the Actual World is further foregrounded because they can only ever influence the Textual Actual World from a position outside of that domain. Thus an exaggerated ontological dichotomy is established before the narrative is begun. Not only does the {Navigation} lexia list the different options, but the chosen configuration is presented at the head of each destination lexia. Readers are always aware of the role they have played in the construction of the text.

While the structure adds to the staccato style of the narrative, the resultant disjointed scenes are also responsible for generating humour in the novel. Its structure is reminiscent of a comedy sketch-show – a series of relatively short but witty episodes. Accordingly, the Eastgate catalogue describes *Figurski* as 'a comic, frantic narrative that recalls Monty Python in its absurdity and erudition' (Eastgate Systems, 2008). In a review of *Figurski* which was conducted by Michael Tratner, one of Holeton's contemporaries, the reader also perceives an integral relationship between the episodic structure of the text, the self-reflexivity that it generates and the comedic impression that it gives. He suggests that:

> the focus on humor was directly tied to the work's computerized form, in several ways: 1) the work consists of numerous small pieces, and so tends to create small literary experiences such as a good laugh, rather than building up 'character' or a compelling plot; 2) the computer screen presents many elements in the book as borrowed from elsewhere – particularly from popular culture – and the borrowing has the feel of parody and mockery. (Tratner quoted in Holeton, 1998)

While Tratner primarily connects the episodic structure with the comedy that results, he also notes that the text's comedy is self-conscious and dependent on the reader's familiarity with many of the references. Hinderaker (2002) provides substantial evidence to show that the characters 'all have some real-life basis', suggesting also that there is an integral connection between the Actual World and Textual Actual World of *Figurski*. Thus, an association between the episodic structure of the narrative, self-reflexivity and comedy are recurrent themes in readings of the text.

The Absurd World of *Figurski*

As a consequence of its episodic structure, playful self-reflexivity and humour, *Figurski* represents a fitting example of what Slocombe (2006) defines as a postmodern 'absurd situation novel' (106–14). He explains that 'in such novels, narrative action revolves around an irrational series of events' (108) so rather than a coherent narrative, the fictional domain is, like *Figurski*, sporadic and fragmented, comprised of episodes which are often only tenuously connected. In further defining the category, Slocombe identifies an important relationship between the reader's experience of reality and the world that is constructed by the text, suggesting that 'the absurd situation novel … places the reader in a world that mirrors their own, but in a funhouse of mirrors, twisting and distorting the image' (108) so that what might first appear to be a familiar ontological domain is then subverted to become a world that is simultaneously familiar and strange.

This chapter will show how the interaction between the episodic structure, humorous content and resultant destabilised ontology that Slocombe identifies in some postmodernist novels is also evidenced in *Figurski*. It will begin by analysing the relationship between the familiar and the unfamiliar to show that while the Actual World is important for the construction of the Textual Actual World, elements are also amended, added or deleted in order to present a setting that is also very unusual. The novel is funny because of the various situations in which the characters find themselves, but humour is also generated by the frequency with which they occur as well as the varied qualities they have. As Slocombe suggests of absurd situation novels, *Figurski* houses a Textual Actual World that is full of epistemological clashes. Thus, in addition to showing how a world is generated that is often incompatible with the Actual World, the analysis will then show how the various episodes in which the characters are presented are used to disrupt the ontological dichotomy that is enforced by other parts of the text. The second part of the chapter will show how the epistemological clashes manifest most forcefully by analysing the use of images in the text. This part of the chapter will also begin the process of developing a theoretical framework through which images can be analysed using Possible Worlds Theory. As this is an enormous task and one that cannot be satisfactorily completed in one chapter of one book, the scope of the project will be limited to considering how images in hypertext fiction work *ontologically*. That is, it will consider how the images work with the rest of the text to determine a particular ontological landscape. Finally, this chapter will consider how the images contribute to or uphold the overall dialogue in the novel between familiar and bizarre elements. It will conclude that while the situations that are presented foreground the artificiality of the Textual Actual World, in showing how they are related to the Actual World, they also draw attention to the strangeness of the world that the reader inhabits.

Familiar versus Unusual Locations

As a consequence of the episodic nature of *Figurski*, the locations from which the reader must choose are important for creating some sense of cohesion in the text. However, Findhorn, Shower-Lourdes and the Holodeck also epitomise the epistemological incongruities that are found throughout the novel. As the title suggests, the most important location in the novel is Findhorn. This is the location at which the protagonist, Frank Figurski, settles on his release from prison. It is also where he happens upon the mechanical pig which forms the starting point for the novel's quest narrative. The introductory lexia describes Findhorn as:

> A New Age intentional community on the Moray Firth in Scotland established in 1962 by Peter and Eileen Caddy and Dorothy Maclean in a trailer park near the fishing village of Findhorn. ... The community attracted spiritual seekers from all over the world. In the 1980s residents established educational programs and began planning an Eco-Village based on principles of sustainability, renewable energy, and harmony with natural systems. The Findhorn Foundation promotes values of spirituality, ecology, and community. ... {Findhorn 1.x}.

As has been seen in other parts of this book, Ryan's (1991) principle of minimal departure can be used to explain how readers utilise their knowledge of the Actual World when reading a fictional text. The principle states that readers assume that a Textual Actual World will reflect the Actual World unless the text specifies otherwise. In this instance also, rather than introducing a completely novel and imaginary Textual Actual World location, the narrative of *Figurski* utilises information from the Actual World. In *Figurski*, the lexia provides a number of Actual World references which connect the fictional location with the Actual World. It refers to the Actual World locations, Moray Firth, Findhorn and Scotland, and three Actual World individuals, Peter Caddy, Eileen Caddy and Dorothy Maclean. Temporally, events are dated according to the familiar Gregorian calendar. The definition also provides information about the Findhorn Foundation which represents feasible activities in the Actual World. Spiritual communities do exist and were certainly not uncommon in the 1960s. Indeed, if readers were to research this location, they would find that the description of Findhorn is historically accurate. The Findhorn Foundation does exist as an independent spiritual community in Scotland and it was founded by Caddy and Maclean. Findhorn, therefore, represents a location that departs relatively minimally from the reader's experience of the Actual World.

Similarly, like Findhorn, the location of Shower-Lourdes in *Figurski* does have an Actual World basis. It is defined as:

> Popular name for trailer-park shrine near Port St. Lucie, Florida, where in 1990 an apparition of Jesus appeared to one-time Wal-Mart cashier Adnarim Lorac while she showered. ... The apparition glowed and spoke to the naked, portly Mrs. Lorac: "Love one another." Jesus commanded her to return for another shower on the same day each month, when he would deliver more messages. As word of the phenomenon spread, a growing cadre of believers, seekers, and groupies gathered in the trailer park for the monthly event. ... {Shower-Lourdes 1.x}.

As the extract shows, the description of Shower-Lourdes refers to an Actual World location: Port St. Lucie in Florida. It also refers to an Actual World concept: the supermarket brand Wal-Mart. Events are dated, like the Findhorn definition, according to the Gregorian calendar. These are all facts which link the Textual Actual World location of Shower-Lourdes with locations in the Actual World. That Port St. Lucie and Wal-Mart are referred to without further elucidation also implies that these entities have a basis in the Actual World and, to some extent, this is true. Port St. Lucie and Wal-Mart do exist in the Actual World.

Yet while some of the locations and concepts have a basis in the Actual World, the character, Adnarim Lorac, her apparition, and the resulting designation of 'Shower-Lourdes' is entirely fabricated. This information is therefore entirely constructed in the Textual Actual World. Although Mrs. Lorac's experience is rather extraordinary the type of apparition that she experiences is not unknown in the Actual World. Many supposed apparitions have been approved by the Roman Catholic Church, including several in the twentieth century. This lexia therefore utilises a hybrid of factual information and invented material.

The principle of minimal departure can be used to explain how readers compute the information from the {Shower-Lourdes 1.x} lexia. They assume that Port St. Lucie and Wal-Mart of the Textual Actual World resemble Port St. Lucie and Wal-Mart in the Actual World and they then add information to the Actual World template about Adnarim Lorac and her apparition. This process is not necessarily challenging to readers and occurs every time they encounter new information in a text. It represents a rather conventional mixture of the familiarity of the Actual World and the constructed domain of a Textual Actual World.

While Findhorn and Shower-Lourdes can be constructed through applying the principle of minimal departure relatively unproblematically, the Holodeck location requires a much more significant adjustment. It is defined as:

> Holographic Environment Simulator on *Star Trek: The Next Generation,* *Deep Space Nine*, and *Voyager*, where people and places are recreated for a variety of recreational and training purposes. 3-D holographic projectors, combined with matter replicators (a version of Star Trek's innovative matter-to-energy transporter technology), create simulations essentially indistinguishable from reality. ... Users can create their own simulations or customize existing programs from a large library of holodeck software. ... {Holodeck 1.x}.

As the definition states, the Holodeck is a machine that simulates environments and it is largely responsible for generating many of the scenarios in which the characters find themselves in *Figurski*. As the lexia also states, it is a machine that was first shown in the various incarnations of the science-fiction films and television series of *Star Trek*. Thus while Findhorn and Shower-Lourdes are both locations which have an Actual World basis, the Holodeck is a location with a basis in another Textual Actual World.

The extra-textual origin of the Holodeck is significant for two reasons. First, while information about the machine is given in the {Holodeck 1.x} lexia, the text also alerts readers to the origin of the machine. The Holodeck originates in the Textual Actual World of *Star Trek*. As the analysis of *Patchwork Girl* shows (see Chapter 5), the principle of minimal departure can be used to explain how other texts can act as potential sources of information for the construction of a Textual Universe. Put simply, when readers are alerted to the significance of another text, they gather information from another Textual Actual World as well as using the Actual World as a source of information. Thus, as Ryan (1991) notes, 'reading is a compromise between minimal departure and intertextuality' (56).

Doležel (1998a) also provides an explanation of how readers use intertextual references. Expanding Eco's (1979) work on the role the reader plays in the construction of fictional worlds, Doležel suggests that when readers read, they consult different types of knowledge – what he calls different types of 'encyclopaedic knowledge' (177). Encyclopaedic knowledge is according to Doležel 'our store of knowledge' (176) about a particular domain. Like Ryan's principle of minimal departure, Doležel's concept of encyclopaedic knowledge assumes that fictional world construction is achieved by two sources of knowledge: the knowledge given by the text and the knowledge that readers bring with them to the text. If and when a text does not provide details or explanations about particular aspects of its fictional world, Doležel suggests that readers utilise their 'actual-world encyclopaedia' (177) to fill in the gaps.

Yet while Doležel suggests that the Actual World remains the principal source of knowledge for readers, he also claims that readers can draw upon a range of 'fictional encyclopaedias' (177), which are constructed according to 'knowledge about a possible world constructed by a fictional text' (177). He explains:

> in order to reconstruct and interpret a fictional world, the reader has to reorient his cognitive stance to agree with the world's encyclopaedia. In other worlds, knowledge of the fictional encyclopaedia is absolutely necessarily for the reader to comprehend a fictional world. The actual-world encyclopaedia might be useful, but it is by no means universally sufficient. ... The readers have to be ready to modify, supplement, or even discard the actual-world encyclopaedia (181).

Like Ryan, Doležel recognises that readers will approach a text with a vast array of previous experience and knowledge which has come from various different sources. Some of their knowledge will come from their experience of the Actual World, but some will come from their experience of reading about other domains – in particular other fictional worlds. When they read, they will take clues from the text as to which source of knowledge will be most appropriate.

Applying Ryan's and Doležel's conjectures to *Figurski* explains how readers compute the reference to the Holodeck. The text signals that knowledge about the Textual Actual World of *Star Trek* is required by making explicit reference to it as the origin of the Holodeck. Readers will therefore use any knowledge they have about that domain – or to use Doležel's terminology, their fictional encyclopaedia of *Star Trek* – and apply it to the Holodeck in *Figurski*. Yet whether readers gain information about the Holodeck from the intertextual reference or through the description of the machine given in *Figurski*, they are alerted to the fact that the entity is borrowed from another Textual Actual World and, thus, they are asked to look beyond the Textual Actual World of *Figurski*. The ontological boundary between the Actual World and the Textual Actual World is accentuated because readers must either reach across the boundary in order to access information about the subsumed location or, through relying on information from the {Holodeck 1.x} lexia, they are explicitly told that this machine exists in an alternative ontological domain. Thus, even if readers are not aware of the *Star Trek* notoriety of the Holodeck, they will still be alerted to its ontological separateness because the text explicitly specifies that it is borrowed from another Textual Actual World.

Yet, while *Star Trek* represents a site of intertextuality, the fact that the Holodeck is borrowed from another Textual Actual World is not solely responsible for the ontological foregrounding in this case. The Holodeck is also significant because it introduces concepts that deviate dramatically from the expectations that are established by the other locations in the novel. The {Holodeck 1.x} lexia tells readers about a machine that is impossible according to current Actual World technology. The 'matter replicators' that the lexia describes are without basis in the Actual World and the creation of realms that are 'indistinguishable from reality' represent an operation that is unknown in the Actual World. These elements therefore frame the location as inherently fictional. Temporally also, as opposed to the more familiar Gregorian calendar given at Findhorn and Shower-Lourdes, the events on the Holodeck are dated using less familiar 'Stardates'. Thus, this location operates according to laws, principles and conventions that are, at least to some extent, alien to a reader's experience of the Actual World.

Importantly, the existence of the Holodeck as a location for a fictional narrative does not necessarily lead to ontological foregrounding. As Ryan (1991) notes:

> even if readers reject these entities [ghosts, UFOs, ESPs, miracles etc. from their personal representation of reality, the possibility remains that the sender renders them as real, and so their occurrence in a text does not constitute an absolute sign of fictionality. Still greater is our disagreement concerning the inventory of the real world, and the properties of its members. It is consequently easy for a text to … introduce nonexisting individuals, while claiming nevertheless that TAW [Textual Actual World] reflects AW [Actual World] (46).

As Ryan points out, the ontological disparity between the Actual World and a Textual Actual World is not necessarily foregrounded by epistemological incongruities. In fact, she suggests that incompatibility between the species, technology or physical environment of a Textual

Actual World and those of the Actual World can be a source of debate. In addition, as Ryan's observations suggest, entities, concepts and individuals that do not exist in the Actual World are relatively common in fiction, and the principle of minimal departure can be used to explain how readers are able to supplement their knowledge of the Actual World relatively easily in order to accommodate any additional components that a Textual Actual World might contain.

In addition to the reader's willingness to integrate the unfamiliar, Ryan also notes that our experience of reading teaches us that some genres are likely to depart more dramatically from our experience of the Actual World than others. 'Reading a fairy tale,' she states, 'we know right away that we may find dragons and flying horses, foxes and frogs. ... We *expect* some animals to be able to talk. ... We *expect* some suspension of the real world laws of human psychology' (55, my italics). Ryan suggests that while the Actual World acts as a default source of information, texts which belong to a particular genre presuppose particular practices so that readers of a fairy tale are not necessarily surprised to encounter a dragon in that kind of Textual Actual World because their experience of previous fairy tales sanctions such a possibility. Consequently readers' experiences of particular types of text lead to scenarios in which 'generic landscapes predict what will be shown and hidden in a certain type of text, what will be given or denied significance' (57) so that readers anticipate the nature of a particular Textual Universe before or shortly after they begin reading a text.

Ryan's conjectures provide a useful means of conceptualising the generic expectations that a reader might have but her theory requires some qualification before it can be applied to *Figurski*. First, the geographical, sociological and educational background of readers will certainly inform their individual and collective expectations of a particular genre so that cultural and ideological implications must be acknowledged in any theory and analysis of reader expectations. In addition, if we accept that generic landscapes can be used to *predict* the inventory of a Textual Universe, then we have to accept that information about a Textual Actual World can be gained before reading has begun. Ryan acknowledges that her stance 'involves a rejection of the view that textual universes are created *ex nihilo*, and that textual meaning is the product of a self-enclosed system' (55) and thus recognises that the concept of generic landscapes is dependent on preconceived intertextual information. She substantiates this by asserting that 'generic landscapes solidify through a process of filtration: we gather elements from themes and objects characteristic of a certain corpus' (55). While generic expectations can be, and likely are, utilised in the reading of many texts, the genre to which a text belongs may not always be available in advance. Contextual information, such as the reputation of the author, the sentiments of the title, the impression given by the cover illustration or blurb can be used to prepare the reader for the type of Textual Universe a book contains. However, the peculiarity of the Textual Universe is sometimes only apparent once readers begin to experience the Textual Universe that is constructed and that occurs *within* the text. While readers may use their intertexual knowledge as a basis for comparison, the construction of a Textual Universe does take place within the text and, as will be shown, can be undermined.

Despite these provisos, Ryan's conjectures about generic expectations are useful because they explain the epistemological interplay between Actual World and Textual Actual World knowledge. Rather than being two distinct processes, the principle of minimal departure *and* knowledge of generic landscapes can be seen as simultaneously activated by a text, limited only by the reader's own knowledge of each. According to this premise, readers apply the principle of minimal departure but also have pre-formed generic expectations which might override their knowledge of and access to their Actual World template. Thus, while the principle of minimal departure and the associated correlation between Textual Actual World and Actual World can explain how readers adjust their epistemological template, generic conventions can also influence the effect that a text can have on a reader.

Pavel (1986) also notes that an increased epistemological incongruity between a Textual Actual World and the Actual World does not necessarily lead to an increased ontological perceptibility. Instead he claims that the artificiality of a fictional domain can be highlighted by 'the *amount* of new information absorbed ... but also the general *quality* of the alternate world' (90, my italics). According to Pavel ontological foregrounding can be caused by two related things: the magnitude of new information that the reader has to add to their experience of the Actual World and the characteristics of that new information. While some texts describe domains that contain a whole host of entities and events that are incompatible with the reader's experience of the Actual World, Pavel suggests that as long as the text maintains an illusion of similarity, the ontological separateness can be lessened. He claims that 'impersonation works only so long as the fictional setting is taken seriously, imagined as real. In order to make fiction function smoothly, the reader and the author must pretend that there was no suspension of disbelief, that travel to the fictional land did not occur' (89). Pavel's conviction that the ontological boundary between a Textual Actual World and the reader in the Actual World can be hidden is important because it explains how texts which describe unusual situations are not necessarily interpreted as more artificial than those that do not. Like Ryan, therefore, Pavel suggests that a Textual Actual World that is not based on the Actual World is not necessarily more obviously artificial than a text that is, but rather that it is the attention that is drawn to the fictional nature of the world that is consequential.

One of the ways in which Pavel suggests texts can draw attention to their artificiality is through epistemological clashes. Although he does not refer to 'genre' explicitly, he does pay attention to epistemological incongruities that are generated when expectations that are associated with particular types of text are undermined. In particular he notes that 'stories about the most common individuals are sometimes framed in such a way as to ... suggest a world of mystery and ritual, better fitted for supernatural characters than for the wretched protagonists of these texts' (93). Pavel's distinction between 'common individuals' and 'a world ... better suited for supernatural characters' compares two different types of ontological domain: those that contain elements that resemble the Actual World and those that do not. He suggests that when a text contains elements of each, an implicit incongruity is generated and, like Ryan, he suggests that reading involves a tussle between Actual World knowledge and expectations of what a particular type of Textual Actual World should contain.

Applying these hypotheses to Kafka's *The Castle*, Pavel notes that:

> contradictory clues seem to suggest that the world we attend is sometimes similar to ours and sometimes obeys alien logic. Too well-structured to be simply oneiric, too realistic to accept a mythical framework, the nature of the fictional surroundings remain elusive. ... Distance indicators are wilfully jammed, leaving indeterminate the choice between familiarity and infinite remoteness (93).

Pavel suggests that the world that Kafka presents in *The Castle* resembles the Actual World in many respects and thus departs minimally from the reader's experience of this domain. However, he also notes that the fictional world generated by *The Castle* also contains elements which differ much more dramatically from the reader's experience of the Actual World. Thus, the Textual Actual World is simultaneously accessible and opaque and the epistemological oscillation between the familiar and the unknown has eventual ontological implications. As readers become less able to *systematically* reconcile the domain described by the text with their experience of the Actual World, its artificiality becomes much more apparent.

Ryan's and Pavel's theories of reading are important because they can be used to explain the way in which a reader is affected by the different experiences within the same text. If we accept, as they both argue, that both the principle of minimal departure *and* generic expectations are utilised in the act of reading, then both the principle of minimal departure *and* generic expectations can also be undermined or subverted by a text. Texts can present scenarios that deviate from a reader's knowledge and experience of the Actual World – what Doležel calls their 'actual-world encyclopaedia' – and they can also present scenarios that deviate from their knowledge, experience and expectations of a particular genre.

Applying these conclusions to the analysis of *Figurski*, the peculiarity of the text is revealed. The use of the Holodeck as a key location is not striking because of its degree of fictionality or because of the generic expectations with which it is associated. Rather, the Holodeck is marked as a bizarre location in *Figurski* by its difference to the other locations that it appears alongside. Findhorn and Shower-Lourdes are based, either completely or to a large extent, on Actual World locations and practices. They therefore depart minimally from readers' experience of the Actual World and encourage them to access their encyclopaedic knowledge of that domain. Using this information, readers apply the principal of minimal departure and assume that the Textual Actual World of *Figurski* is largely based on the Actual World. Conversely, however, while 'Holographic Environment Simulator[s] which create simulations essentially indistinguishable from reality' {Holodeck 1.x} exist as fictional objects in the Actual World, they are not associated with Actual World conventions or practices. Thus, the Holodeck presents a concept and a location that departs from readers' experience and associated encyclopaedic knowledge of the Actual World to a larger degree than that of Findhorn or Shower-Lourdes. This is significant because the reader experiences a conflict of expectations. There is an incongruity between what some locations prepare us to expect and what another actually delivers. As Ryan puts it, the text 'call[s] to mind the principle of minimal departure – only to block its operation' (Ryan, 1991: 58) so that a two-way process occurs. In some parts of the text, Actual World knowledge is identified as relevant for the construction of the Textual Actual World but in other parts of the text, this knowledge proves to be useless. In some parts of the text, it demands one type of encyclopaedic knowledge and in other parts of the text, it demands another. The expectations that the text instils are thereby simultaneously subverted.

Related to this is the text's subversion of the reader's generic expectations. The text tells us that the Holodeck originates in *Star Trek* and this detail stimulates generic expectations that are associated with science fiction. In science fiction, we are not surprised by Holographic Environment Simulators or Stardates. However, the science fiction expectations that the Holodeck generates are incongruous with the realist expectations that are provoked by the events that occur at Findhorn and to some extent Shower-Lourdes.

The reason that the combination of the three locations is significant is that readers must apply a different set of generic expectations – and different encyclopaedia – to different parts of the same text or, more accurately, different generic expectations and encyclopaedia – to different parts of the same Textual Actual World. Rather than acting as 'complementary sources of information' (Ryan, 1991: 56) which result in 'a compromise between minimal departure and intertextuality' (Ryan, 1991: 56), in *Figurski*, 'distance indicators are wilfully jammed' (Pavel, 1986: 93) because generic expectations are instated and particular encyclopaedic knowledge is signalled as relevant, only to be concurrently challenged. There is no epistemic compromise, only incongruity and the Textual Actual World that is generated is vastly unpredictable.

Incongruent Text Types

The incongruity between the familiarity of Findhorn and Shower-Lourdes and the extraordinariness of the Holodeck is indicative of the way in which *Figurski* simultaneously establishes and challenges our expectations of its Textual Actual World. The epistemological clashes that the differences in these spaces cause are also reflected in the episodes and scenarios that occur within them. More specifically, what initially appear to be familiar Actual World conventions are invoked before subsequently being distorted.

While much of the novel is written in prose, a whole host of other text types are also evident. These include fictional forms such as epic poems, haikus, children's stories, dramatic texts, as well as non-fictional texts often associated with academic discourse, such as conference abstracts and library catalogue entries. The melange of texts contributes to the episodic feel of the novel by presenting a number of vastly diverse incidents and situations as well as largely incongruous forms of representation from both fictional and non-fictional contexts. In addition, the different text types also facilitate clashes between form and content.

There are numerous examples within the text, but one analysis can be used to illustrate how the others function as a whole. In each case the activities are used, like the various locations, to invoke and subsequently challenge the reader's expectations of the entity with which they are confronted. Numerous lexias are distributed throughout the text which contain study questions or comprehension activities. In the {1.3.08} lexia, the screen is divided into two sections, one headed 'Talking about the Ideas' and the other headed 'Things to Do' with instructions asking for a critical engagement with a novel.

The appearance of study questions within a novel is not necessarily significant. The study questions could represent one of the many different activities in which the characters are involved – of which there are many. However, the questions invite a response to a novel called *Figurski at Findhorn on Acid* and therefore ask for an interpretation of the novel in which they also occur. For example, under 'Things to Do', readers are asked to adopt one of the characters from *Figurski* and 'analyze, from his or her character's own perspective, the cultural message in the text about drugs or luncheon meat' {1.3.08}. The questions are self-reflexive and ontologically significant because readers are asked to see them, not as an activity in which the characters are engaged, but as an activity in which they should engage in the Actual World. To answer them, they must remain outside of the Textual Actual World and recognise that domain as an artificial construction.

While self-reflexivity does contribute to exposing the artificiality of the Textual Actual World, however, it is the epistemological incongruity between style and content that is responsible for generating the generic clashes. The way in which readers are asked to 'analyze' the text is typical of the critical activities which take place in classrooms. The style of many of the questions emulates that of academic discourse. The use of 'drugs' and 'luncheon meat' as opposed to the more colloquial 'Acid' and 'Spam' shown in the extracts above is indicative of a stylistic shift towards a high register. Yet while some of the questions adhere to the scholarly conventions, many of the instructions are entirely inappropriate for the context in which they occur. In the 'Talking about the Ideas' section, one question asks: 'seen any good movies recently?', which is an enquiry that is entirely incongruous with the academic discourse invoked by other parts of the same lexia. This question is associated with informal, phatic discourse rather than intellectual enquiry. Stylistically also, the omission of the second person pronoun, 'you', and the auxiliary verb, 'have', means that the question is grammatically incomplete. It introduces a level of informality that conflicts with the formality of the other instructions.

The style, tone and familiarity of the questions in this part of the lexia are therefore inconsistent with the generic expectations that are simultaneously invoked by the study questions format. As was seen in the analysis of the different locations, the principle of minimal departure and generic expectations are invoked while also subsequently subverted. The result is a scenario that, like the other parts of the Textual Actual World, is very obviously artificial.

The juxtaposition of the familiarity of the narrator and the formality of the academic questions in {1.3.08} is indicative of the generic clashes that are evident throughout the novel. Epic poems, which are conventionally associated with grand and heroic deeds, tell tales of eating Spam; haikus, which are traditionally considered to be a serious form of poetry, take baked goods as their focus; stories written in a style that emulates children's literature include reference to LSD and contain various profanities which are entirely unsuitable topics for the intended audience that their form might predict.

Yet while the clashes work in a similar way throughout the text, the focus on the academic practice is particularly pertinent in this case. Since the questions parody typical academic practice, *some* of the instructions would be appropriate in a particular context and therefore be relevant to a particular type of audience. That the texts are associated with academia is particularly significant in the context of *Figurski* because, as a hypertext, it is likely that academics comprise a large proportion of its readership. As studies have shown (e.g. Pope, 2006; Ensslin, 2007), the distribution of hypertext fiction is limited to a relatively small, niche market which mainly includes other writers of hypertext fiction and university students. It is taught on university syllabi and many hypertext authors, including the author of *Figurski*, Richard Holeton, are university professors or academic researchers. It is likely therefore that at least some readers will have direct experience of the academic discourse that is presented. Consequently, they will be more receptive to the generic clashes that *Figurski* introduces within those practices. The mixture of the familiar and the bizarre is particularly relevant therefore because of the likely nature of the audience to which it is directed. Subsequently, the self-reflexivity of the academic discourse is more than just playful. It asks the reader to evaluate the practice in which many of them may well engage.

Rewriting History

As the analysis above suggests, the incongruous locations and practices that *Figurski* presents are responsible for establishing much of the absurdity in the text. Epistemological clashes are also caused by the placing of the characters within re-representations of relatively well-known historical events. Since the Holodeck is a machine that simulates scenarios, it is largely responsible for generating the various different scenarios in which the characters find themselves.

A recurring simulation transports the characters to a scene which simulates Princess Diana's fatal car accident that took place in the Actual World in 1997. In a lexia which combines 'Figurski and the No-Hands Cup Flipper on the Holodeck with Spam and Rosellini's 1737 Mechanical Pig', the following scene is described:

[Dim lights, twinkling stars, Parisian skyline. Inside speeding black Mercedes driven by Henri Paul. Sky disappears as car enters tunnel. ... Nguyen "Trevor Rees-Jones" Van Tho holds mechanical pig and small bag in front passenger seat, Frank "Dodi Al Fayed" Figurski cuddles with Princess Diana in the back. Car spins out of control and begins slow motion crash. ... Diana throws up eggs and Spam, which sprays off air bags and splatters on leather seats. Passengers scream.]
   Henri: Merde! Merci. Merci-des. Merde-cedes. Mercedes ... [repeats].
   [Paparazzi pick through wreckage, cameras flash while passengers make dying moans. Nguyen feels hands poking through broken windows, tugging mechanical pig from his grasp] {2.2.06}.

The scene described in the {2.2.06} lexia is based on an Actual World event. Princess Diana was chased by a group of paparazzi photographers and was killed in a road accident, in Paris. She was a passenger in a black Mercedes and was accompanied by Dodi Al Fayed, Trevor Rees-Jones and a driver named Henri Paul. The scene presented in the {2.2.06} lexia thus represents a Textual Actual World based on an event in the Actual World. As the extract shows, the scene is presented as a format with stage directions given in square brackets and speech prefixes preceding the dialogue. In this particular episode therefore, an Actual World event is fictionalised using conventions associated with dramatic texts.

It is important to note that the use of an Actual World event represents a slightly different epistemological mechanism to the use of Actual World locations such as Findhorn and St. Lucie in Florida. Whereas Findhorn and St. Lucie draw upon the reader's knowledge of Actual World locations, the {2.2.06} lexia utilises the reader's knowledge about individuals and events and therefore a specific historical moment. While each utilises a reader's knowledge of the Actual World, it is a different type of knowledge in each. The events in {2.2.06} utilise Actual World counterparts as well as Actual World locales. In addition, whereas an Actual World location such as Findhorn can be directly experienced by a reader, the fictionalisation of Diana's car accident involves events to which a reader has no *direct* access.

The use of an Actual World counterpart in a Textual Actual World and the fictionalisation of a historical event do not necessarily represent unusual devices. As was discussed in the analysis of *Victory Garden* (see Chapter 4) both are essential for historical fictions. However, in some cases events can be presented in such a way that ontological ramifications are felt. McHale (1987) explains that '"classic" historical fiction ... tries to make the transgression [between the real and the fictional] as discreet, as nearly unnoticeable' (90) so that the ontological boundary between the Actual World and Textual Actual World is unmarked. This is the case in historical fictions which are loyal to Actual World events. However, McHale also recognises that some texts make the distinction between the Actual World and the Textual Actual World very apparent. He suggests that this can be done by texts which 'visibly contradict the public record of "official" history' either by '*supplement[ing]* the historical record, claiming to restore what has been lost or suppressed; or ... *displac[ing]* official history all together' (90). McHale makes a distinction between historical fictions which remain relatively loyal to the original but which add a neglected component or point of view, and historical fictions which alter the original narrated version of the event to the point where the original version becomes radically different to the episode on which it is based. These two approaches to storytelling therefore differ in terms of the respective emphasis that is placed on alternative epistemological perspectives and alternative ontological domains. The first type of historical fiction adds information to the record, whereas the second changes the record altogether.

The distinction between supplementation and displacement made by McHale represents the difference between the use of the historical in *Figurski* and the use of the historical in *Victory Garden* (see Chapter 4). *Victory Garden* uses the Gulf War as a backdrop against which the entire novel is situated. It does not replace the official public record of events with alternatives but provides extra information or, to use McHale's terminology, presents 'suppressed' or unknown perspectives within that context. Within the Textual Actual World of *Figurski*, the changes that are made to the 'public record of "official" history' are so extreme however that, although it does resemble the original on which it is based, it also creates an entirely different episode. In McHale's terms, it displaces history. Moreover, as the analysis will show, it supersedes the official record quite dramatically.

Clearly there are some epistemological issues in terms of establishing the 'public record of "official" history'; McHale's use of quotation marks acknowledges that this is problematic, if only implicitly. Cultural, political and social factors can influence the documentation of events so that the 'official' public record can be difficult to define. Related to this is the question of the 'visibl[e] contradict[ion]' of a public record. The extent to which a version must 'contradict' the 'public record' for it to constitute a significant and therefore noticeable departure from the 'official' public record is debateable. In Possible Worlds Theory, at least, any change to the original constitutes an alterative version which will always contradict the other(s), but the point at which that becomes noticeable is perhaps less easy to define.

Yet while it is important to recognise the plurality of perspectives and experiences in the Actual World, it is also necessary to classify historical events as fact. Carried to its ultimate fruition, a reliance on plurality and relativism renders any recounting of events extremely difficult, if not impossible. Similarly, in a literary critical context, discounting the existence of historical fact can unnecessarily impede the analysis of historical fiction because if events cannot be said to have happened definitively then historical fictions can be said to have no epistemological basis – a position which, as the analysis below will show, is considerably problematic, if not unjustifiable. Thus, while an awareness of the subjectivity of historical accounts is prudent, a belief in concrete facts is also sensible, realistic and in many cases absolutely necessary for the documentation of significant Actual World events.

Similarly, while philosophical debates exist regarding its epistemological availability, Possible Worlds Theory is founded on the basis that the Actual World does exist. The public record of official history can therefore be seen as the components of the Actual World on which a Textual Actual World draws when a historical event is fictionalised. While sometimes difficult to define absolutely, a parallel can be justified by drawing correlations between the events described in a text and the events known to have happened in the Actual World.

Returning to the analysis of *Figurski*, the public record of official history on which the {2.2.06} lexia in *Figurski* draws includes information about the participants (Diana, Dodi Al Fayed, Trevor Rees-Jones, Henri Paul), the location (Paris) and other prevalent details such as the time at which it occurred (night-time) and the vehicle that was involved (a black

Mercedes-Benz passenger car). As McHale observes in relation to other texts, *Figurski* invokes this information but then replaces it with another version so as to 'juxtapose the officially accepted version of what happened and the way things were, with another, often radically dissimilar version of the world' (90). In the {2.2.06} lexia, Diana is accompanied, not by Dodi Al Fayed and Trevor Rees-Jones, but by Frank 'Dodi Al Fayed' Figurski and Nguyen 'Trevor Rees-Jones' Van Tho. The mixing of the Actual World and Textual Actual World in these cases is signalled linguistically through the merging of proper names. 'Dodi Al Fayed' and 'Trevor Rees-Jones' are used as rigid designators which invoke individuals from the Actual World. However, in the Textual Actual World of *Figurski*, Frank Figurski and Nguyan Van Tho enact their roles so that while the text invokes Actual World counterparts it also replaces them with fictional characters. The characters, which are overtly incongruous with the originals from the Actual World scene, begin to supersede official history.

Events are also presented which are dramatically different to the original accident. At the point of impact in *Figurski*, Diana 'throws up eggs and Spam'. While we do not have any evidence on which to assess the historical accuracy of this episode, the contents of her vomit are incongruous with usual expectations of a royal diet. Similarly, as an inexpensive Anglo-American foodstuff, it is unlikely that Spam would be served in the fine-dining hotels and restaurants of Paris. The events that take place immediately after the accident are entirely incongruous with Actual World events. An unknown figure reaches into the car to steal the mechanical pig – a rather unusual item which was not reported as being present in the Actual World events which took place in 1997.

Epistemologically, therefore, the episode draws upon an event from the Actual World. Readers must utilise their knowledge of Diana's fatal car accident in the Actual World in order to see how it is changed in the Textual Actual World. However, rather than using the Actual World event as a backdrop to which to add detail, the text also dramatically changes that event. Readers must utilise knowledge of the Actual World while simultaneously acknowledging the new version's incongruity with the original. McHale acknowledges this apparent duality, noting that 'the tension between these two versions induces a form of ontological flicker between two worlds: one moment, the official version seems to be eclipsed by the apocryphal version; the next moment, it is the apocryphal version that seems mirage-like, the official version appearing solid, irrefutable' (90). McHale suggests that the two versions – the Actual and the Textual Actual – exist in an ontological tussle, each competing for epistemological dominance.

In *Figurski* readers must use and retain their knowledge about the original incident in the Actual World so that they can see its bearing on the current scene. In addition, because the changes are so extreme, they are forced to acknowledge its epistemological and therefore ontological separateness in order to see the difference between the two versions. While the official version is needed as a basis on which the new version is built, it is also made partially redundant by the version which seeks to replace it. Moreover, because the events in *Figurski* are incongruous with our experiences of the Actual World, our encyclopaedic knowledge of the Actual World is not entirely useful in this context. Readers have to use the Actual World as an epistemological template but then depart from the expectations that this generates to accommodate the incongruous details that the text provides.

Epistemologically, it is not absolutely critical for readers to recognise that this scene invokes an Actual World event – the scene is still somewhat unusual regardless of its reliance on previous events. However, once noticed, the boundary between the Actual World and the Textual Actual World is accentuated because the changes make explicit the event's origin in an ontological domain outside of the Textual Actual World. The ontological trickery or, to invoke McHale's vocabulary, the 'ontological flicker' is lessened, if not unnoticed, without a knowledge of the events on which it is based.

Visualising *Figurski*

As the analysis of the texts above suggests, *Figurski* comprises an episodic Textual Actual World, presenting a number of different locations, scenarios, characters, artefacts and text types. It also draws on the reader's knowledge of the Actual World in order to reveal its dependence upon and deviance from that domain. In addition to the textual narrative, the novel also contains a number of images which add to or supplement the events described verbally elsewhere. Visuals include photographs, hand-drawn pictures, screen-shots and diagrams as well as eclectic collages. The novel exists, then, not just as a stylistic and generic medley, but also as an amalgam of different media. Importantly, just as the different locations, events and artefacts are used to signal a complex epistemological and ontological relationship between the Textual Actual World and the Actual World, the images also represent an equally powerful narrative device.

The use of visual images within texts is not a recent phenomenon, developed only in response to the technological advances with which hypertext is associated. Children's print fictions are littered with drawings and photographic images, and William Blake's sketches are an example from the realm of adult literature. Visual images are not necessarily challenging or ontologically disruptive to a reader's experience of a text. On the contrary, they are often used to add to the authenticity of a narrative. However, as the analysis below shows, different types of image are used within *Figurski* as a means of manipulating the onto-logical landscape of the text, penetrating, moving and foregrounding the boundary between the Actual World and Textual Actual World in a number of different ways.

Images in Possible Worlds Theory

Before the analysis of the images in *Figurski* proceeds, it is first necessary to outline the logical debates that exist within Possible Worlds Theory regarding the ontological status of images because it is on such con-jectures that the subsequent discussion draws. Of the extremely small amount of attention paid to visual images within Possible Worlds Theory in literary studies, Ryan's (1991, 2006) relatively short discussions prove to be the most fruitful. Analysing the truth-value of photographs and pictures, in both a logical and literary context, she recognises that while the ontological intricacies of *textual* fictionality are well debated within Possible Worlds Theory, 'the question of fictionality is much more difficult to assess in pictorial and other types of visual communication (sculpture, cartoons, photography)' (Ryan, 1991: 97). The difficulty arises, argues Ryan, because 'there is an element of make-believe inherent to all pictures: the sender (artist, photographer, etc) presents spectators with a surface covered with lines and colors, and asks them to regard these marks as an object – to pretend that they see this object' (97). Ryan sug-gests that because an image is only ever a representation of the object, person or scene, it can only ever be reached through an imaginative process. Whereas in prose fiction the text conjures a Textual Actual World, an image is never the object, but only ever a means of present-ing the object.

Concentrating primarily on photographs and paintings, Ryan does foresee problems with categorising an entire form of communication as fundamentally 'real' or 'fictional' in its representational capacity and, instead, she constructs a more flexible proposal. Conflicting with her conjectures above, she acknowledges that 'pictures, when compared to words, have a unique ability to conjure up the presence of their referent. The picture of an object can be mistaken for this object, while a word can never be mistaken for its referent' (98). Under this proposal, Ryan suggests that visual media are somehow less artificial than textual representations because of their mimetic capacity to reflect an object almost exactly – something that is textually impossible. Thus, while images are logically non-actual, they do have the intrinsic capacity to depict extremely accurate representations of their subjects. This confliction is what makes it difficult, if not impossible, to classify a visual medium as *either* fictional or non-fictional in its representational capacity.

Seeking a resolution, Ryan suggests that in order to determine the relative fictionality of any image, a distinction has to be drawn between 'pretended *presence* and pretended *existence*' (98). She explains that 'even if one admits that all pictures conjure up make-believe presence … the existence of the referent is not necessarily established by the act of make-believe. When we look at a portrait of Napoleon, we may face him in make-believe, but it takes no act of pretense to believe in his historical existence' (98). Rather than stressing the innate fictionality of all pictorial representations, Ryan suggests that the nature of the subject itself should be ontologically determinant. A photograph of Napoleon may well be inherently fictional, but the image can actually connote non-fictionality because of the ontological status of the Actual World subject. According to this principle, if the subject exists in the Actual World, the image can also imply Actual World existence to the extent that its fictionality is lessened, if not lost.

Thus, as a potential solution to her own debate, Ryan proposes three different conditions which constitute fictionality in pictorial representations and suggests that 'a picture is fictional when … 1) … it is offered as the illustration of a fictional text. … 2) … it represents a nonexistent object located in an APW [Actual Possible World]. … 3) … when pretense and role-playing are involved on the level of the scene depicted by the artist' (99). Each of Ryan's three definitions uses simulation as an indicator of fictionality and in each case an image is considered fictional if it depicts an ontological space that is separate from the Actual World. In her first condition, an illustration of a fictional text corresponds to a depiction of a Textual Actual World; in her second, a nonexistent object can only ever exist in a possible world; in her third, while in role-play the participants are located in the Actual World, they create a scene which exists in another ontological domain. Fictional texts, nonexistent objects and role-playing are each deemed 'fictional' by Ryan because they constitute ontological domains that are separate from the Actual World, and, consequently the images that depict them must also be considered as a form of fictional representation.

Unfortunately, Ryan's preliminary theory is too underdeveloped to account for all instances of nonverbal communication within or outside of a fictional text. Similarly, without a range of analyses to accompany her account, it remains rather speculative. This is primarily because she does not acknowledge the vast array of visual communicative methods. All types of what are quite different forms of non-verbal media are grouped together under the umbrella term 'picture', so that the representational capacity of a photograph is judged alongside that of painting, for example. This is problematic because, according to Ryan's own conjectures, the fictional capacity of each communicative media is judged according to whether it is verbal or nonverbal. It is likely therefore that nonverbal media requires a similar degree of subdivision for its interpretation.

More importantly, while Ryan's proposal for what comprises pictorial fictionality provides a theoretical basis for the analysis of literary images, it adheres too strictly to possible-worlds logic to be usefully applied to all examples. While any picture used as an 'illustration of a fictional text' is inevitably fictional in nature, its inclusion in a fictional text can be used for a number of different purposes. To categorise all images as fictional merely because of their location in a fictional text is to ignore the individual resonance and purpose of each image.

Ryan (2006) remedies some of these theoretical shortfalls in subsequent work, making a distinction between different types and different uses of visual media (37–42). Speaking of photography, for example, she argues that it 'makes a determinate and *almost* irrefutable truth claim: "What I am showing really existed." The only way to refute this claim would be to prove that the photograph has been manipulated, or that the recorded scene had been faked' (38). Unless subject to deliberate human interference, argues Ryan, photographic images always attempt to depict 'truth', at least in the logical sense because photographs reflect the scene in front of the lens exactly. The capacity for representing reality exactly, she suggests, is due to 'the objectivity inherent to the technology' (38). In addition to the somewhat problematic media essentialism exhibited in her discussion, Ryan's conjectures require at least some modification for their application to fictional texts. This is because Ryan discusses the truth-value of photographs in relation to the Actual World and not a Textual Actual World.

While she does not make a distinction between fictional and nonfictional images in photographs, however, Ryan does discuss the ontological peculiarity of 'man-made pictures' (40). Crucially, Ryan's agenda here is to 'coax paintings, drawings, and sculptures into expressing statements capable of being true or false' (40) and therefore her focus is the propositional capacity of visual representation as opposed to their hermeneutic function within a fictional text. However, her conjectures are relevant for the analysis of images in fiction because of the distinction between fictionality and non-fictionality that she posits. In particular, she suggests that:

> man-made pictures are not inherently fictional or nonfictional, but they can inherit these properties from other objects. Rather than applying to all pictures, the features of fictionality and nonfictionality would only concern those artworks that either refer to texts or are included in books. An illustration in an anatomy textbook would be nonfictional because the text, as a whole, is offered for belief; while an illustration in a fairy-tale book would participate in the act of make-believe mandated by the story. This proposal leaves a large number of paintings outside of this dichotomy, while most if not all films, photos, and texts can be classified as either fictional or nonfictional (40–1).

Ryan suggests here that the ontological status of an image must be defined according to its context. By her own admission, her assertions are not completely satisfactory and 'leave a vast number of artworks outside the dichotomy of fiction/nonfiction' (42), but they do acknowledge that the circumstances within which an image is placed influence its ontological status.

While clearly relevant, Ryan's (1991, 2006) examinations of visual images are not sufficiently developed to account for *all* uses of images within fiction. Implicitly, however, she does endorse an approach that is based on the analyses of individual examples. As Ryan suggests, all images have some degree of fictionality because of their intrinsic representational capacity. However, there is a danger that in adhering too closely to the logic of Possible Worlds Theory the literary element is lessened, if not neglected. Crucially, it is not my intention here to devise a comprehensive visual component for Possible Worlds Theory. Neither is it to suggest that *all* images can be judged as fictional or non-fictional simply through a process of contextual analysis. My goal is to show how Possible Worlds Theory can be used to analyse visual elements in texts, such as *Figurski*, which use images as a means of self-consciously problematising ontological and epistemological distinctions.

Images in *Figurski*

Paralleling the text's episodic structure, the images within *Figurski* depict a range of scenarios and events. As the analysis will show, some are overtly artificial and resonate with the parts of the text in which bizarre situations occur. Others are more representational of Actual World events and therefore link to the parts of the narrative that depict more familiar situations. The interaction between these two types of image is important because it is within this visual medium that the overall message of the novel presents itself.

In the pictures which are overtly artificial, the intrinsic fictionality of images that Ryan identifies can be seen most clearly. The {3.1.07} lexia, for example, contains a text and image sequence as shown in Figure 6.1.

As the screenshot shows, the {3.1.07} lexia contains a series of images with accompanying text above. The title describes this series of lexias as 'The Figurski, No-Hands Cup Flipper, and Fatima Michelle Vieuchanger at Shower-Lourdes on Acid Picture Book' and the entire sequence offers a short self-contained narrative in which the three central characters are involved. In this lexia, Figurski, the No-Hands Cup Flipper and Fatima set up camp in a Florida trailer park. Figurski produces 'a tiny piece of film' and they each eat a portion – the insinuation being that the characters are taking the 'Acid' of the lexia title. Visually, the first image is highlighted and subsequent images are presented with a frosted effect.

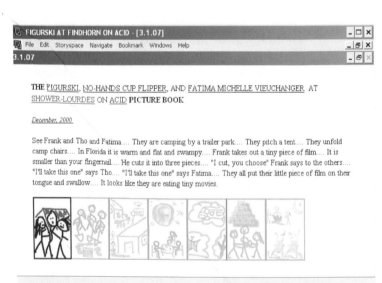

Figure 6.1   Screenshot of {3.1.07}

Following the default path, the next image in the sequence is highlighted and described by associated text until the narrative sequence is complete.

Evidently there is a reciprocal relationship between the images and the text in the sequence. In the {3.1.07} lexia, the use of an imperative, 'see Frank and Tho and Fatima', in the first sentence explicitly instructs the reader to consult the drawing below. Deictically, therefore, the text draws attention to the iconic relationship between the textual description and visual representation of the Textual Actual World. However, the strikingly artificial style of both the text and the images exposes its ontological status. Since the images appear to be hand-drawn, they are unquestionably artificial. The graphical representation therefore sets a certain tone as soon as the lexia is reached. In the body of the text, the child-like style of the narrative compounds the fictionality that is instigated by the visuals above. Linguistically, the consistent use of simple sentence constructions gives the text a rather unsophisticated style. Noun phrases, such as 'a trailer park', 'a tent' and 'camp chairs', appear without modifying adjectives and the entire text lacks figurative embellishment. The minimal style is reminiscent of a children's story. The images are also very obviously artificial. The majority comprise simple, hand-drawn shapes which are presented in the three primary colours. Basic structures are used to depict the people and their surroundings with very little detail of the landscape.

Ontologically, the use of an image that has quite obviously been *created* in the Actual World foregrounds the ontological divide between that domain and the Textual Actual World. In addition, because the accompanying text tells us that this drawing is of the Textual Actual World, the fictionality of the entire novel becomes even more apparent. Thus, it is not just the materiality of the image that is ontologically foregrounding here; the domain that it depicts is also significant.

While the {3.1.07} lexia contains a very obviously artificial drawing of the Textual Actual World, some visuals within *Figurski* offer more realistic representations. As Figure 6.2 shows, the {030} lexia contains a photographic image accompanied by text.

The image is quite opaque and it is therefore difficult to establish from the image alone what is being represented. The text below aids our interpretation however by declaring that the image depicts the 'apparition of Jesus in shower stall of Adnarim Lorac, Port St. Lucie'. Since the image appears in a novel in which an apparition on a shower curtain is described verbally, we can assume that the image is intended as a visual depiction of some part of the Textual Actual World. In particular, it depicts the events that are described within one of the location lexias, namely {shower-lourdes 1.x}.

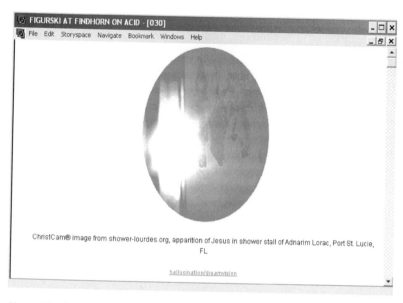

Figure 6.2   Screenshot of {030}

In the Actual World, the image is not a genuine photograph of the events described by *Figurski* because the Textual Actual World of *Figurski* does not actually exist; it is only a fictional construction. Within the context of the Textual Actual World, however, readers can interpret the image as providing a faithful representation of the shower stall at Port St. Lucie. The photograph makes the 'determinate and *almost* irrefutable truth claim' (2006: 38) that Ryan describes because, while the image in {030} must have been taken in the Actual World, it is used as a photographic illustration of the Textual Actual World. In the Actual World, the events at Port St. Lucie did not occur. However, several apparitions have taken place within the Actual World. Thus, readers only have to depart relatively minimally from their experience of the Actual World to account for the events depicted in {030}. This lexia does not cause significant ontological disruption because it functions as a relatively plausible pictorial representation of the Textual Actual World and because, in this instance, the Textual Actual World presents a scene which, if not familiar, is at least compatible with the reader's experience of the world to which she or he belongs.

While the {030} lexia appropriates a photographic image and accompanying textual explanation as a means of faithfully depicting the

Figure 6.3   Screenshot of {063}

Textual Actual World and causing minimal ontological disruption, other images within *Figurski* are more obviously bogus.

Like the photograph in {030}, the image shown in {063} depicts a space that is described elsewhere within the novel (see Figure 6.3). More specifically, in one of the Holodeck's simulations, the text states that a 'section [of the Great Wall of China] is really constructed of millions of cans of Spam' {1.1.10}. Thus, the photograph offers another iconic depiction of a particular part of the Textual Actual World. However, unlike the photograph in {030}, the {063} lexia foregrounds the artificiality of *Figurski* because it presents a situation that is completely incongruent with the reader's experience and comprehension of the Actual World.

The photograph shows an eminent Actual World location – the Great Wall of China – but, unlike its Actual World equivalent, the structure is built from cans of Spam. While the image represents a scene that is, though unusual, both logically and physically possible in the Actual World, it also deviates dramatically from the reader's experience of that domain to the point that it becomes ontologically significant. Like the photograph in the {030} lexia, the image in {063} originates in the Actual World. However, because it has been quite obviously 'manipulated' (Ryan, 2006: 38) it invalidates its *'almost* irrefutable truth claim' (38). Its status as an artificial construction is exposed because the changes that are implemented are so radical that its resemblance to the original is invalidated. Thus, this image achieves visually what much of the rest of the novel does textually. To invoke Ryan's conjectures from the discussion of the verbal narrative above, it invokes an Actual World location and thereby 'call[s] to mind the principle of minimal departure – only to block its operation' (Ryan, 1991: 58). While there is an epistemological likeness between the image in {063} and the reader's Actual World encyclopaedia, there is also an obvious disparity and the degree of the difference causes the ontological boundary between the reader and the Textual Actual World of *Figurski* to become significant.

In addition to the visual photograph, the accompanying text also produces its own form of ontological play. This is because the quotation, taken from *Scouting for Boys*, is an explicit intertextual reference to a text in the Actual World. While the quotation is used within the context of the Textual Actual World, it is borrowed from another source. The citation below the quotation refers to the source explicitly and consequently attention is drawn to the boundary between the Textual Actual World and the Actual World. Thus, the image in {063} highlights its artificiality by depicting a scene that is incongruous with our experience of the world, but the accompanying text compounds the associated ontological foregrounding by referring to a source beyond the boundaries of its current position.

While the analysis of the text and image in {063} highlights their respective self-reflexive functions, it is also important to consider how they operate collectively. Although both image and text take 'walls' as their focus, there is no apparent epistemological relation between the image of the Great Wall of Spam and the metaphorical claims in the Baden-Powell quotation. The image provides a visual depiction of an aspect of the Textual Actual World but the accompanying text represents a dramatic deviation from it. In addition to the ontological foregrounding that is caused by each individual component, therefore, their combined incongruity intensifies it. Rather than working together, the image and text in {063} work as a form of what McHale (1987) calls 'anti-illustration' (189). According to McHale, when illustration is used in postmodern fiction, it is often used as a means of foregrounding the ontological status of the Textual Actual World. He suggests in particular that 'the absence of any apparent relation between the illustration and the verbal text turns ... visual materials into pure demonstrations of the *visuality*' (190) and thus a form of self-reflexivity. The image–text relationship in *Figurski* can be seen to act in this way. It may be used as an illustration, but it also represents another tool that causes epistemological incongruities and consequential ontological foregrounding.

The analysis of the {063} lexia above shows how images are used within *Figurski* to foreground the artificiality of the text and maintain the unpredictability of the Textual Actual World that it constructs. In {063} an Actual World image is manipulated in order to illustrate an element of the Textual Actual World. Thus, like many of the other images, it is used as another means of representing scenes that are described elsewhere. In her analysis of images in *Figurski*, Ensslin (2007) also notes that 'graphics and photographs mostly illustrate elements mentioned in the text, as well as adding comic, surprising pastiche features to the novel. … It has to be conceded, however, that pictographic and photographic elements only occasionally carry their own, isolated meaning' (129). Ensslin's observations reflect the fact that most images work in the same way: as a means of illustrating something that is described textually elsewhere in the text. Yet the elements that 'carry their own meaning' are perhaps the most important because of the message that they, like many other elements within the text, very subtly convey.

The most striking of images is shown in lexia {058}. It is placed amongst many of the other images within the 'Notes' section and shows a pig, flying through the air above a pool of water. As Figure 6.4 shows, the image suggests that the pig has jumped from a rock platform into the water. The text below describes the animal as 'Ralph the Swimming Pig' and gives its apparent Actual World location as 'Aquarena Springs, San Marcos' in Texas, USA.

The image that {058} displays is striking – if not comical – because it depicts a scene which likely departs significantly from most readers' experience of the Actual World. In the Actual World, pigs live in pigsties rather than water pools; pigs wallow in mud rather than fly through the air; pigs do not generally partake in aerial manoeuvres.

As the analysis has shown, throughout the text readers are exposed to a number of situations which contradict their experiences of the Actual World. This produces a simultaneous invocation and blocking of the principle of minimal departure. Yet while this process can be used to explain a reader's initial response to *Figurski*, the frequency with which Actual World knowledge is thwarted also means that they will be increasingly unsurprised by the appearance of events or scenes that contradict their experience of the Actual World. Readers begin to become immune to, if not expectant of, epistemological incongruities between the Textual Actual World and the Actual World. Pavel (1986)

World Famous Ralph the Swimming Pig, Submarine Theatre, Aquarena Springs, San Marcos, TX (1993)

Figure 6.4   Screenshot of {058}

suggests that when texts consistently challenge our knowledge of the Actual World 'we do not consistently apply the principle of minimal departure in these cases. On the contrary, when confronted with fictions of this kind, we seem to anticipate a maximal departure' (93). He suggests that, after habitual exposure to unusual or unexpected situations, readers begin to expect this pattern to be repeated. He suggests in particular that 'mimetic principles are supplemented with antimimetic expectations' (93) so that once they learn the futility of applying Realist expectations, readers begin to utilise a different kind of knowledge. Pavel's observations are significant because they suggest that it is possible to identify an 'antimimetic' or 'unnatural' pattern or genre (cf. Richardson, 2006; Alber, 2009), although the degree to which a text must deviate from mimetic principles before it instates 'antimimetic expectations' or becomes 'unnatural' is debateable. More importantly in the context of this analysis, because readers have to apply different sets of expectations to different parts of the text, after some experience of reading *Figurski*, they may well adjust their expectations accordingly.

Returning to the analysis of *Figurski*, because the image of the flying pig occurs in a text which contains events and locations which may well conflict with the reader's experience of the Actual World, it is likely that she or he will categorise the image in {058) as fictional. Importantly, the text anticipates a sceptical response to the image because in the subsequent lexia, entitled 'Frequently Asked Questions about Ralph the Swimming Pig' {059}, a detailed explanation of the pig's legitimacy is provided. The questions that are answered include 'what is Aquarena Springs?' and 'can Ralph really swim?'.

Ontologically, therefore, the {058} image might well be categorised by readers as an Actual World image which has been manipulated for the purpose of the novel. However, the accompanying {059} lexia contradicts any such conclusion because it functions as a means of qualifying Ralph the Flying Pig's Actual World existence. While readers might initially place this image within the Textual Actual World, they need only consult the 'Acknowledgements' section of the hypertext to see that it actually originates in and refers to an animal from the Actual World. Though unusual and perhaps incredulous, the image does present an Actual World entity. The boundary between the Textual Actual World and the Actual World becomes distorted because what we might initially conclude to be another example of *Figurski*'s absurd fictionality ultimately materialises as fact.

While also a means of generating humour, the image of the flying pig is an embodiment of the novel's overall message. The text contains various locations, episodes and accompanying images which show the epistemological incongruity of the Textual Actual World of *Figurski* from the Actual World. However, this image shows the epistemological similarity between the two domains. Thus, while the Textual Actual World of *Figurski* is nonsensical, ridiculous and illogical, it ultimately uses the Actual World as its point of departure. The implication is perhaps, therefore, that the ubiquitous absurdity that is to be found in the Textual Actual World of *Figurski* is just as applicable to the Actual World on which it is based.

Conclusion

As the analysis above shows, the Textual Actual World of *Figurski* is both episodic and eclectic. In the Actual World, this fragmentation gives the text a feeling of discontinuity and disjointedness. Readers get a glance into a variety of different scenes and scenarios, but they constitute brief visits. In addition, the absurd scenarios in which the characters often find themselves mean that the Textual Actual World is an unpredictable ontological domain. It may be a domain that resembles the Actual

World in which the reader resides, but it is not long before an element is introduced that makes it somewhat incompatible and therefore incongruent. Both the structure and the style of the text contribute to the absurdity within the text and therefore the ontological foregrounding that is a product of that atmosphere.

The use of familiar locations, individuals and events is one of the many ways in which the familiar is invoked in *Figurski* only to be simultaneously subverted. Bizarre situations are often the result of simulation, either physical through the use of the Holodeck or mental with the use of Acid. However, this does not lessen their impact or their relevance to the Actual World. Ultimately, the relationship between the Textual Actual World of *Figurksi* and the Actual World of the reader is ontological and epistemological and, as the analysis has shown, the text takes advantage of both. As Slocombe (2006) argues in his discussion of absurd postmodern fiction, a dialogue between the familiar and the bizarre 'forces the reader to question their own awareness, to question the world in which they live as well as themselves' (108). This results, he suggests, in the 'destabilization of "ontological boundaries"' (108) because they are asked to consider the extent to which they can engage with the situation, both the typical and the strange. *Figurski* makes that dialogue explicit throughout and problematises ontological boundaries with dramatic epistemological consequences. However, as Slocombe shows in his analysis of print narratives, 'the gap between our expectations of reality' (109) and what we eventually discover to be true 'whilst opening the door to despair, can also lead to laughter' (109). *Figurski* encourages readers to laugh at its Textual Actual World while also inviting them to laugh at the Actual World to which they belong.

7
Conclusion: Future Worlds

Drawing together a number of consistencies found within the four hypertext fiction novels, this concluding chapter outlines the theoretical and analytical implications of this book and evaluates the effectiveness of its Possible Worlds Theory approach. Offering directions for future research, it will also suggest that other forms of digital fiction might benefit from the approach profiled in this book. Finally, it will suggest areas in which Possible Worlds Theory requires further development for its application more generally.

Opening Conclusions

The first two chapters of this book showed how the first wave of hypertext theory over-generalised the structural, poetic and aesthetic capabilities of hypertext. A reliance on poststructuralist abstraction, anecdotal descriptions and an overestimation of the reader's role within the text led to a critical stalemate from which few analyses of individual works were born.

As a more productive approach, Chapter 2 showed how more realistic observations have led some second-wave hypertext theorists to recognise reader alienation as being a salient feature of hypertext reading. Since the reader is integrally involved in the construction of the hypertext, they have a role in the physical construction of the text as well as the associated Textual Actual World that the text describes. Since the construction of the text is an act that must be undertaken in the Actual World, the reader's role is one of the ways in which they are alerted to the separateness of the Textual Actual World and consequently the artificiality of that domain. In addition to the reader's role, a number of hypertext theorists have also recognised that Storyspace novels often contain narrative devices which draw further attention to the ontological peculiarity of their Textual Actual Worlds.

The extensive analyses within this book have revealed a number of specific instances of self-reflexivity in hypertext fiction. In particular, Chapters 3, 4, 5 and 6 have shown that narrative contradictions, impossible forms of fictional communication, the embedding of ontological domains, explicit intertextual references to other works, overt utilisation of counterparts, and the construction of impossible situations and events are some of the many ways in which each novel self-consciously draws attention to the artificiality of the domain it simultaneously constructs. While the two aspects of hypertext reading are distinct – the role of the reader working outside the text and narrative devices working within the text – the analyses have shown how both work mutually to foreground the ontological divide between the Textual Universe and the reader in the Actual World.

Methodological Conclusions

In addition to identifying and analysing a number of self-reflexive devices within four texts, this book has also profiled a theoretical method for the analysis of Storyspace hypertext fiction more generally. With a focus on modality, reference and ontology, the ongoing theoretical expositions have shown that Possible Worlds Theory provides an appropriate framework and accompanying terminology with which to analyse the self-reflexive narrative devices found in some Storyspace hypertext novels. Since Possible Worlds Theory is an approach which is primarily concerned with the relationships between ontological domains and their constituents, it provides tools which can be used to analyse the reader's relationship with the text including negotiating, locating and interrogating the borders between the Actual World and the Textual Actual Worlds as well as the ontological structures contained therein. Ryan's (1991) model of Possible Worlds Theory was identified as a methodological point of departure. The analyses that proceeded then examined a selection of narrative devices to show the dexterity of Possible Worlds Theory.

The analysis of *afternoon* in Chapter 3 showed how Possible Worlds Theory can be used to justify narrative contradictions in terms of conflicting ontological domains. It also showed how a second-person address to the reader can be examined as the transgression of an ontological boundary. Within this chapter, Ryan's framework was amended so that such ontological transgressions could be modelled more accurately in a hypertext context. In addition, the World View category was added in order to accommodate the epistemological conflicts that exist as a consequence of the multiple narrators that narrate in *afternoon*.

The analysis of *Victory Garden* revealed how Possible Worlds Theory can be used to analyse historical fiction. In particular, the principle of minimal departure, transworld identity and counterpart theory were examined and applied. The chapter showed how Possible Worlds Theory can accurately examine intertextual references. In particular, an analysis of quotations in the novel showed how Possible Worlds Theory can be used to expose the epistemological ambiguities that their inclusion introduces to a fictional text.

The analysis of *Patchwork Girl* illustrated how Possible Worlds Theory can be used to analyse literary pastiche and self-conscious rewrites of canonical works. Transworld identity and counterpart theory were again examined and subsequently applied to reveal the ontological and epistemological mechanisms on which rewrites rely. The analysis also showed why the ontological mechanics of a fictional author figure can be effectively examined using Possible Worlds Theory.

Finally the analysis of *Figurski* showed how Possible Worlds Theory can be used to examine the absurdist humour in the novel. More specifically, it showed how *Figurski*'s playfulness relies on a switch between expected and subverted generic expectations. This analysis also showed how Possible Worlds Theory can be used in the analysis of visual images in fiction and has furthered the development of Possible Worlds Theory as a tool for multimodal texts.

Generic Conclusions

While generically categorising the four novels was not the principal aim of this book, the use of self-reflexive narrative devices within each work has allowed comparisons to be made with other genres and/or period styles throughout. The analyses have shown that many of the ontologically self-conscious narrative devices identified by McHale (1987, 1992) in his extensive examination of postmodernist print fiction can be found within the Storyspace novels. Narrowing the categorisation further, in drawing attention to the attributes that historical and fictional narratives share, *Victory Garden* relies on devices which are associated with 'historiographic metafiction' (Hutcheon, 1988, 1989). Since *Patchwork Girl* simultaneously relies upon and self-consciously reworks a canonical text, it contains features which can be cross-identified with Doležel's (1998a) definition of the 'postmodern rewrite'. Finally, in showing the ease with which the Actual World can be aligned with an absurd Textual Actual World, *Figurski* can be categorised as an 'absurd situation novel' (Slocombe, 2006).

Importantly, while generic connections have been made throughout the book and appropriate discussions invoked, affiliations have only been made possible via analysis. Unlike the first wave of hypertext theory which sought to categorise hypertext fiction according to its extra-textual structural capacity, this investigation has shown how each novel uses the form for a particular thematic purpose. Consequently, while medium-wide connections are certainly appealing and in some cases appropriate, they cannot always be justified. Individual hypertext novels can only be categorised according to genre or period style by basing conclusions on substantiating evidence – something that can only be gathered as a result of close textual analysis. In order to establish if other – if not all – Storyspace novels can be categorised according to pre-determined literary categories, examinations of individual works are essential. Not only will a more transparent and systematic approach to hypertext fiction help to ensure that the second wave of hypertext theorists avoid the methodological pitfalls of their predecessors, but the associated analyses will also expand the field of hypertext criticism more generally.

Future Directions

While this book has shown how Possible Worlds Theory can be used for the analyses of four Storyspace works, further applications are required to establish and refine the approach. The theoretical expositions that run throughout this study are intended to provide a method that can be replicated within other analyses and it is hoped that it will be adopted by others in their exploration of other works. This study has been limited to four Storyspace novels, but the Eastgate catalogue contains a number of others. Hypertext fictions that are produced using alternative forms of software such as HyperCard as well as those published in HTML on the Web also require theoretical and analytical attention.

In addition, while this study has been limited to what Ensslin (2007) defines as 'hypertext fiction', Chapter 1 has shown that other types of digital literature also exist. As many of them share structural similarities with hypertext fiction, they might also benefit from a Possible Worlds Theory approach. Hypermedia fictions rely on similar structuring mechanisms to hypertext fiction in that they demand reader agency and sometimes contain multiple reading paths. Yet because they utilise additional media such as sound and visual images they will likely require additional media-specific tools if their analysis is to be comprehensive. Ryan's (2006) application of Possible Worlds Theory to Michael Joyce's hypermedia fiction, *Twilight, a Symphony*, shows how hypermedia fiction can be analysed using a similar approach to that advocated in this book, but additional analyses of other works will help to determine the dexterity of such a method.

In addition to digital fiction, Possible Worlds Theory might also be used as an analytical approach for other forms of digital literature. The digital canon is rapidly expanding to incorporate an increasingly diverse range of genres. The *Electronic Literature Directory*, a database which provides a 'descriptive guide to over 2,000 works, 1,000 authors, and 150 publishers' (Electronic Literature Organisation, 2009) of electronic literature, catalogues a vast array of different forms ranging from hypertext poetry to codeworks – literary texts which incorporate programming code into the work – and machinima movies – short films that are produced when real-time graphic engines such as video games are recorded.

The medial and generic multiplicity of the emerging digital literature canon is also reflected by the contents of the *Electronic Literature Collection* (Hayles et al., 2006). The collection, which contains 60 works and is available online and on CD-ROM, is intended 'for reading, classroom use, sharing, and reference' and thus is marketed at general readers as well as scholars of electronic literature. Importantly, users can navigate the collection according to 'title' or 'author' but the works are also catalogued according to 'keyword' and this latter means of navigation provides valuable insight into the way in which electronic literature is challenging if not successfully altering more traditional definitions of 'literature'.

Many of the categories do draw on well established generic distinctions such as 'Fiction', 'Poetry', 'Children's Literature' and 'Women Authors'. In addition, however, categories such as 'Games', which include both video games and computer games, and 'Interactive Fiction', in which 'players use text commands to control characters and influence the environment' (Hayles et al., 2006) include works with ludic elements. Similarly, in addition to the convention of categorising literary works according to genre, some of the works in the Electronic Literature Collection are also categorised according to the software package in which they have been produced; 'Flash' and 'Virtual Reality Modelling Language' represent two such examples. While software does not necessarily dictate content, a process of categorisation which foregrounds technological distinctions does at least acknowledge that certain affordances are associated with specific media (cf. Hayles, 2002).

As the examples of the *Electronic Literature Directory* and the *Electronic Literature Collection* show, a vast array of electronic literature is now available for reading and analysis. Each genre, form or technological manifestation is not necessarily suited to a Possible Worlds Theory analysis. It is worth noting, however, that many electronic texts require readers to interact with the works or make reference to their ontological peculiarity in some way. Consequently, the analytical tools that Possible Worlds Theory offers might well be useful to scholars seeking to understand these texts.

Potentially legitimising such a hypothesis, Ryan's (2006) analysis of Talan Memmott's codework poem, *Lexia to Perplexia*, concludes that it offers 'a new twist ... on self-reference' (219) because of the way in which program code is incorporated within the poem. She also suggests that some computer games 'play with the levels of world and code' (224) and 'exploit the contrast between the player's real and fictional identities' (224). In both instances, Possible Worlds Theory could be used as a means of differentiating between the various ontological domains that are constructed within such works and thus systematically analyse the ontological mechanics of this device. Similarly, in applying Ryan's (1991) Possible Worlds Theory framework to the video game, *Myst*, Van Looy (2005) demonstrates the flexibility of the theory's narratological remit. While he recognizes that the use of 'narratological concepts and theory to describe digital media is not always unproblematic', he does conclude that 'it can deliver valuable insights' and as such advocates similar experimentation in other areas.

While this book has focused on hypertext fiction, which relies on the digital medium as a tool for aesthetic expression, an increasing number of texts, which are created on the World Wide Web, utilise this vast hypertextual network as a means of compilation and dissemination. In Wright's (2004a) *In Search of Oldton*, for example, fact and fiction enmesh in a '90% true story'. Created over the course of a two-year writing project, *In Search of Oldton* was created in an attempt to 'make sense of what happened' during the author's formative years. The resultant narrative is comprised of stories and artefacts collected from 'people – online and offline – [in order] to build up digital evidence of a town that never really existed' (Wright, 2004b). In addition, the final version of the hypertext narrative, Wright's work in progress is available on his personal blog (Wright, 2004c) and Oldton playing cards can be bought from Wright's website. Adding a further dimension to the intertextual mélange, *In Search of Oldton* was also later produced and broadcast as a radio play (Wright, 2006).

Like Wright's personal writing project, online fan fictions also exist within an intertextual network within which the relationship between works of art is essential. Websites such as *FanFiction.net* host thousands of stories written as parodies, prequels, sequels or alternatives to the original canonical print works. Fan fiction works thus very much rely on their epistemological connection to their sources and influences. Fan fiction texts can be written in print and, as such, the phenomenon is not dependent on digital media. Yet as Thomas (2007b) observes, 'fanfiction websites encourage readers to browse and to read more than one story, grouping them together by genre, title, character pairings etc. so that the concept of an individual piece of fiction as a fixed entity gives way to a more fluid conception of "text"'. As Thomas's analysis suggests, by providing a repository for fan fiction narratives, the World Wide Web makes their fundamental intertextual connections more evident, immediate and traceable and a means of analysing those connections is likely to be essential for understanding the texts that result.

As the examples of *In Search of Oldton* and fan fiction show, many online narratives exist within a whole network of intertexts with constituent connections problematising the ontological status of and epistemological relationship between a particular work and its sources. While Possible Worlds Theory may not be able to answer all of the questions that these new narratives pose, it does offer some relevant tools. The preceding discussion suggests that ontological boundaries are becoming increasingly blurred or malleable in online publishing environments and Possible Worlds Theory could provide an appropriate means of negotiating, locating and interrogating them.

Future Analyses

The preceding survey suggests that the analysis of a number of different digital text types may well benefit from a Possible Worlds Theory approach. However, general conclusions must not be made about its benefits for entire genres without the accompanying analyses of individual works that are necessary to substantiate such claims. Chapter 2 of this book accuses the first wave of hypertext theory of fostering a schism between theory and practice. In order to ensure that is not continued into the second wave, substantiating close readings must accompany all analyses of digital texts.

Similarly, while this book provides one approach to hypertext fiction, others need to be developed. Primarily this will ensure that the multifarious intricacies of all types of digital text are addressed, but it will also ensure that scholars of digital fiction have access to a range of theoretical and analytical tools.

Finally, the scholars of hypertext fiction and digital texts generally must publicise their work to the wider academic community. A failure to disseminate work more widely will mean that this area of research remains detrimentally niche. The fascinating narrative experiments that digital texts are capable of will be kept hidden and the methodological advances that will inevitably be made within hypertext theory will remain undisclosed. Both scenarios will disadvantage both print and digital scholarship.

The Future of Possible Worlds Theory

As the preceding methodological conclusions show, Possible Worlds Theory has the potential to illuminate the ontological mechanics of a number of devices in a number of different texts which are written and read in various media. The dexterity of Possible Worlds Theory, at least for texts which play with ontology, is a consequence of its logical loyalty and transparency. Yet while its robustness is certainly attractive, the logical axioms on which Possible Worlds Theory rests are sometimes prohibitive and therefore unsuitable for the field of literary studies.

Primarily, the Law of Non-Contradiction and the Law of the Excluded Middle – both of which prohibit contradictions in a logical context – are ineffective whenever narrative contradictions occur. As the analyses have shown, in the context of Storyspace hypertext fiction analysis, this is a particularly pertinent issue because much of it does contain incongruous narrative paths. This book has chosen to negotiate some of the theory's logical restrictions in order to maintain its commitment to analysing the narrative devices of the novels. However, further work might expand this area so as to reconcile the two fields without making such dramatic compromises.

In addition, while the method has proved effective for the analysis of hypertext fiction, Possible Worlds Theory does have limitations. First, the field continues to be divided by an irreconcilable conflict regarding the ontological status of possible worlds. Theorists who subscribe to an Abstractionist perspective are guided by their conviction in the ontological exclusivity of the Actual World which means that possible worlds according to this perspective are only ever hypothetical. Concretists, on the other hand, are committed to a system of reality in which both the Actual World and possible worlds are ontologically compatible. Finally, though less pervasive or influential, the Constructionist position refutes the notion that our system of reality is organised around a single Actual World centre and instead opts for a more subjective form of categorisation.

Throughout this text, it has been shown that each theoretical perspective can provide valuable tools to a fictional context and, consequently, concepts have been taken from each, sometimes simultaneously. Primarily, since a Textual Actual World is a particular type of possible world, the Abstractionist perspective has been adopted when categorising fictional worlds ontologically. Indeed, this text rests on the principle that a Textual Actual World does not materially exist beyond the imagination of the author, reader and words on the page. While theoretically incongruous with an Abstractionist ontological position, the Concretist conviction in the autonomy of possible worlds and their constituents is useful for analysing the relationship between one Textual Actual World and another. It has therefore been used in this capacity. Granting each Textual Actual World – as a special type of possible world – with ontological autonomy means that the significance of counterparts in fiction can be analysed more appropriately. Similarly, the ontological plurality of the Constructionist perspective can be used as a means of analysing epistemological incongruities in novels which use multiple narrators. It is on this perspective that the World View category takes most influence. The World View category provides a means of distinguishing between epistemological perspectives and ontological domains which is something that the conflicting voices in *afternoon* require in particular. The World View term has also been invoked in the analyses of *Victory Garden* and *Patchwork Girl*. Additional studies are required to establish its suitability and applicability to other texts as well as other types of literature.

The World View category represents just one example of the numerous theoretical modifications and supplementations that have been suggested throughout this study. In Chapter 3, Ryan's (1991) framework was modified so that it could more visibly accommodate the alienation caused by particular self-reflexive devices in the Storyspace works. The chapter showed why it is necessary to label both the textual and actual addressees that take part in fictional communication, particularly during some instances of second-person narration. For this purpose, a 'narratee' role was introduced into Ryan's model and the Textual Actual World split into two constituent parts: the narrating space of the Textual

Actual World and the narrated space of the Textual Actual World. The split was necessitated in order to model the peculiar ontological position of the narrator in a Textual Universe. While the model was used throughout the subsequent analyses, further theoretical discussion and future application of the amended framework will help to establish its applicability further.

During the analyses of *Victory Garden* and *Patchwork Girl* theoretical debates established the respective benefits of using transworld identity and counterpart theory in a literary context. The debate concluded that both concepts were useful in the analysis of historical fiction and rewrites or parody. While their simultaneous application necessitates a logical compromise, it remains faithful to the narratological remit of this book and, as such, has been justified in the context of this study.

Conclusion

As the conclusions that have been made in this chapter show, this book has contributed to the second wave of hypertext theory as well as Possible Worlds Theory in literary studies. Hypertext fiction may have been less influential than its earliest proponents had hoped. It is perhaps not surprising therefore that the critical field which surrounds it is still undergoing significant developments. Similarly, while Possible Worlds Theory remains relatively influential within narrative theory, applications are still being refined. This book contributes to the field by providing an approach for the analysis of one type of digital literature but, as the preceding discussion shows, both disciplines still have work to do. It is hoped that the progress made within this study will prove useful to the second wave of hypertext scholarship, the ongoing development of Possible Worlds Theory and, most importantly, their future methodological synergy.

References

Aarseth, E. J. (1994) 'Nonlinearity and Literary Theory.' In: G. P. Landow (ed.), *Hyper/Text/Theory*. Baltimore, MD: John Hopkins University Press, pp. 53–86.

Aarseth, E. J. (1997) *Cybertext: Perspectives on Ergodic Literature*. Baltimore, MD: John Hopkins University Press.

Abbott, H. P. (2002) *The Cambridge Introduction to Narrative*. Cambridge: Cambridge University Press.

Alber, J. (2009) 'Impossible Storyworlds – And What To Do With Them.' *Storyworlds: A Journal of Narrative Studies* **1**(1).

Amerika, M. (1998) 'Stitch Bitch: The Hypertext Author as Cyborg-Femme Narrator.' *Telepolis* [online], February/March 1998. Last accessed 1 July 2009 at URL: http://www.heise.de/tp/r4/artikel/3/3193/1.html

Ashline, W. L. (1995) 'The Problem of Impossible Fictions.' *Style* **29**(2): 215–34.

Barthes, R. (1990) *S/Z* [1974] (trans. R. Miller). Oxford: Blackwell.

Baum, L. F. (1990) *The Patchwork Girl of Oz* [1913]. New York, NY: Dover.

Bell, A. (2007) '"Do You Want to Hear About it?" Exploring Possible Worlds in Michael Joyce's Hyperfiction, *afternoon: a story*.' In: M. Lambrou and P. Stockwell (eds), *Contemporary Stylistics*. London: Continuum, pp. 43–55.

Bell, A. (forthcoming) 'Ontological Boundaries and Methodological Leaps: The Significance of Possible Worlds Theory for Hypertext Fiction (and Beyond).' In: R. Page and B. Thomas (eds), *New Narratives: Theory and Practice*. Lincoln, NE: University of Nebraska Press.

Bennett, C. (2001) 'eNarrative Spotlight 4: A Chat with Richard Holeton.' At: *eNarrative.org* [online]. Last accessed 3 March 2009 at URL: http://www.stanford.edu/,holeton/publications/Bennett.pdf

Berners-Lee, T. (1999) *Weaving the Web: The Past, Present and Future of the World Wide Web by its Inventor*. Britain: Orion Business.

Bernstein, M. (2002) 'Storyspace 1.' *Hypertext '02: Proceedings of the Thirteenth ACM Conference on Hypertext and Hypermedia*, 11–15 June 2002, College Park, MD, pp. 172–81.

Bolter, J. D. (1991) 'Topographic Writing: Hypertext and the Electronic Writing Space.' In: P. Delany and G. P. Landow (eds), *Hypermedia and Literary Studies*. Cambridge, MA: MIT Press, pp. 105–18.

Bolter, J. D. (2001) *Writing Space: Computers, Hypertext and the Remediation of Print* (2nd edn). Mahwah, NJ: Lawrence Erlbaum Associates.

Bolter, J. D. and Joyce, M. (1987). 'Hypertext and Creative Writing.' *Proceedings of the First ACM Workshop on Hypertext (Hypertext '87)*, 13–15 November 1987, University of North Carolina, Chapel Hill, NC: ACM Press, pp. 41–50.

Ciccoricco, D. (2004) 'Tending the Garden Plot: *Victory Garden* and Operation Enduring …' *The Electronic Book Review* [online]. October 2004. Last accessed 13 June 2009 at URL: http://www.electronicbookreview.com/thread/internetnation/operational

Ciccoricco, D. (2007) *Reading Network Fiction*. Tuscaloosa, AL: University of Alabama Press.

Cixous, H. (1991) *Coming to Writing and Other Essays* (trans. S. Cornell et al.), D. Jenson (ed.). Cambridge, MA: Harvard University Press.

Connolly, D. (2000) 'A Little History of the World Wide World Wide Web.' At: *The World Wide World Wide Web Consortium* [online]. Last accessed 14 March 2009 at URL: http://www.w3.org/History.html

Coover, R. (1969) 'The Babysitter.' In: *Pricksongs and Descants*. New York, NY: Grove Press, pp. 206–39.

Coover, R. (1994) *Hypertext Hotel* [online]. Last accessed 18 March 2009 at URL: http://hyperdis.de/hyphotel/

Cortazar, J. (1966) *Hopscotch*. London: The Harvill Press.

Coverley, M. D. (2000) *Califia* [CD-ROM]. Watertown, MA: Eastgate Systems.

Delany, P. and Landow, G. P. (1991) *Hypermedia and Literary Studies*. Cambridge, MA: MIT Press.

Deleuze, G. and Guattari, F. (1988) *A Thousand Plateaus: Capitalism and Schizophrenia* (trans. B. Massumi). London: Athlone Press.

Derrida J. (1979) 'Living On.' In: J. Hulbart (ed.), *Deconstruction and Criticism: A Continuum Book*. New York, NY: Seabury Press, pp. 75–176.

Derrida, J. (1981) *Dissemination* (trans. B. Johnson). Chicago, OH: University of Chicago Press.

dichtung-digital [online]. Last accessed 18 March 2009 at URL: http://www.dichtung-digital.de/

Divers, J. (2002) *Possible Worlds*. London: Routledge.

Doležel, L. (1976) 'Narrative Semantics.' *PTL* 1: 129–51.

Doležel, L. (1980) 'Truth and Authenticity in Narrative.' *Poetics Today* 1: 7–25.

Doležel, L. (1985) 'Pour une typologie des mondes fictionnels.' In: H. Parret and H. Ruprecht (eds) *Exigences et Perspectives dans la Semiotique Recueil d'hommage pour Greimas*. Amsterdam-Philadelphia: Benjamins, pp. 7–23.

Doležel, L. (1989) 'Possible Worlds and Literary Fictions.' In: S. Allen (ed.), *Possible Worlds in Humanities, Arts and Sciences: Proceedings of Nobel Symposium 65*, New York, USA: De Gruyter, pp. 221–42.

Doležel, L. (1998a) *Heterocosmica: Fiction and Possible Worlds*. Baltimore, MD: John Hopkins University Press.

Doležel, L. (1998b) 'Possible Worlds of History and Fiction.' *New Literary History* 29(4): 785–809.

Douglas, J. Y. (1992) 'What Hypertexts Can Do That Print Narratives Cannot.' *Reader* 28: 1–22.

Douglas, J. Y. (1994) '"How Do I Stop This Thing?" Closure and Indeterminacy in Interactive Narratives.' In: G. P. Landow (ed.), *Hyper/Text/Theory*. Baltimore, MD: John Hopkins University Press, pp. 159–88.

Eastgate Systems (2008) Catalogue entry for *Figurski at Findhorn on Acid* [online]. Last accessed 4 March 2009 at URL: http://www.eastgate.com/catalog/Figurski.html

Eco, U. (1979) '*Lector in Fabula*: Pragmatic Strategy in a Metanarrative Text.' In: *The Role of the Reader: Explorations in the Semiotics of Texts*. London: Hutchinson, Chapter 8.

Electronic Book Review [online]. Last accessed 18 March 2009 at URL: http://www.electronicbookreview.com/

Electronic Literature Directory [online]. Last accessed 20 August 2009 at URL: http://directory.eliterature.org/

Electronic Literature Organisation (2009) 'Introduction to the Directory' at *Electronic Literature Organisation* [online]. Last accessed 15 September 2009 at URL: http://eliterature.org/dir/index.php

Ensslin, A. (2007) *Canonizing Hypertext: Explorations and Constructions*. London: Continuum.

Ensslin, A. (forthcoming) 'From (W)reader to Breather: Cybertextual Retro-intentionalisation in Kate Pullinger et al.'s *Breathing Wall*.' In: R. Page and B. Thomas (eds), *New Narratives: Theory and Practice*. Lincoln, NE: University of Nebraska Press.

Ensslin, A. and Bell, A. (eds), (2007) 'New Perspectives on Digital Literature: Criticism and Analysis.' Special Issue of *dichtung-digital* [online] 37. Last accessed 18 March 2009 at URL: http://www.dichtung-digital.de/

FanFiction.net [online]. Last accessed 15 September 2009 at URL: http://www. fanfiction.net

Gaggi, S. (1997) *From Text to Hypertext: Decentering the Subject in Fiction, Film, the Visual Arts and Electronic Media*. Philadelphia, PA: University of Pennsylvania Press.

Gardner, C. (2004) 'Meta-Interpretation and Hypertext Fiction: A Critical Response.' *Journal Computers and the Humanities* 37: 33–56.

Genette, G. (1980) *Narrative Discourse* [1972] (trans. J. E. Lewin). Oxford: Blackwell.

Genette, G. (1988) *Narrative Discourse Revisited*, (trans. J. E. Lewin). Ithaca, NY: Cornell University Press.

Geyh, P., Lebron, F. G. and Levy, A. (eds), (1997a) *Postmodern American Fiction: A Norton Anthology*. New York, NY: W. W. Norton.

Geyh, P., Lebron, F. G. and Levy, A. (eds), (1997b) *Postmodern American Fiction: A Norton Anthology* [online]. New York, NY: W. W. Norton. Last accessed 13 July 2009 at URL: http://www.wwnorton.com/pmaf/hypertext/aft/index.html

Goodman, N. (1978) *Ways of World Making*. Indianapolis, IN: Hackett Publishing Company.

Goodman, N. (1983) *Fact, Fiction and Forecast* (4th edn). Cambridge, MA: Harvard University Press.

Goodman, N. (1984) *Of Mind and Other Matters*. Cambridge, MA: Harvard University Press.

Hayles, N. K. (2000) 'Flickering Connectivities in Shelley Jackson's *Patchwork Girl*: The Importance of Media-Specific Analysis.' *Postmodern Culture* [online] 10 (2). Last accessed 1 July 2009 at URL: http://www.iath.virginia.edu/pmc/text-only/ issue.100/10.2hayles.txt

Hayles, N. K. (2002) *Writing Machines*. Cambridge, MA: MIT Press.

Hayles, N. K; Montfort, N; Rettberg, S. and Strickland, S. (eds) (2006) *Electronic Literature Collection Volume One* [online]. College Park, Maryland: Electronic Literature Organization. Last accessed 15 September 2009 at URL: http:// collection.eliterature.org/1/index.html

Higgason, R. E. (2003a) 'A Body of Criticism.' S. Tosca and J. Walker (eds) *Journal of Digital Information* [online] 3(3). Last accessed 26 October 2009 at URL: http://journals.tdl.org/jodi/article/view/117

Higgason, R. E. (2003b) 'A Scholar's Nightmare.' S. Tosca and J. Walker (eds) *Journal of Digital Information* [online] 3(3). Last accessed 26 October 2009 at URL: http://journals.tdl.org/jodi/article/view/117

Hinderaker, A. (2002) 'It Has No Beginning, It Has No End: a Novel Approach Plays Havoc with Literary Convention.' *Stanford Magazine* [online] **6**. Last accessed 11 July 2009 at URL: http://www.stanfordalumni.org/news/magazine/2002/ novdec/showcase/review.html

Hintikka, J. (1967) 'Individuals, Possible Worlds, and Epistemic Logic.' *Nous* **1**: 33–62.

Hintikka, J. (1989) 'Exploring Possible Worlds.' In: S. Allen (ed.), *Possible Worlds in Humanities, Arts and Sciences: Proceedings of Nobel Symposium 65*. New York, NY: De Gruyter, pp. 52–73.

Holeton, R. (1998) 'Don't Eat the Yellow Hypertext: Notes on *Figurski at Findhorn on Acid.' Kairos* [online] 3(2). Last accessed 3 March 2009 at URL: http:// english.ttu.edu/kairos/3.2/response/Kendall/holeton/

Holeton, R. (2001) *Figurski at Findhorn on Acid* [CD-ROM]. Watertown, MA: Eastgate Systems.

Hutcheon, L. (1988) *A Poetics of Postmodernism: History, Theory, Fiction*. London: Routledge.

Hutcheon, L. (1989) *The Politics of Postmodernism*. London: Routledge.

Hutcheon, L. (1996) '"The Pastime of Past Time": Fiction, History and Metafiction.' In: M. J. Hoffman and P. D. Murphy (eds), *Essentials of the Theory of Fiction* (2nd edn). London: Leicester University Press, pp. 472–95.

Jackson, S. (1995) *Patchwork Girl; Or, a Modern Monster* [CD-ROM]. Watertown, MA: Eastgate Systems.

Jackson, S. (1998) 'Stitch Bitch: The Patchwork Girl.' *Paradoxa* 4(11): 526–38.

Joyce, E. (2003) 'Sutured Fragments: Shelley Jackson's *Patchwork Girl* in Piecework.' In: J. Van Looy and J. Baetens (eds), *Close Reading New Media: Analyzing Electronic Literature*. Louvain: Leuven University Press, pp. 39–52.

Joyce, M. (1987) *afternoon: a story* [CD-ROM]. Watertown, MA: Eastgate Systems.

Joyce, M. (1988) 'Siren Shapes: Exploratory and Constructive Hypertexts.' *Academic Computing* 3: 10–14.

Joyce, M. (1997) 'Nonce Upon Some Times: Rereading Hypertext Fiction.' In: N. K. Hayles (ed.), *Modern Fiction Studies* 43(3): 579–97.

Koskimaa, R. (2000) *Digital Literature: From Text to Hypertext and Beyond* [online]. Unpublished PhD Thesis, University of Jyväskylä, Finland. Last accessed 13 June 2009 at URL: http://users.jyu.fi/~koskimaa/thesis/thesis.shtml.

Kripke, S. (1963) 'Semantic Analysis of Modal Logic.' *Zeitschrift für Mathematische Logik und Grundlagen der Mathematik* 9: 67–96.

Kripke, S. (1972) *Naming and Necessity*. Oxford: Blackwell.

Laccetti, J. (2006) 'Review of *Figurski at Findhorn on Acid*.' At: *The Resource Center for Cyberculture Studies* [online]. Last accessed 3 March 2009 at URL: http://rccs. usfca.edu/bookinfo.asp?ReviewID = 419&BookID = 338

Landow, G. P. (1992) *Hypertext: the Convergence of Contemporary Critical Theory and Technology*. Baltimore, MD: Johns Hopkins University Press.

Landow, G. P. (1994) 'What's a Critic to Do? Critical Theory in the Age of Hypertext.' In: G. P Landow (ed.), *Hyper/Text/Theory*. Baltimore, MD: John Hopkins University Press, pp. 1–48.

Landow, G. P. (1997) *Hypertext 2.0: The Convergence of Contemporary Critical Theory and Technology*. Baltimore, MD: John Hopkins University Press.

Landow, G. P. (2006) *Hypertext 3.0: Critical Theory and New Media in an Era of Globalization*. Baltimore, MD: John Hopkins University Press.

Larsen, D. (1993) *Marble Springs* [CD-ROM]. Watertown, MA: Eastgate Systems.

Larsen, D. (2003) 'You Can Get There From Here.' S. Tosca and J. Walker (eds) *Journal of Digital Information* [online] **3**(3). Last accessed 26 October 2009 at URL: http://journals.tdl.org/jodi/article/view/117

Leibniz, G. W. (1952) *Essays on Theodicy: Of God's Goodness, Man's Freedom and the Origins of Evil* [1710] (trans. E. M. Huggard). London: Routledge & Kegan Paul.

Lewis, D. (1973) *Counterfactuals*. Oxford: Blackwell.

Lewis, D. (1983a) 'Anselm and Actuality.' In: *Philosophical Papers: Volume 1.* Oxford: Oxford University Press, pp. 175–88.

Lewis, D. (1983b) 'Postscripts to "Counterpart Theory and Quantified Modal Logic".' In: *Philosophical Papers: Volume. 1.* Oxford: Oxford University Press, pp. 39–46.

Lewis, D. (1986) *On the Plurality of Worlds*. Oxford: Blackwell.

Liestol, G. (1994) 'Wittgenstein, Genette, and the Reader's Narrative in Hypertext.' In: G. P. Landow (ed.), *Hyper/Text/Theory*. Baltimore, MD: John Hopkins University Press, pp. 87–120.

McDaid, J. (1992) *Uncle Buddy's Phantom Funhouse* [HyperCard]. Watertown, MA: Eastgate Systems.

McHale, B. (1987) *Postmodernist Fiction*. London: Routledge.

McHale, B. (1992) *Constructing Postmodernism*. London: Routledge.

Maître, D. (1983) *Literature and Possible Worlds*. Middlesex: Middlesex Polytechnic Press.

Margolin, U. (1989) 'Structuralist Approaches to Character in Narrative: State of the Art.' *Semiotica* **75**(1/2): 1–24.

Margolin, U. (1990) 'Individuals in Narrative Worlds: An Ontological Perspective.' *Poetics Today: Narratology Revisited II* **11**(4): 843–71.

Margolin, U. (1996) 'Characters and Their Versions.' In: C. Mihailescu and W. Hamarneh (eds), *Fiction Updated: Theories of Fictionality, Narratology, and Poetics*. Toronto, ON: University of Toronto Press, pp. 113–32.

Miles, A. (2003a) 'Reviewing versus Criticism.' S. Tosca and J. Walker (eds), *Journal of Digital Information* [online] **3**(3). Last accessed 26 October 2009 at URL: http://journals.tdl.org/jodi/article/view/117

Miles, A. (2003b) 'There's No Need to Bite the Breast.' S. Tosca and J. Walker (eds) *Journal of Digital Information* [online] **3**(3). Last accessed 26 October 2009 at URL: http://journals.tdl.org/jodi/article/view/117

Moulthrop, S. (1989) 'Hypertext and the Hyperreal.' In: N. Meyrowitz (ed.), *Proceedings of ACM Hypertext 89 Conference*, 5–8 November 1989, Pittsburgh, PA, pp. 259–68.

Moulthrop, S. (1991a) *Victory Garden* [CD-ROM]. Watertown, MA: Eastgate Systems.

Moulthrop, S. (1991b): 'Beyond the Electronic Book: A Critique of Hypertext Rhetoric'. In: J. Walker (ed.), *Proceedings of ACM Hypertext 91 Conference*, 15–18 December 1991, San Antonio, TX, pp. 291–8.

Moulthrop, S. (1991c) 'Reading from the Map: Metonymy and Metaphor in the Fiction of Forking Paths.' In: P. Delany and G. P. Landow (eds), *Hypermedia and Literary Studies*. Cambridge, MA: MIT Press, pp. 119–32.

Moulthrop, S. (1994) 'Rhizome and Resistance: Hypertext and the Dreams of a New Culture.' In: G. P. Landow (ed.), *Hyper/Text/Theory*. Baltimore, MD: John Hopkins University Press, pp. 299–319.

Moulthrop, S. (1995) *Hegirascope, Version 2* [online]. Last accessed 14 March 2009 at URL: http://iat.ubalt.edu/moulthrop/hypertexts/hgs/

Murray, J. H. (1997) *Hamlet on the Holodeck: the Future of Narrative in Cyberspace.* New York, NY: The Free Press.

Nelson, T. (1965) 'A File Structure for the Complex, the Changing, and the Indeterminate.' *Proceedings of the Twentieth National Conference of the Association for Computing Machinery,* 24–26 August 1965, Cleveland, OH, pp. 84–100.

Nelson, T. (1970) 'No More Teachers' Dirty Looks.' *Computer Decisions* 9(8): 16–23.

Nelson, T. (1974) *Computer Lib/Dream Machines.* Redmond, WA: Tempus Books.

Nelson, T. (1981) *Literary Machines.* Swarthmore, PA: Self-published.

Nolan, D. P. (2002) *Topics in the Philosophy of Possible Worlds.* London: Routledge.

Page, B. (1999) 'Women Writers and the Restive Text: Feminism, Experimental Writing, and Hypertext.' In: M. L. Ryan (ed.), *Cyberspace Textuality: Computer Technology and Literary Theory.* Bloomington, IN: Indiana University Press, pp. 111–36.

Page, R. and Thomas, B. (eds) (forthcoming) *New Narratives: Theory and Practice.* Lincoln, NE: University of Nebraska Press.

Palmer, A. (2004) *Fictional Minds.* Lincoln, NE: University of Nebraska Press.

Pang, A. (1998) 'Hypertext, the Next Generation: A Review and Research Agenda'. *First Monday* [online]. 3(11). Last accessed 29 April 2009 at URL: http://firstmonday.org/htbin/cgiwrap/bin/ojs/index.php/fm/article/view/628/549

Parker, J. (2003) 'The Museum of Hyphenated Media.' *Electronic Book Review* [online]. Last accessed 3 March 2009 at URL: http://www.electronicbookreview.com/thread/electropoetics/quilted

Pavel, T. G. (1975) 'Possible Worlds in Literary Semantics.' *The Journal of Aesthetics and Art Criticism* 34(2): 165–76.

Pavel, T. G. (1979) 'Fiction and the Casual Theory of Names.' *Poetics* 8: 179–91.

Pavel, T. G. (1986) *Fictional Worlds.* London: Harvard University Press.

Penguin (2007) *A Million Penguins* [online]. Last accessed 18 March 2009 at URL: http://www.amillionpenguins.com/wiki/index.php/Welcome

Phelan, J. and Maloney, E. (1999) 'Authors, Readers, and Progression in Hypertext Narrative.' *Works and Days* 33/34(17) & 35/36(18): 265–77.

Plantinga, A. (1974) *The Nature of Necessity.* Oxford: Clarendon Press.

Plantinga, A. (1979) 'Transworld Identity or Worldbound Individuals.' In: M. Loux (ed.), *The Possible and the Actual: Readings in the Metaphysics of Modality.* Ithaca, NY: Cornell University Press, pp. 146–65.

Plantinga, A. (2003) *Essays in the Metaphysics of Modality.* Oxford: Oxford University Press.

Pope, J. (2006) 'A Future for Hypertext Fiction.' *Convergence: The International Journal of Research into New Media Technologies* 12(4): 447–65.

Pressman, J. (2007) 'Digital Modernism: Making it New in New Media.' Unpublished PhD Thesis. University of California, Los Angeles, USA.

Pressman, J. (2009) 'Modern Modernisms: Young-hae Chang Heavy Industries and Digital Modernism.' In: S. Yao, M. Gillies and H. Sword (eds), *Pacific Rim Modernisms.* Toronto, ON: University of Toronto Press, pp. 443–65.

Prince, G. (1980) 'Introduction to the Study of the Narratee.' In: J. P. Tompkins (ed.), *Reader-Response Criticism.* Baltimore, MD: Johns Hopkins University Press, pp. 7–25.

Pullinger, K., Schemat, S. and babel (2004) *The Breathing Wall* [CD-ROM]. UK: self-published.

Punday, D. (1997) 'Meaning in Postmodern Worlds: The Case of *The French Lieutenant's Woman.*' *Semiotica* **115**(3/4): 313–43.

Punday, D. (2004) 'Involvement, Interruption, and Inevitability: Melancholy as an Aesthetic Principle in Game Narratives.' *SubStance* 33(3): 80–107.

Rescher, N. (1975) *A Theory of Possibility.* Pittsburgh, PA: Pittsburgh University Press.

Rescher, N. (1979) 'The Ontology of the Possible.' In: M. Loux (ed.), *The Possible and the Actual: Readings in the Metaphysics of Modality.* Ithaca, NY: Cornell University Press, pp. 166–81.

Richardson, B. (2006) *Unnatural Voices: Extreme Narration in Modern and Contemporary Fiction.* Columbus, OH: Ohio State University Press.

Ronen, R. (1994) *Possible Worlds in Literary Theory.* Cambridge: Cambridge University Press.

Ryan, M. L. (1991) *Possible Worlds, Artificial Intelligence and Narrative Theory.* Bloomington, IN: Indiana University Press.

Ryan, M. L. (1992) 'Possible Worlds in Recent Literary Theory.' *Style* **26**(4): 528–52.

Ryan, M. L. (1998) 'The Text as World Versus the Text as Game: Possible Worlds Semantics and Postmodern Theory.' *Journal of Literary Semantics* 27(3): 137–63.

Ryan, M. L. (2001) *Narrative as Virtual Reality: Immersion and Interactivity in Literature and Electronic Media.* Baltimore, MD: John Hopkins Press.

Ryan, M. L. (2006) *Avatars of Story: Electronic Mediations.* Minneapolis, MN: University of Minnesota Press.

Ryan, M. L. (forthcoming) 'The Interactive Onion: Layers of User Participation in Digital Narrative Texts.' In: R. Page and B. Thomas (eds), *New Narratives: Theory and Practice.* Lincoln, NE: University of Nebraska Press.

Saporta, M. (1963) *Composition No. 1* (trans. R. Howard). New York, NY: Simon & Schuster.

Sawhney, N. and Balcom, D. (1997) *HyperCafe* [online]. Last accessed 10 June 2004 at URL: http://www.lcc.gatech.edu/gallery/hypercafe/

Shelley, M. (1998) *Frankenstein; Or the Modern Prometheus* [1818]. Oxford: Oxford University Press.

Slocombe, W. (2006) *Nihilism and the Sublime Postmodern: The (Hi)Story of a Difficult Relationship from Romanticism to Postmodernism.* London: Routledge.

Snyder, I. (1996) *Hypertext: the Electronic Labyrinth.* New York, NY: New York University Press.

Stafford, B. M. (1991) *Body Criticism: Imaging the Unseen in Enlightenment Art and Medicine.* Cambridge, MA: MIT Press.

Taylor, C. and Pitman T. (2007) *Latin American Cyberliterature and Cyberculture.* Liverpool: University of Liverpool Press.

Thomas, B. (2007a) 'Stuck in a Loop? Dialogue in Hypertext Fiction.' *Narrative* **15**(3): 357–72.

Thomas, B. (2007b) 'Canons and Fanons: Literary Fanfiction Online'. Ensslin, A. and Bell, A. (eds). Special issue of *dichtung-digital* [online] **37**. Last accessed 15 September 2009 at URL: http://www.dichtung-digital.de/

Tosca, S. and Walker, J. (2003) 'Hypertext Criticism: Writing about Hypertext.' S. Tosca and J. Walker (eds), *Journal of Digital Information* [online] **3**(3). Last accessed 26 October 2009 at URL: http://journals.tdl.org/jodi/article/view/117

Traill, N. H. (1991) 'Fictional Worlds of the Fantastic.' *Style* **25**(2): 196–210.

Van Looy (2005) 'Virtual Recentering: Computer Games and Possible Worlds Theory.' *Image and Narrative* **12**. Last accessed 6 November 2009 at URL: http://www.imageandnarrative.be/tulseluper/vanlooy.htm.

Van Looy, J. and Baetens, J. (eds) (2003) *Close Reading New Media: Analyzing Electronic Literature*. Leuven: Leuven University Press.

Walker, J. (1999) 'Piecing Together and Tearing Apart: Finding the Story in *Afternoon.*' *Proceedings of the Tenth ACM Conference on Hypertext and Hypermedia*, 21–25 February 1999, Darmstadt, Germany, ACM Press, pp. 111–17.

Waugh, P. (1984) *Metafiction: The Theory and Practice of Self-Conscious Fiction*. London: Methuen.

Wright, T. (2004a) *In Search of Oldton* [online]. Last accessed 15 September 2009 at URL: http://www.oldton.com/index.html

Wright, T. (2004b) 'In Search Of Oldton' at *trAce Online Writing School* [online]. Last accessed 15 September 2009 at URL: http://tracearchive.ntu.ac.uk/writersforthefuture/view/InSearchofOldton.htm

Wright, T. (2004c) 'inresidence' blog [online]. Last accessed 15 September 2009 at URL: http://timwright.typepad.com/inresidence/

Wright, T. (2006) *In Search of Oldton*. Memory Experience season (2006). BBC Radio 4. Monday 24 July, 2.15pm.

Index